The Morphogenesis of the Norwegian Educational System

Based in the philosophy of critical realism, this book employs a range of Margaret Archer's theoretical concepts to investigate temporal and spatial aspects of Norwegian education. Stemming from Archer's engagement as visiting professor from 2017 to 2019 in the Department of Education at UiT The Arctic University of Norway, the book explores a new area for critical realist theorizing by asking how different spatial contexts affect the workings of the system. The various chapters employ diverse sets of Archer's theoretical concepts; from morphogenetic cycles and the emergence of educational systems at the macro level, to the exercise of reflexivity among individual school leaders and students at the micro level. In contrast to the focus on educational homogeneity and similarity among Nordic and Scandinavian countries, and promotion of the conception of the 'Nordic Model', this book draws attention to differences between these nations as well as regional differences within Norway. As such, it will appeal to scholars with interests in education, sociology, critical realism, educational sciences and pedagogy, education history and political science as well those with a specific interest in the Nordic region.

Margaret S. Archer is Emeritus Professor at the University of Warwick, UK. Her books include *Social Origins of Educational Systems*; *Culture and Agency: The Place of Culture in Social Theory*; *Realist Social Theory: The Morphogenetic Approach*; *Being Human: The Problem of Agency*; *Structure, Agency and the Internal Conversation*; *Making our Way Through the World*; *The Reflexive Imperative*; *Late Modernity: Trajectories towards Morphogenic Society*; *Generative Mechanisms Transforming the Social Order*; *Morphogenesis and the Crisis of Normativity*; and *Morphogenesis and Human Flourishing*.

Unn-Doris K. Bæck is Professor of Sociology in the Department of Social Sciences at UiT the Arctic University of Norway. Her main research interests are within the sociology of education and the sociology of youth, with special emphasis on social and spatial inequalities. She has published extensively in journals and anthologies within these fields.

Tone Skinningsrud is Professor Emeritus in the Department of Education at UiT the Arctic University of Norway. Her research contributions are in the areas of educational history, the sociology of education, comparative education, and field work methods. She has published in journals of educational history comparative education and visual anthropology. Currently, she is co-authoring a comprehensive history of Norwegian education applying Margaret Archer's morphogenetic approach.

Routledge Studies in Critical Realism

Critical Realism is a broad movement within philosophy and social science. It is a movement that began in British philosophy and sociology following the founding work of Roy Bhaskar, Margaret Archer and others. Critical Realism emerged from the desire to realize an adequate realist philosophy of science, social science and of critique. Against empiricism, positivism and various idealisms (interpretivism, radical social constructionism), Critical Realism argues for the necessity of ontology. The pursuit of ontology is the attempt to understand and say something about 'the things themselves' and not simply about our beliefs, experiences or our current knowledge and understanding of those things. Critical Realism also argues against the implicit ontology of the empiricists and idealists of events and regularities, reducing reality to thought, language, belief, custom or experience. Instead, Critical Realism advocates a structural realist and causal powers approach to natural and social ontology, with a focus upon social relations and process of social transformation.

Important movements within Critical Realism include the morphogenetic approach developed by Margaret Archer; Critical Realist economics developed by Tony Lawson; as well as dialectical Critical Realism (embracing being, becoming and absence) and the philosophy of metaReality (emphasizing priority of the non-dual) developed by Roy Bhaskar.

For over 30 years, Routledge has been closely associated with Critical Realism and, in particular, the work of Roy Bhaskar, publishing well over 50 works in, or informed by, Critical Realism (in series including Critical Realism: Interventions; Ontological Explorations; New Studies in Critical Realism and Education). These have all now been brought together under one series dedicated to Critical Realism.

The Centre for Critical Realism is the advisory editorial board for the series. If you would like to know more about the Centre for Critical Realism, or to submit a book proposal, please visit www.centreforcriticalrealism.com.

Explaining Morality
Critical Realism and Moral Questions
Steve Ash

For more information about this series, please visit: https://www.routledge.com/Routledge-Studies-in-Critical-Realism-Routledge-Critical-Realism/book-series/SE0518

The Morphogenesis of the Norwegian Educational System
Emergence and Development from a Critical Realist Perspective

**Edited by
Margaret S. Archer, Unn-Doris K. Bæck
and Tone Skinningsrud**

LONDON AND NEW YORK

First published 2022
by Routledge
2 Park Square, Milton Park, Abingdon, Oxon OX14 4RN

and by Routledge
605 Third Avenue, New York, NY 10158

Routledge is an imprint of the Taylor & Francis Group, an informa business

© 2022 selection and editorial matter, Margaret S. Archer, Unn-Doris K. Bæck and Tone Skinningsrud; individual chapters, the contributors

The right of Margaret S. Archer, Unn-Doris K. Bæck and Tone Skinningsrud to be identified as the authors of the editorial material, and of the authors for their individual chapters, has been asserted in accordance with sections 77 and 78 of the Copyright, Designs and Patents Act 1988.

All rights reserved. No part of this book may be reprinted or reproduced or utilised in any form or by any electronic, mechanical, or other means, now known or hereafter invented, including photocopying and recording, or in any information storage or retrieval system, without permission in writing from the publishers.

Trademark notice: Product or corporate names may be trademarks or registered trademarks, and are used only for identification and explanation without intent to infringe.

British Library Cataloguing-in-Publication Data
A catalogue record for this book is available from the British Library

Library of Congress Cataloging-in-Publication Data
A catalog record has been requested for this book

ISBN: 978-0-367-75677-2 (hbk)
ISBN: 978-0-367-75679-6 (pbk)
ISBN: 978-1-003-16352-7 (ebk)

DOI: 10.4324/9781003163527

Typeset in Times New Roman
by KnowledgeWorks Global Ltd.

Contents

Notes on contributors vii

1 **Introduction** 1
MARGARET S. ARCHER, UNN-DORIS K. BÆCK AND TONE SKINNINGSRUD

PART I
Morphogenetic cycles, the contextualization of education and educational development 11

2 **The structures of state educational systems and why they matter: Norway and Denmark compared** 13
MARGARET S. ARCHER AND TONE SKINNINGSRUD

3 **A letter by the Sámi Lutheran missionary Thomas von Westen: A critical realist perspective on contextualization** 38
RANDI SKJELMO

4 **Vindicating Archer's concepts of educational systems – centralized and decentralized – as exemplars of critical realist theorizing** 53
TONE SKINNINGSRUD

PART II
The spatial context of educational mechanisms 77

5 **Towards a critical realist ontology for spatial education analysis** 79
UNN-DORIS K. BÆCK

6   Structural constraints on teachers' work: Comparing work
    experiences in rural and urban settings in Northern Norway   98
    DANIEL ANDRE VOLL RØD

7   Reflexivity and educational decision-making processes
    among secondary school pupils   122
    ANNA-MARIA STENSETH AND DANIEL ANDRE VOLL RØD

PART III
**External and internal conditioning of educational interaction
and practice**   145

8   The impact of PISA on education in Norway: A morphogenetic
    perspective on structural elaboration in an education system 147
    TERJE ANDRÉ BRINGELAND

9   School leaders' reflexive mode in their internal conversations
    on PISA   181
    TERJE ANDRÉ BRINGELAND

10 The worldwide language issue in education   211
    BIRGIT BROCK-UTNE

    Index   231

Notes on Contributors

Margaret S. Archer is Emeritus Professor at the University of Warwick, UK. Her books include Social Origins of Educational Systems; Culture and Agency: The Place of Culture in Social Theory; Realist Social Theory: The Morphogenetic Approach; Being Human: The Problem of Agency; Structure, Agency and the Internal Conversation; Making our Way Through the World; The Reflexive Imperative; Late Modernity: Trajectories towards Morphogenic Society; Generative Mechanisms Transforming the Social Order; Morphogenesis and the Crisis of Normativity; and Morphogenesis and Human Flourishing.

Unn-Doris K. Bæck is a professor of sociology at UiT the Arctic University of Norway, Department of Social Sciences. Her main research interests are within the sociology of education and the sociology of youth. A common denominator in her research has been an interest in social and spatial inequalities. This has led her to investigate different systems, such as education and the labor market, and different variables, such as social background, gender, ethnicity and place, as well as the intersections between these, in order to reveal how inequalities are produced and reproduced. Dr. Bæck has conducted comparative studies in a number of different countries.

Terje André Bringeland is PhD candidate in Education at UiT The Arctic University of Norway, Department of Education. His main research interest are systemic structures, education policy, tests, power-relations, autonomy, accountability, leadership, and professionalism. His interests have led him to investigate the Norwegian education system and how the PISA (Programme for International Student Assessment) test has affected systemic structures and school personnel in order to understand their professional autonomy, concerns and actions with the test.

Daniel Rød is PhD-candidate in sociology at UiT the Arctic University of Norway, Department of Social Sciences. His background is in social anthropology, sociology and pedagogy, and he is currently finishing a PhD in the sociology of education. His main research interests are tied to structural inequalities in rural education, focusing especially on educational systems and education politics.

Tone Skinningsrud is professor emeritus in education at The Department of Education, University of Tromsø, The arctic University of Norway. Her research contributions are in the areas of educational history, the sociology of education and comparative education, with a special emphasis on educational policy and politics. The theoretical perspectives of her research contributions are inspired by Roy Bhaskar's philosophy, critical realism, and Margaret S. Archer's morphogenetic approach, in particular Archer's foundational study of 'Social origins of educational systems'.

Randi Skjelmo is Associate Professor in Education at University of Tromsø, in the Department of Education. Her field of expertise is History of Education. Among her publications are the article 'Education of Teachers for Northern Norways before 1826. Skjelmo har in 2017, together with Professor Liv Helene Willumsen, published the book *Thomas von Westens liv og virke [Thomas von Westen's life and work]*. Additionally, Skjelmo is the leader of the research project, The beginning of Teacher Education in the North.

Anna-Maria Stenseth is a PhD-candidate in pedagogy at UiT The Arctic University of Norway, Department of Education. Her main research interests are within education and the sociology of youth. In her PhD study, she investigates how gender and ethnicity are actualized according to space, and in which ways the intersection between gender, ethnicity and place affect educational opportunities and orientations.

Birgit Brock-Utne is affiliated to the University of Oslo as a Professor in Education and Development (http://www.uv.uio.no/iped/english/people/aca/bbrock/index.html). Her main research interests are within the field of socio-linguistics, especially the language of instruction in developing as well as in the Nordic countries. She was a Professor at UDSM, Tanzania (1988–1992). She has been a Visiting Professor at several universities and colleges in the US, in South Africa, in Britain, Japan, Austria, Spain and in New Zealand. In 2011 she was the President of BAICE. She was the Norwegian coordinator of the Language of Instruction in Tanzania and South Africa project which ran from 2001 until 2013.

1 Introduction

Margaret S. Archer, Unn-Doris K. Bæck and Tone Skinningsrud

Introduction

The present volume is a result of Margaret S. Archer's engagement as visiting professor from 2017 to 2019 in the Department of Education at UiT The Arctic University of Norway. While in Tromsø, professor Archer worked with the research group Space and Time in Education (STED), whose research interest has been to investigate temporal and spatial aspects of educational change. The numerous seminars and workshops where members of the research group had the opportunity to present and discuss their work resulted in the chapters presented in this book. The chapters revolve around the employment of concepts and analytic approaches from critical realism and the morphogenetic approach in education analysis of developmental traits and the state of different parts of the Norwegian education system.

UiT The Arctic University of Norway is placed in the North of Norway, a region with distinctive characteristics compared to other parts of the country, notably its dispersed population, i.e., the prevalence of rural settlements and the historical presence of the Sami people, who have inhabited the land and used it for reindeer herding. As a Nordic and Scandinavian country, Norway is often associated with 'The Nordic Model', a label used to designate both its social structure, political organization and its educational system. Since Scandinavian languages and cultures are similar, and to outside observers may seem almost identical, the differences between these countries are often not appreciated. In addition, internal regional (geographical/spatial) differences in each of the countries are often overlooked.

One aspect of Norwegian history that is almost forgotten in contemporary discussions on the present, and possibly the future, is that Norway was united with Denmark for several hundred years. From the time of the Lutheran reformation, in 1536, and until the end of the Napoleonic wars, in 1814, Norway was a province of Denmark, ruled by the Danish monarch. The uneven development of 'the Norwegian province' and the rest of the Danish conglomerate state did not start with the dissolution of the union. However, development might be seen to increasingly diverge after 1814, when the countries were established as distinct political entities. Norway

DOI: 10.4324/9781003163527-1

adopted a modern Constitution in 1814, at the time of the separation from Denmark, while Denmark remained an absolute monarchy until 1849.

The present volume directs attention to two aspects of educational systems that are often overlooked, namely the spatial (geographical) situatedness of educational institutions and the temporal dimension of educational development, accounting for how current changes are conditioned by pre-existing structures.

Another aspect of the history of the Northern region of Europe, which is often overlooked, is the educational history of the Sámi people. The Sámi, originally a dispersed group of hunters inhabiting the northern inland of Norway, Sweden, Finland and parts of Russia, during the Viking Age and the early Middle Ages, emerged as a consolidated ethnic group with its distinct source of livelihood, culture and language (Hansen and Olsen 2014, 732). The area historically inhabited by the Sámi people transcends past and present political borders between the northern regions of Norway, Sweden, Finland and Russia, and does not include Denmark. The northern border between the kingdoms of Denmark-Norway and Sweden-Finland was not settled until 1751, and the Norwegian border with Russia was not until 1826. Thus, with the consolidation of state powers in the 17th and 18th centuries in Denmark-Norway and Sweden-Finland, the citizenship of the Sámi nomads who moved their herds over large stretches of land, part of which were contested by the nation states in the region, became an issue.

In 1716, when Thomas von Westen, the Lutheran Missionary, was appointed by the Danish-Norwegian king Frederik IV's Missionary Collegium to lead the Sámi mission, the border in the north was not yet settled. One of the reasons why a mission among the Sámi was initiated is assumed to have been the competition between the Danish-Norwegian and Swedish-Finnish states for land and tax-paying subjects in the north. Of course, the missionaries themselves had other motives, and their work had other consequences than strengthening Sámi loyalty to the Danish-Norwegian crown. Chapter 3 in this book tells parts of the story and achievements of Thomas von Westen, who initiated and lead the early mission among the Sámi for eleven years. His work resulted in the establishment of several elementary schools for the Sámi long before the rest of the population in the north were provided with organized schooling.

Morphogenetic cycles, the contextualization of education and educational development

The first chapter, written by Margaret S. Archer and Tone Skinningsrud, makes two major points: firstly, that state educational systems (SES) have causal effects on how education operates and develops, and secondly, that the widespread conception of 'The Nordic Model' is an oversimplification that obscures the differences between educational systems in the Scandinavian and Nordic countries. The authors raise the question: why did Denmark

Introduction 3

become a copybook example of a *decentralized* SES whilst Norway exemplified structural *centralization*? The chapter compares the processes resulting in the emergence of the Norwegian centralized and the Danish decentralized educational system, starting with Archer's definition of an SES and specifying their structures: Unification, Systematization, Differentiation and Specialization. The distinction between centralized and decentralized educational systems is explicated, and an analytical narrative is provided of educational development during the 19th century in both countries, at the end of which the Danish and the Norwegian systems emerged. The narrative suggests that the Danish system was established through the incorporation of existing independent educational networks that were *specialized* and *differentiated* upon which *unification* and *systematization* were superimposed. The Norwegian system, on the other hand, was gradually constructed from above, forging the unification of a bifurcated structure by means of a policy of restriction. The Danish thriving 'third' sector consisting of partly private real schools had no equivalent in the Norwegian context. The endurance, in Denmark of the real schools and free schools, at the primary level, ensured a sizable sector of private schools, which endured throughout the 20th century. Even today Denmark has a larger sector of private schools than the other Scandinavian countries, while Norway has virtually been without private schools for the major part of the 20th century. Norway is still the Scandinavian country with the lowest percentage of private schools. The chapter, towards the end, points to two external influences that affect most educational systems during the 20th and 21st centuries, including Denmark and Norway, i.e., the international chains of production adopted by multinational companies and the educational competition instigated by the international testing regime, which includes Program for International Student Assessment (PISA) and its parallels. The authors point out that international production chains tendentially require specialized skills and knowledge at the national level, while educational competition promotes the homogenization and standardization of knowledge. How these conflicting influences play out in the two countries remains to be seen.

The second chapter, written by Randi H. Skjelmo, goes back one century, from Norway's magical year 1814, and the century during which both Norway's and Denmark's educational systems emerged, to the 1700s, when Norway was still a Danish province. The chapter gives an account of early educational establishments associated with missionary work among the Sami population in the north of Norway. Skjelmo uses Archer's model of the morphogenetic cycle (structural conditioning → interaction → structural elaboration) to frame Thomas von Westen's accomplishments in his missionary work among the Sami and the conditions that made them possible. Focusing on a recently recovered letter written by von Westen in 1718 to his superiors in the Royal Ministry of Missions (*Collegium de cursu Evangelii promovendo*) in Copenhagen, Skjelmo points out that von Westen's accomplishments were enabled partly by his official appointment by the Ministry as leader of the Sami mission, partly by his incumbency of positions as a teacher at the Cathedral School and *notarius publicus* in the Norwegian city of Trondheim. In addition, von Westen spent his wealthy wife's entire fortune on building up the Sami Mission in the North. The result of his work at the time of his death in 1727, at the age of 45, was the establishment of 13 Missionary districts covering the whole area of Norway north of Trondheim, each district furnished with its own officially appointed and ordained missionary, 37 elementary schools for the spread of literacy in the mission districts and finally, schools for the education of missionaries, catechists, schoolmasters and assistant catechists, located in Trondheim, the administrative centre of the Sami mission in the North. The schools for the Sami population, established by von Westen, were the first common schools in the North of Norway, providing for the Sami population before schools for the Norwegian inhabitants in the region were established.

In the third chapter, Tone Skinningsrud points out that Margaret Archer's definitions of educational systems – centralized and decentralized – are real definitions in contrast to nominal definitions, i.e. they denote essential characteristics of educational systems rather than just assigning a linguistic meaning to the term 'educational system'. In establishing real definitions, Archer's conceptualizations correspond to Roy Bhaskar's claim that working out real definitions is the basic ambition in all scientific investigations. The chapter gives a short presentation of Archer's definitions and theory of educational systems – centralized and decentralized – focusing on their explanatory power through their identification of mechanisms. Following this, other definitions of educational centralization and decentralization, prevalent in the current international research literature, are presented and discussed. These conceptualizations generally conceive of educational centralization and decentralization as the redistribution of decision-making authority and of decentralization, specifically, as delegation of authority. Also, current definitions of centralization/decentralization as strategies of governance and as degrees of school autonomy are presented and discussed. These other conceptions of educational centralization and decentralization have been applied in recent analyses of Norwegian education, and analyses of the Norwegian educational system using these alternative conceptions of educational decentralization are compared with an analysis using Archer's concepts. The comparison demonstrates that Archer's concepts account for a broader range of phenomena and, therefore, have greater explanatory power than other conceptions of educational centralization and decentralization in current use.

The spatial context of educational mechanisms

The second part of the volume includes three contributions that focus on the spatial context of educational mechanisms. Education is a key factor in the development of any society: economically, socially and culturally. As described above, the education system in Norway can be characterized as centralized, meaning that in theory, teachers, students and their parents shall encounter the same education system no matter where they are or who they are. The societies in which this centralized education system function are rarely, however, uniform in the same way. Even though Norway on the surface may come across as a homogenous society, a progressive welfare state with a value base rooted in egalitarian ideals, with equality and equal rights as important values, it still represents dissimilarities making it heterogenous in many ways. One such heterogeneity is connected to geographical variations, which among other things imply variations when it comes to industrial structures, livelihoods, etc. In Norway (and many other countries), variability of educational performance and trajectories related to geographic location is well documented. While urban education research has had precedence over research focusing on education in rural areas (Bæck, 2015), the three contributions in the second part of the volume focus on rural areas as important areas for investigation. The contributions are especially preoccupied with how space becomes actualized in certain ways in rural and remote areas. However, even though the focus here is on rural and remote, spatialized understandings of educational issues are obviously also relevant in urban and suburban areas.

Spaces are dynamic, changing and temporal. The role of education in societies and the contents of education – the education system itself – changes over time, whether it is through educational reforms (intentional) or as a result of various other factors, for example, through the emergence of international agencies impacting national education systems, or other societal or economic events. Processes affecting space and processes affecting the education system create a complex interplay of events that may produce spatially distinct effects, relevant in order to understand the functioning of the education system, and also educational outcomes, opportunities, achievements, experiences and preferences at the individual level. The three contributions in the second part offer analyses of empirical data collected in different locations in Norway; locations that constitute different educational landscapes or educational spaces. Changes in the national educational system as well as social processes on a global and local scale are important for understanding the production of regional educational spaces. The analyses in the three chapters make it clear that educational phenomena are embedded and unfold in space.

The second part opens with Unn-Doris K. Bæck's chapter entitled 'Towards a Critical Realist Ontology of Spatial Education' (Chapter 4). As the title suggests, Bæck seeks to investigate how the problem of spatial variations and spatial inequalities in education and educational outcomes can be analysed by use of insights from critical realism, thereby contributing with theoretical analyses in a research field, rural education, that is in need of theoretical discussions and advances. The starting point is a critique of what she sees as a tendency to employ explanations focusing primarily on individual characteristics in research on attainment differences in education, thereby overaccentuating the role of the individual as the principal analytic entity. Bæck, therefore, calls for an increased analytical focus at the level of schools, classrooms, local communities, regions or nations. Her starting point, and the empirical basis for the theoretical outlines, is the problem of geographical differences in early school leaving and educational attainment in Norway. Empirical data on upper secondary school students' experiences with the education system are presented. Bæck then goes on to propose an analysis where she uses the interplay between actor and structure as a basis for explaining individual action. By focusing on the material and structural conditions under which young people act and conduct their choices, she shows how societal structures work as causal factors in this regard. Bæck identifies three main generative mechanisms that she sees as particularly significant for explaining spatial differences in educational attainment: the centralized education system, various decentralization reforms and neo-liberal education policy.

In Daniel Andre Voll Rød's chapter, the work experiences of teachers residing in two different locations, one characterized as rural and the other as urban, are compared. Rød takes as his starting point that while the Norwegian educational system is centralized in terms of power distribution, with highly unified educational laws, curriculum and funding models, the uniformity of national policy has not resulted in similar working conditions for all teachers. From interviews with teachers in the rural case municipality, Rød finds that the teachers experienced insufficient school funding, which resulted in a scarcity of necessary equipment and a cutting down of activities that were not seen as strictly needed. Teachers in the urban case municipality, on the other hand, had observed that educational leaders in the municipality used their power in a way that made the teachers question whether their professional authority as teachers were respected and appreciated by the leaders. This was in contrast to the rural teachers who experienced a lack of involvement from their municipality.

With Anna-Maria Stenseth and Daniel Andre Voll Rød's chapter entitled *'Reflexivity and educational decision-making processes among young pupils'*, the focus moves from teachers to pupils. The chapter is based on interview data collected among pupils in two lower secondary schools in one rural and one urban municipality in the north of Norway. The pupils were interviewed on two occasions; first during their final year of lower secondary school, and then followed up a few months after their transition to upper secondary education. Stenseth and Rød employ Archer's understanding of reflexivity to analyse educational decision-making processes among pupils in the transition from lower to upper secondary education. The concept of reflexivity and different modes of reflexivity, as outlined by Archer (2007), are used to analyse how young people conduct choices within existing structures, e.g., educational options and future work opportunities. The analysis suggests that the school system is better suited for certain modes of reflexivity over others, which again might affect future social trajectories.

External and internal conditioning of educational interaction and practice

The final part of the volume takes up the analysis where Chapter 2 left-off, namely with international influences. These are obviously macroscopic in kind, especially when one focus of its chapters is upon the OECD's PISA, whose testing programme Norway joined in 2,000. However, PISA's causal consequences are not confined to the macro level but require attention to the meso level through those processes and practices which are not only affected but also transmit them further downwards to the micro level of individual schools and their teachers whose agents ultimately determine whether they are met by resistance, compliance, or complicity. Fortunately, each of these last chapters deals predominantly with different educational strata – with higher education and academia; with educational establishments in relation to other social institutions; and with lower secondary education and its 'school leaders', reflexively evaluating this novel influence as individual members of the teaching profession. This three-by-three representation could be extremely complex because there is no guarantee of congruence between the cells in terms of processes and practices and, above all, pressures exerted upwards or downwards. Nevertheless, we began in Chapter 2 by defending the historical view that the Norwegian SES emerged and continued to develop as a centralized system, and this gives us certain theoretical expectations. The final part of the volume can helpfully stand as a test for whether or not such hypotheses are corroborated in practice. This will not command consensus amongst students of Norwegian education but it will make our approach and account in this book coherent.

Analytically, three processes for introducing (or blocking) change are expected to be of importance in *decentralized* educational systems as responsible for morphogenesis; *External Transactions* conducted directly with other interested parties outside formal education, *Internal Initiation* introduced directly by teaching personnel in schools and universities and *Political Manipulation* where external demands are affected indirectly through alliances putting pressure on the central polity. All these processes are of roughly equivalent importance in *decentralized systems* (although this statement cannot be metrified), whereas *Political Manipulation* predominates in *centralized systems*. As Bringeland writes in Chapter 8, 'PISA is being marketed as a non-curriculum-based study that tests students' generic knowledge and skills independent of geographic location or national education system, and this ensures PISA's success'. He notes two important omissions here on the part of PISA. First, it neglects the structuring of any SES as was the case for Bernstein and Bourdieu and second, that the spatial distribution of both the 'parts and people', as accentuated in Part 2, is treated as equally irrelevant. Instead, Bringeland adduces evidence that, on the contrary, PISA's 'impact depends on each country's educational structures, disaffections and perceived needs'. Yet, even prior to Norway's participation, the 'OECD advised central Norwegian authorities to reclaim their control of education and make the system more uniform'. This was already in train during the 1990s and one of the prime impacts was to reduce the scope for *Internal Initiation*. The 'side-lining of educational expertise at the municipal level reduced professional input in municipal decision-making and fragmented the local professional community. Professional influence and self-determination in school matters were reduced'. So too were *External Transactions*, with the reinforcement of a national curriculum and a parallel reduction in the municipalities' ability to respond flexibly to local demands. Bringeland illustrates how by corollary *Political Manipulation* of the political parties increased in importance as the avenue for introducing educational change, although he (rightly) refuses to hold PISA solely responsible for this.

In his second chapter (9), Bringeland recognizes the need to examine how PISA, in reinforcing centralized powers, was received and responded to by those proximately involved in implementing complementary changes in the classrooms of Norway, namely the 'School Leaders'. To begin this enterprise he examined the reflexivity of a tiny group of such Leaders and their internal conversations about PISA's findings and recommendations. Although he did not encounter virulent hostility towards this OECD influence, perhaps of greater significance was the general incomprehension of these experienced teachers about what was meant to change in classroom practice that would reap the promised benefits for their pupils. They were willing to attend courses to discover the answers and despite this possibly indicating a compliant if not complicit attitude; it did encourage the expectation that the teaching profession would not be a major pressure group in the initiation of an alternative classroom agenda for everyday teaching practice. Much further research is required here concerning this rather passive response, as Bringeland recognizes, but were such studies to provide substantiation, then this induced attitudinal subordination would contribute immensely to the reduced significance of internal initiation.

The last chapter (10) by Birgit Brock-Utne, well known for her global experience and influence, returns to the macro level and argues passionately that something almost parallel is effectively muting the influence of Norwegian academics. This effect derives from the fact that 'Norwegian as an academic language is increasingly being threatened by English at masters and doctoral levels', with knock-on consequences for publishing and international recognition of research. Although the use and survival of the Sami indigenous language had been given legal protection, this was refused for Norwegian after a considerable political battle at the start of the new millennium. At times, the reasoning became crystal clear; learning in English from the reception class onwards, would, it was claimed, give pupils easier access to the global labour market. This consideration seemed to completely override the distinction between learning a language as a subject and having that language convey all instruction. Not only did this weaken social integration (with children communicating less fluently with their grandparents) but the confluence of external influences (including the EU's Bologna Declaration [1999], plus the market motivated policy of Publishing houses and the League Tables for Journals all worked in the same direction – intensifying intellectual commodification).

Academics were not passive recipients of these influences, and in 2006, 223 distinguished professors in the Humanities and Social Sciences launched a petition stating that universities have a responsibility to defend Norwegian as an academic language. However, not only was the petition unsuccessful, but decade after decade saw more Masters' theses and PhDs submitted in English. It is sad that Birgit Brock-Utne could not have given us a modern, academic version of David and Goliath for she has fought against the strong tendency that she describes for us.

In sum, what the chapters making up this book serve to underscore is how difficult it is for a country of 5 million people to resist such a confluence of concerted external influences from organized blocks of other nations, as we speculated at the end of Chapter 1. What then has this volume added? The answer is no more cheerful but, at least, we hope it has demonstrated how the existence and persistence of a centralized Educational System is a structure whose generative mechanism supports standardization and is deaf to demands for policies and practices in response to those seeking diversification.

References

Archer, M. S. (2007). *Making Our Way through the World: Human Reflexivity and Social Mobility*. Cambridge, UK: Cambridge University Press.

Bæck, U.-D. K. (2015). Rural location and academic success: Remarks on research, contextualisation and methodology. *Scandinavian Journal of Educational Research*. doi:10.1080/00313831.2015.1024163

Hansen, L. I. and B. Olsen. (2014). *Hunters in Transition: An Outline of Early Sámi History*. Leiden/Boston: Brill.

Part I
Morphogenetic cycles, the contextualization of education and educational development

2 The structures of state educational systems and why they matter

Norway and Denmark compared

Margaret S. Archer and Tone Skinningsrud

Introduction

There are two basic misunderstandings that will be examined in this chapter and then put together because they seem to account for the contradictory and chaotic understandings of educational policy and its generative mechanisms today. Both can largely be explained by the unhelpful desertion of what used to be known as 'comparative and historical' analysis of social institutions in sociology and 'the dry delights of educational administration' by those tracing the regulatory changes in the governance of schools, colleges, and universities. These will be called 'The Neglect of the Educational System' and 'The over-generalization of the "Nordic Model"'.

The argument is that these two are closely related, and for our purpose, which is the explanation of millennial transformations of Norwegian education, reference to social structure, culture, and agency (SAC)[1] are necessary in accounting for shifts in educational policy and practice, it is indispensable to correct them. This is undertaken from the critical realist ontological and methodological approaches that Tone Skinningsrud has summarized in the next chapter.

The neglect of educational systems

Why this negligence?

Unlike social institutions, such as the 'family', 'religion' or 'stratification', whose existence was taken for granted by anthropologists, state educational systems (SESs) are historical and structural newcomers. Of course, there was always 'induction' and 'imitation' among hunter-gatherers, becoming more formalized with pastoralism. Obviously, too, we can date formal schooling back to the medieval Cathedral Schools of various religious orders. But there were no national educational systems. These were novelties, emergent in critical realist terms from certain State leaders[2] accepting that they could derive advantages from them whilst other collective agents – especially the Catholic Religious Orders and Craft Guilds – viewed this as trespassing

DOI: 10.4324/9781003163527-3

on their very different definitions of instruction. Surely, the 'arrival' of a new social institution should have intrigued the early sociologists and posed a barrage of questions such as why, for what ends, consonant or complementary with what other *étatiste* goals, against what opposition? (This especially in cases such as Emperor Napoléon, fully preoccupied with the conquest of Europe, but ready to give extremely explicit answers to those questions.)[3] Although historians supplied details of how particular schools such as Oxford and Cambridge eventually developed into universities, the social scientists remained silent.

SESs were held causally irrelevant

The silence became prolonged. This was nowhere more evident in the 20th century than for Bernstein and Bourdieu, neither of whom ever acknowledged the SES as a distinct stratum of education with its own properties and powers. Instead, it was once more neglected, and education was treated as a permeable membrane. Both Bernstein and Bourdieu, for all their insights, had universalized their theorizing as if the systemic contexts from which these SESs had originated (and to which they were then applied) were irrelevant and could be treated as a common bland background, like magnolia paintwork.

Both theories were based on a set of assumptions, which served to occlude differences between educational structures and how they relate to their social contexts. These assumptions can be distilled into three propositions:

a The *penetrability* of educational institutions by definition (by 'class codes' and 'cultural arbitraries', respectively).
b The universal *complementarity* between education and social stratification.
c The consequent *homogenization* of SESs.

The effect of (a) was to eliminate the differential *penetrability* of different structures of SESs and their components, in favour of accentuating educational adaptation to general social change – thus, explaining the absence of educational politics in both theories. The effect of (b), *complementarity* between education and social stratification, was to stress functional similarities at the expense of structural differences, thus highlighting universal not variable processes of change. The effect of (c) was the universalization of processes linking educational and social stratification across educational systems. This is illustrated in Figure 2.1 below, where two of the most different SESs, in terms of origins, operations and outcomes, namely France and England, were treated as alike in their sins of omission and commission by the two theorists.

At that time (the early 1970s), Margaret Archer's main resort was to educational historians (such as Antoine Prost in France and Brian Simon in

Structures of state educational systems

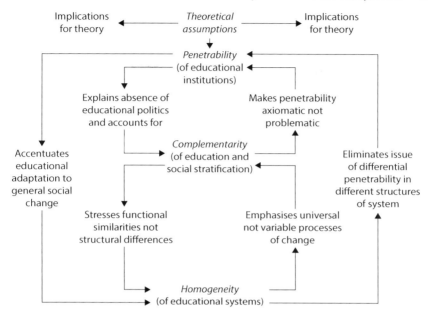

Figure 2.1 Theories making educational systems unimportant.

Source: Archer, 'process without system', 1983, *Archives Européennes de Sociologie*, 219.

England) and their recognition of the ubiquity of educational power struggles, vested interests and increasingly articulate grievances – before, during and after the formation of any country's SES. Just as important was their acknowledgement that parties (mainly the Churches) which previously enjoyed control through their ownership of educational property and provision of teaching personnel may have lost out in the struggles but still battled on and stayed in the educational game.

Morphogenesis as an alternative to homogenization

As co-authors, we both recognized that specific accounts are required in our two countries to explain how particular parts of the social order originated and came to stand in a particular relationship to one another. It was important to ask, whose actions were responsible for this, through which interactions, when and where and with what consequences? In all of this, the practising sociologist has to know a great deal about the historical origins and current operations of each SES.

In response to these questions, the morphogenetic approach was developed in *Social Origins of Educational Systems* (1979 [2013]), stressing the critical realist credo that every social form and its transformation is *activity-dependent* (reliant on agents attempting to realize their goals), *concept-dependent* (their knowing, fallibly under their own descriptions, what they were trying to achieve) and *context-dependent* (on the prior circumstances that defined their capacities and their liabilities when seeking the re-structuring of formal education). The outcomes of this morphogenetic cycle, during which SESs emerged *for the first time* and with distinctive characteristics, are economically presented by Tone Skinningsrud in Chapter 2. All it is necessary to add is a summary of the differences between those SES that emerged in countries where the State successfully dominated in this emergence (that are termed *centralized systems*), as in France and Russia, where the respective States took on the role as the leading educational part) compared with those (termed *decentralized systems* which emerged through incorporating existing networks of educational organizations and then seeking to integrate these parts into a system – as in England and Denmark.) Although all four features in Figure 2.2 are present in any SES, in centralized systems, *Unification* and *Systematization* are strong whilst *Differentiation* and *Specialization* remain weaker. The reverse is the case for decentralized systems.

Lastly, it is essential to remedy certain errors that have attended the understanding of morphogenetic cycles – of which this is only the *first* in relation to SESs, but not the last. In other words, these cycles are plural and sequential, with each earlier one influencing later ones. Therefore, it is a serious mistake to assume that any SES remains identical in its characteristics to those they manifested at their initial point of emergence. Why? In a nutshell because all the SAC relations impinging upon educational systems (their activity-dependence, concept-dependence and context-dependence, as already outlined, are likely to change and not necessarily in synchrony with one another). That is true of any social institution whatsoever; none have unchanging eternal life. Thus, each cycle comprising [$T^1 \rightarrow \{T^2 - T^3\} \rightarrow T^4$], means that T^4 is the new T^1 of a subsequent cycle. Whether given conditions are considered as T^1 or T^4 depends upon the investigator and his/

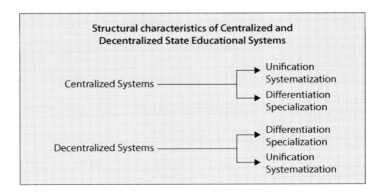

Figure 2.2 By the end of morphogenetic Cycle 1.

her research question and there are justifiable substantive reasons why different cycles should be designated by researchers in dealing with distinctive problems.

The over-generalization of the 'Nordic Model'

Reluctance to endorse the Nordic Model is based strictly though timorously[4] on educational grounds. Namely, the aim is to contrast the Norwegian and the Danish SESs rather than homogenizing the two as co-executors of social policies known variously as promoting 'progressive schooling for all'[5] or 'pioneering the Comprehensive School'. Perhaps being British is not such a bad thing because it forewarns researchers and commentators not to generalize about the four countries making up the UK, especially where education is concerned.

- An SES is defined as 'a nationwide and differentiated collection of institutions devoted to formal education, whose overall control and supervision are at least partly governmental, and whose component parts and processes are related to one another'.[6] This definition stresses that both the political and the systemic aspects should be present together for an SES to exist because either characteristic alone was not unknown in European history. Accounts need to begin here because the emergence of SESs was an institutional novelty occurring at different times in different countries and marking a new boundary between the State and civil society. The main argument is that at their origins in the first decade of the 20th century, Denmark's SES was *decentralized* whilst that of Norway was *centralized*, and the main question examined here is whether *centralization* and *decentralization* made a significant difference to the role that other parts of civil society could play in subsequent educational transformation? This question cannot even arise if the two systems are not differentiated from one another at their point of origin.[7]
- In the rest of the West when social scientists explained what they meant by the 'Nordic Model' they took refuge in generalizations, such as 'endorsing neither unbridled capitalism nor coercive State socialism'; somewhat later as 'Welfare states'; and considerably later as the actualization of Giddens' 'Third Way'. None of these are helpful for institutional analysis since many social forms could fit the bill as falling into these three different notions of being in 'the middle'. If sociologists collectively, though somewhat reluctantly, accepted that historically there were multiple forms of capitalism,[8] then it logically followed that they could not have had identical 'middles'. The point is where did this leave their SESs?

Each social science discipline seemed to offer different accounts and explanations. Most hinged on the role of the respective national Social Democratic Parties. Educationalists accentuated their increased responsiveness to the global market by the 20th century and are epitomized in the following overview. '(T)he almost uniform view amongst educationalists is that market-led reforms are a result of the increasing power of the Right, which has gained sufficient power to push through reforms aiming at creating a quasi-market for education'.[9] This summation was fraught with the problem that different trajectories were followed by the various Social Democratic Parties in Scandinavia. Indeed, the authors of the previous quotation were forthright in remarking that Norway has been the least affected by neo-liberal reforms.[10] In turn, that now leads to three questions – one about the SESs, the second about the particular nature of Social Democracy in Nordic countries and the third concerns the temporal relations between the two institutions. These can only be answered by backtracking to the Cycle 1 analysis of the SES, the nature of Social Democratic politics at the time and the subsequent relations between them. It is not possible to provide a serious analysis within a single chapter.

- The explanatory quest is to identify the generative mechanism(s) responsible for change over more than a century. Ontologically, these are real, even if we fail to discover them fully. It is never a substitute for the investigator to impose their own teleology upon their own descriptions, which is merely a version of the epistemic fallacy. In particular, and desirable as they might be, the pursuit of normative goals such as the 'maintenance of social solidarity' or the establishment of 'equality of educational opportunity or outcomes' can only be attributed to historic agents – if they had said so and attempted to do so. That being the case, we are returned to the original set of questions, who wanted such changes, for what reasons, against the opposition of which other groups and with what outcomes. Since the consequential results are more likely to be the results of negotiated compromise than of unimpeded zeal for transformation by one party, the analysis of institutional relations is inevitable throughout Cycle 1.

Next, much the same issues are considered during 'late' modernity. In Norway and Denmark, SESs had always operated in the context of representative democracy but now globalization began seriously to intrude, which was far from being the case at their origins. The concluding section focusses briefly on the new millennium and asks whether the novel, global structural and cultural transformations, whose most obvious effect was to generate digitalization, may have distinctive impacts on education, modifying the SESs of Norway and Denmark still further from their initial differences in structuring and from one another? In short, does it remain valid to regard the former as centralized and the latter as decentralized? Much of this is sketchy and tentative. Any conviction that it carries is predicated upon the assumption that it is now possible to discern the first signs of modernity being superseded – a prospect which the 'Centre for Social

Ontology' examined in five volumes, under the general title of 'Social Morphogenesis'.[11]

Emergence of State educational systems: Norway and Denmark contrasted

This section merely summarizes the key points held to explain why the two countries arrived at the end of Cycle 1 with different structures of SESs by the last decade of the 19th century (following the break-up of the Union between the two countries in 1814). Why did Denmark become a copybook example of a *decentralized* SES whilst Norway exemplified structural *centralization?* These points are presented in order of importance with each linked to its successor. Unsurprisingly, they start with 'context dependence', which was found educationally when the Union split because some social sector of each society had previously considered them worth founding and maintaining. In other words, that section had an interest in a particular form of instruction, which could have been material, ideal or usually both.

At the end of the union, the major types of educational institutions were largely the same in the two countries. They were run, financed, and staffed by very different groups in terms of prestige and purpose:

- Elementary schools, mainly serving catechetical goals, but regulated by the state and with state church clerical staff as overseers and super-ordinates.
- The Learned Schools and universities, whose land, and buildings at the time of the Reformation had been expropriated from the Church, became more dependent on fees from professionals, richer burghers and state officials of the landowning political elite, and concentrated upon a classical academic curriculum. This confirmed the status of the landed gentry (especially in Denmark) and formed traditional servants of the State.
- Private Proprietary Schools opened and operated by the commercial classes (town burghers). These prepared for careers in business and were the only type of higher-grade school in urban areas.

Though the major types of educational institutions were largely the same, the volume of provisions and coverage were more uneven in Norway than in Denmark. There were fewer Learned Schools and the provision of elementary schooling was uneven in rural areas. In Denmark, in 1814, after more than three decades of work invested by the 'Great School Commission' (established in 1789), five separate acts on elementary education were passed: for rural areas, the townships, Copenhagen (the capital), the Jewish population in Denmark and the German Duchies of Schleswig-Holstein (which until 1864 were part of the Danish conglomerate state). Obviously, Norway was left out among the Danish 'regions' and groups that received new elementary school legislation in 1814. The 1814 political events interrupted the work of an appointed commission for a new act on Norwegian elementary schooling, which was not resumed. Yet, the 'Norwegian Constitution of 1814 gave no indication as to how the country's education system ought to be organized and developed. Though a preliminary act for elementary education in rural and urban areas, consisting of three paragraphs, was passed by the new Parliament (*Storting*) in 1816, the Primary School Act of 1827 for rural areas was the first comprehensive piece of legislation to establish compulsory education in a democratically governed Norway'.[12] The Act was comprehensive in the sense that it covered the whole country with uniform requirements for all geographical areas as opposed to legislation during the later phase of Danish absolutism which had often targeted specific regions.[13]

Major political events affected social and educational development in Denmark during the first half of the 19th century. Firstly, on 5 January 1813, the Danish state declared bankruptcy caused by the financial burdens of participating on the losing side in the Napoleonic Wars. The Danish currency was devalued, which negatively affected commerce, industry, and the population at large. The commercial class and wealthy town burghers who had financed many burgher (proprietary) schools during the previous couple of decades were no longer able to do so. Many of these schools were closed or merged with public Latin (Learned) Schools. The 1814 elementary education act for the merchant towns had included the option of establishing local Real Schools (secondary schools) conditional on the willingness of parents to cover the costs. But the general crisis turned these into 'paper promises' and such schools did not become economically viable until the 1830s.[14]

A major political event was the abolition of absolutism and Denmark's adoption of a modern democratic Constitution in 1849, with serious educational consequences for the Lutheran church. The Danish Constitution was modelled after the Belgian, which was considered more liberal and democratic than most constitutions at the time. Under absolutism there was no religious freedom, a Danish citizen was automatically a member of the evangelical-Lutheran church and parents were obliged to teach their children the principles of the state church. The new Constitution altered this. Now, members of any religion could participate in the political process, and in 1850, a bill concerning freedom of belief was passed by the Parliament (*Rigsdagen*), which granted the parents of a child the right to decide in which faith it should be raised.

The Free School Act of 1855 was a direct consequence of the new Constitution, which guaranteed freedom of religion. This was also seen to guarantee the right for people to set up their own schools, subject to supervision from the authorities. Thus, the basic principle of parental rights in choice of schooling was established. The duty to attend the common school (*skolepligt*) was replaced by the duty to receive education (*undervisningspligt*). Parents could educate their children themselves at home or organize a school together with other parents.[15] The Free School Act enabled the development of a free-school movement promoting schools named after N. F. S. Grundtvig (*De grundtvigske-koldske friskoler*). Originating in rural areas, the content of the Free schools was defined by the parents and the local community rather than the state. The state provided national guidelines and supervision. Referring to the Danish Constitution and to Grundtvig, the Free school movement, still vital at the end of the 20th century, at that time claimed to uphold two kinds of freedom, parental rights vis à vis the state and the rights of minorities in a democracy.[16]

The Real School movement in Denmark also originated around the mid-19th century. It represented a challenge to the traditional Latin Schools, which had been reformed in 1809, but also some degree of cooperation. The 1809 reform which was implemented in both Norway and Denmark gave the Latin Schools their new name 'Learned Schools' and at the same time established them as secular schools. They were no longer closely affiliated with the church and students and teachers no longer participated in daily church services. The 1809 Learned School Act had represented an attempt to promote a Real School curriculum as an integrated part of their program. This effort was not successful, but it reflected the debate which was ongoing in both countries turning on whether the knowledge sought by the burghers, 'Real' subjects, which included both the sciences and modern languages as well as more trade and vocationally oriented subjects should be offered in separate schools or integrated in the traditional Latin or Learned establishments which excelled in classic languages and literature.

The burgher schools had around the 1790s and at the beginning of the 19th century proliferated in both Norway and Denmark, and their intake of students exceeded the intake in the Latin (later Learned) Schools. However, in Norway, already the 1809 act on Learned Schools was seen by one of the most established burgher schools in the Nordic countries, the 'Trondheim burgher and real school' (*Trondhjem borger og realskole*) (established in 1784), as an opportunity to fit into the structure of public education. This prospect was embraced due to the economic difficulties experienced by the Trondheim school. The 1809 act allowed the lower grades of the Learned Schools (incomplete Learned Schools, also called Middle Schools) to be established as separate institutions, and the course of the burgher school could be made to fit with the requirements of these incomplete Learned Schools.

In the Norwegian capital, Oslo, towards the mid-19th century, an educational reformer, Hartvig Nissen, who was later engaged to work for the Ministry, established a new type of school which included both the program of Real Schools and the classical curriculum, a combined school. This idea was picked up by the Ministry, and at the mid-century it was decided in Parliament that only Learned Schools which had established a combined program, which also included a Real-curriculum, would receive financial support from the state. Soon after, in 1867, a state appointed commission, headed by the same educational reformer and entrepreneur Nissen, delivered a White Paper which recommended that the Learned School should have two tracks in its upper classes, one for science studies and one for classical studies. Both tracks would qualify for university entry. This arrangement was adopted by the Norwegian Parliament in their passing of the 1869 Act on Public Schools for Higher General Formation (*Lov om Offentlige Skoler for den Høiere Almendannelse*). Their new name signalled the broadening of these schools' programme. The Act entailed that 'Realists', i.e., students of the natural sciences were allowed to matriculate at the university. This had formerly been the prerogative of students of classical languages. The previous course of the Learned Schools was sectioned into two distinct levels, i.e., the first six years, called 'the Middle School', which was terminated by a final exam, and would qualify for employment at lower levels of administration and office work, and a three-year course on top of the Middle School, which would qualify for university admission. Thus, the Real (burgher) Schools had been absorbed as part of the Learned Schools. The new Middle School, which was identical with the lower classes of the Learned Schools, proved to be a success in terms of enrolment, and after 1869, the Norwegian state funded numerous Middle Schools in the towns all over the country.

This development in Norwegian education was mentioned to the Danish political authorities in 1867, when the Nissen-commission had presented its proposal. In Denmark as well, opinions differed regarding the institutional setting of the science ('Real') study program, whether it should be offered in separate (Real) schools or as an additional program in the established Learned Schools. Official recognition of scientific qualifications had been acceded in Germany in 1832, by instituting a certificate in science knowledge (real-examen). In Denmark, after the economic crisis in the 1820s, both solutions were tried out, i.e., science departments in classical institutions, like the Sorø Academy in 1837, and the establishment of separate Real Schools. Two Real Schools were established in Århus and Odense in 1839. However, recruiting students to the independent Real Schools proved difficult, and in 1854, a proposal was made in the Danish Parliament to establish science classes in the Learned Schools.[17] This resulted in a legal act, passed in 1855, which established departments of science in the Learned Schools, instituted a public exam (*den almindelige forberedelseseksamen*) and, moreover also permitted private and municipal schools to organize the exam. There was an instant increase in the number of private Real Schools.[18] In 1859, a lower and a higher certificate of science studies were instituted, which secured admission to specific fields of study at the university. In 1867, when it was brought to the attention of the inspector of the Danish Learned Schools, J. N. Madvig, that Norway was about to accept 'Real' students on an equal footing with students of the classical curriculum for university entry, he rejected the idea as irrelevant for Denmark. He claimed that science subjects in the Learned Schools must be considered subsidiary school subjects, which were taught for a limited time-period, thus, they could not be considered as equal to the classical curriculum.[19] However, the Real Schools continued to thrive: from a modest early phase, around 1850, when there were 20 Real Schools, the number increased to more than 138 in 1896. In 1929, there were 250 such schools, and in 1960, more than 800. The Real Schools included a diversity of private, municipal, and state schools, which also varied in terms of content. The main thing which unified them was their publicly recognized exam(s), which changed over the years.

Thus, during the latter part of the 19th century before the Norwegian and the Danish SESs emerged around 1900, the Norwegian educational structure consisted of two major tracks, the schools for general higher formation (*høiere almendannelse*) with their combined programme, which required special private preparatory schools for elementary instruction, and the common elementary school, whose final exam was confirmation in the church, and which had no school above it. This was all changed in 1889, when the name of the common school was changed to 'the school for the people' (*folkeskolen*). Aiming to recruit the whole national age cohort of seven-year-olds, the school's seven-year course was made obligatory, and schools were mandated to organize their own final exam, independent of the church. This reform of the common school was followed in 1896 by a reform of 'the higher school for general formation'. To enable pupils to proceed from the *folkeskole*, the common elementary school, to the higher school for general formation (*høiere almendannende skoler*), the number of grades in the higher schools was truncated. The transformation of education from two tracks (one of them with a dead end) to one ladder was made at the expense of the higher schools. By the end of the 19th century, in Norway, Real Schools of the Danish type had not emerged.

One may speculate about why this was so. One causal factor may be that although Norwegian Middle Schools, established in 1869, were geared to prepare for occupational life, their programs seem to have been more unified than the programs of the Danish Real Schools. Alternatively, the social strata that were recruited to the Norwegian Middle Schools and the Danish Real Schools during the latter part of the 19th century - which seem to have been similar in terms of the qualifications they provided - were less numerous in Norway than in Denmark, and perhaps more lacking in economic resources in Norway. But, however this state of affairs may be explained, the lack of or the presence of a network of intermediate schools, qualifying for largely lower middle-class occupations, affected the processes in the two countries that led to the emergence of the SES, resulting in a centralized system in Norway and a decentralized system in Denmark.

It seems useful to summarize the key features distinguishing the two countries during the 19th century in educational and theoretical terms. That is, *what prior contextual features are held here to have constituted key explanatory factors during the T^1 and $T^2 - T^3$ phases of morphogenesis in education.* These are presented sequentially and based upon the historical digest presented above. They have been condensed into three factors distinguishing between Norway and Denmark in terms of the different conditional influences exerted on educational development by their social structures after the separation of the two countries in 1814.

First, at the time of the split between them, the educational provisions were rather similar in Norway and Denmark and to neither did education appear as a top priority. In Norway, the 1814 Constitution did not provide any blueprints for educational reform, though the Constitutional Assembly had taken a stand on adopting *national* rather than *regional* educational legislation. An initial provisional act (consisting of only three paragraphs) but covering the whole country was passed in 1816 and the first detailed act for common schools in rural areas in 1827. In Denmark, the adoption of the 1849 Constitution, preceded by the emergence of religious revivalist movements opposing the state church, created a favourable climate for greater educational freedom. The Free School Act of 1855, granting parental choice also guaranteed the right of the people to set up their own schools, reflecting their own local persuasions. In this, we can already note *the uniformity of the first Norwegian steps and the freedom for diversity characterizing Denmark's.*

Second, note the neat alignment of the initial three types of educational establishments in Denmark with the divisions of its class structure, which was lacking in Norway where educational provisions worked largely on binary lines. Thus, the educational interaction that began to make headway, although founding an SES was not what motivated Danish interest groups to engage in it. But the protection and advancement of their own networks certainly did – and it did so for all three sections of society involved – the upper classes, the burghers, and active sections among the people. Increasingly these foundational groups sought to outdistance one another. The most thrusting were the burghers in Denmark, mounting a challenge on class lines with their practical Real Schools to the elitist, classicist Learned Schools. This resulted in undiluted competition, with the Real Schools numerically exceeding the Learned Schools by the end of the 19th century. Much less successful in Norway, instead of strengthening *competition*, the protagonists of Real Schooling promoted the *compromise* of a 'combined school', one whose curriculum included Real subjects alongside the classical and the only one to receive state aid, confirmed by the 1869 Act. After this legislation, the first six years were designated as 'Middle Schools', which the state co-funded throughout Norway. In short, the pressure behind the incorporation of the Real definition of instruction represented a major move towards much higher *unification in Norway*, whilst *in Denmark* on the contrary, it fostered a considerable *rise in private schooling*, outside the ambit of the state. The key differences between the centralized and the decentralized SESs-to-be were already being laid down.

Third, the divergences between these national educational provisions were augmented by the Norwegian 1889 transformation of all primary instruction into the one folk-school (*folkeskolen*) for every seven-year-old, followed in 1896 by reform of the 'higher general school' through dovetailing the curricula between primary and secondary levels. Conversely, again, in Denmark, diversity of provisions increased in the mid-century with the spread of Grundtvigian Free Schools in rural areas, whose definition of instruction was supplied by local parents and community rather than the state. Its contents focussed on Grundtvig's philosophy of human relations with nature and the associated folk culture.[20] As their popularity increased, Folk High Schools were developed, thus consolidating a distinctive set of educational values amongst the rural populace.

In sum, not only had educational conflict become associated *with conflict between the political parties in Denmark*, but the former was strong enough to modify the latter into the Union of the Right and of the Left in the same year. The Left supported the rural Folk High schools and put its weight behind the urban Real Schools, whilst the Right supported the Learned Schools and the Universities.

Although *Venstre*, on the left at its inception, could make no inroads in or against Secondary and Higher education, it did furnish increasing Government grants for the rural Folk High schools after 1892, without significant loss of their autonomy; an annual subsidy for the urban *Fri* schools, thus legitimating the private sector, which had found 'school pence are too low for the school but too high for the home'.[21] Hence, *by 1901, when Venstre came to power for the first time, it confronted networks that had been strengthened by 30 years of political checks and balances*[22] *between different interest groups and whose divergent definitions of instruction had remained largely intact despite the development of a State administrative framework*.[23]

Educational and political opposition, thus, tracked one another, with public elementary schools becoming the starting point for most children until 11 years old, with Real Schools as the urban alternative. The Right immediately sought to consolidate the historic role of Learned Schools as the gate keepers to higher education. Although later modifications (1903) made transition possible from the Folk school to a Higher School, *this was effectively a proposal for partition along the lines traced out by the independent networks*. The only party that lost out was the Lutheran Church as clerical supervision had been virtually eliminated, starting in 1809 with the Learned Schools.

Thus, in Denmark, the process of incorporating the various networks was one in which *unification* and *systematization* were superimposed on networks that were *specialized* and *differentiated*. The situation was the reverse in Norway. Upon independence, there was not the same variety or coverage of schooling (which educational historians usually attribute to the geographical dispersal of the population and severity of the climate). Just as important was the Constitution of 1814, *that contained no blueprint for the structure and functioning of education or its control*. The urban mercantile class was small and concentrated in towns. In brief, there were no flourishing networks, each with its sponsoring group, and therefore an absence of the superimposition of vested educational interests and types of schools.

The Primary School Act of 1827 was, thus, the first piece of legislation to establish compulsory education in a democratically governed Norway.[24] Crucially, this set the pattern for central control, not that any group was actively challenging it or that some Nordic Napoleon had clear views about how education could serve the State;[25] the point was to ensure that neither particular material interests nor specific ideological convictions should take over the driving seat.

From the above, it seems that the key feature in Norway was one of *absence* – the lack in 1814 of any broad plan prior to Norwegian Independence of what any potential or aspirant Government sought from education and how they thought to operationalize it institutionally and legally.[26]

What is the relevance of this to Norway in 1814? Is it fair to say that there was an absence of educational planning? Yes, if this refers to the absence of a macroscopic plan for that novelty at that date (a pre-designed SES). No, if the referent is to a general 'respect' for what schools existed and appeared to serve the manifest needs of different sections of the population and to do so fairly. After all, a new State, one of whose first acts was to abolish the aristocracy, and which continued its negativity towards privileged attendance at private schools, did display its general commitment to egalitarianism. It is probably this that later allowed Norwegian education to be swept up (by outside commentators) into the 'Nordic Model'. That is easier to do than to analyse the processes by which the SES was gradually constructed in the absence of a grand plan. It becomes feasible if attention is directed to Figure 2.2 and its accentuation of *unification* and *systematization*.

The emergence of the Norwegian SES by the 1890s had essentially consisted in 'bridging the gap between Primary and Secondary education'. In other words, the Norwegian SES was put together piece meal, *but always from the top down*. Since new legislation was needed for each addition, care was taken that the respective regulations should dovetail with one another, in terms of age groups' eligibility, entrance requirements and to which further forms of instruction graduates could progress.

By 1945, numerous specialized schools were still outside the educational system such as apprenticeship schools, workshop schools, technical schools, trade schools, agricultural schools, schools for the fisheries, for seamen, etc. These schools were traditionally regulated by the various relevant ministries. In the 1974 act on upper secondary schools, several of these schools were included in a common structure, further education, and all regulation was transferred to the Ministry of Education. *This is another way of saying that unification and systematization were imposed from the centre, and thus, diversification and specialization were always conditional upon their conformity to the first pair of characteristics.*

If Norway's centralized SES initially faced difficulties typical to such structures of systems in accommodating sufficient *specialization* to meet local needs, Denmark confronted the opposite problem. Given it had originated by *incorporation* of the independent networks founded by distinct sectors of the population, their *unification* or principled *systematization* was strongly contested. The novel Middle School (*Mellemskole*) was designed to bridge the gap between the Folk School and the gymnasium (the old Learned Schools) and at the same time incorporate the established Real School. Successful in preserving their distinct identity and specialization, organized partly as Real Schools and partly as combined Middle and Real Schools, they continued to thrive and proliferate after 1903.

Venstre was forced to compromise in Denmark since it lacked the parliamentary strength to advance the Folk School by imposing its definition of instruction upon higher levels. Nevertheless, as the governing party, it could impose greater changes on the Learned Schools than those voluntarily conceded by their supporters. Hence, the 'organic connection' that the new Middle School established between them in 1903. These needed not to be self-standing institutions but gave something to both networks. The Folk School became primary schooling for all until the age of eleven and retained its Grundtvigian orientation and knowledge relevant to practical rural life, as state grants were to supply the buildings in every area. Subsequently, pupils could remain there for three more years before transferring to a Gymnasium. Alternatively, they could pursue a Real Secondary education. However, the Gymnasium alone qualified for University entrance, thus maintaining the traditional elitist route. It continued its status-conferring role for the landed elite but added advanced level scientific and linguistic services for industry, administration, commerce and diplomacy. Thus, the politics of the possible shaping incorporation had preserved the diversity of services to different parts of society that educational competition had initiated.

As Korsgaard and Wiborg summed up the difference between the two countries and their emergent SESs at the end of Cycle 1, 'in contrast to the Norwegian Social Democrats, who developed a highly centralized school system and eliminated private schools in the process, their Danish counterparts had supported locally controlled schools, and accepted the existence of private schools as long as these were state-supported and non-selective'.[27]

Systemic developments in the 20th century

Social Origins of Educational Systems dwelt on different structures of SESs in terms of their distinctive processes of change, the agents who could make the most use of them, their guiding ideas and their consequences for patterns of change as causal outcomes. There is no need to repeat this here. As was insisted at the start of this chapter, it is invalid to skip from the end of Cycle 1 (c. 1900) to today for the simple reasons that SESs change over time and so does the world. Thus, there is a need for those with the knowledge and skills (especially linguistic) to work out Cycles 2 or 2 and 3. However, it could well be maintained that it took the full 19th century for the two SESs fully to emerge, as, indeed, was the case in England. Nevertheless, since the Constitution was adopted in 1814, Norway had undergone some important macroscopic contextual changes: by the 1930s, parliamentarianism had been introduced in its political system (1884), political parties had been established (1884), universal franchise had been introduced (for workers in 1898, for women in 1913), industrialization had taken place and an urban working class, as well as entrepreneurs, had emerged – starting during the second half of the 19th century. These cannot be treated as irrelevant to the shaping of the Norwegian SES, even were the process held to be as slow as in England.

The social context confronting these two new SESs was not confined to internal features of their own countries, as these never ceased to filter influences from abroad. The main concern of this section is the interaction between each of the two countries and the wider world. Did external influences prompt further divergence or convergence between their SESs? It involves the point at which the concept of a 'Nordic Model' became widely used, at least retrospectively, to apply to the 1930s onwards. An anodyne version of this is the following argument advanced by Esping-Andersen. He maintained that the Social Democrats not only aspired to create the universal welfare state, this was also a political instrument that paved their way to power. The result of their many years in government was the development of welfare states in which the public sector was envisaged as a tool that pursued social equality through producing services itself and thereby disengaging citizens from market dependence. It is the last proposition that seems particularly contentious: welfare provisions certainly cushioned the populace against market downturns and their unequal impacts (see his concentration on unemployment and benefits), but that is not synonymous with 'disengagement' because it omits the market operating as an incentive to at least some of the better-off.

It is also dubious to attribute such universalizing ambitions to each and every Social Democratic Party over a century, given the variety of alliances they contracted in their respective Parliaments, but more interestingly how it impacted on their SESs. In Norway, the new Constitution's executors had something to prove, namely that the changes introduced were generally welcomed, particularly given the voting system became one of proportional representation, despite the absence of a universal (male) franchise.

The key social feature appears to have been the social composition of the agriculturalists, not landless labourers, but an agrarian 'middle class' in a state where the Norwegian farmer had been elevated to the glorious bearer of the national culture. Social Democratic policy rewarded them because welfare payments were not for the destitute and carried no stigma of the 'deserving poor'. On the contrary, since they were paid from general taxation, this entailed a high rate of income tax, as today. They were not a citizenship right but rather for wage earners, still imbued with the Lutheran work ethic. In short, they were conscientious supporters of the new democratic regime, tempted neither towards Marxism after its initial affinity in the 1920s nor aspiring to join new nobility, when they had successfully seen the old abolished by 1821.[28] The party was a member for ComIntern in the 1920s but was excluded because they allowed party membership for the petty bourgeoisie, i.e., fishermen who owned their boats, and they also allowed collective party membership for Labour Unions. Their radicalism, needless to say, did not endure. In the mid-1930, the Labour party formed a minority government supported by the agrarian party.

However, education was not a key issue among the social policies that were being pursued in the first three decades of the 20th century. Education was not considered and was not an essential part of this large-scale transition from class conflict to class compromise and negotiated agreements in national politics. However, educational politics were high on the Social Democratic Party's agenda from the very beginning. Talk about the 'Nordic Model' in education is something much more recent than the Nordic Model in labour relations. The notion of 'The Nordic Model in Education' was introduced after the millennium as a defence against neoliberal educational reforms – highlighting the threat to egalitarian values.

What is particularly revealing is the pragmatism of the Social Democrats towards the secular extension of the SES which had acceded to old and now to new specialized educational training in Norway. Once the administration of primary and secondary schooling had been determined, involving the local authorities, the permanent teaching staff (appointed by the king) and a representative of the Ministry of Education, attention turned to further education. Since the costs were borne by the State, it was unsurprising that earlier initiatives all concerned primary productive activities (Schools for Forestry and Dairy farming) as well as for those staffing the national infrastructure (railways, post, and telegraph). However, what might puzzle in a centralized SES was the willingness to endorse (and finance) extremely specialized forms of training schools, for instance, that for Canning Technology.[29] It seems this was initially financed by local (Stavanger) owners but gained the support of the Labour Party during postwar reconstruction for its job-creation and the increased viability of the coastal fishing communities. Obviously, this specialized vocational training led only to useful employment and it disrupted no other educational provisions.

Much more important was the elimination of most private provisions among 'higher schools', teacher education, etc., as part of the Labour party's commitment to the abolition of private schools of all kinds in the interests of egalitarianism. Prior to Labour's influence in the 20th century, the private elementary schools had already been radically reduced, despite not being prohibited. Norway has virtually been without private schools for the major part of the 20th century. It is still the Scandinavian country with the lowest percentage of private schools.

Multinational production and global educational competition

What should be mentioned briefly in conclusion are two changes in the world that are undeniable and ineluctably had causal consequences for educational systems globally. Again, their full analysis would involve the same SAC features, which is what makes it intricate, especially when comparative. On the other hand, it is all that saves us from importing of yesterday's 'theory' and superimposing it upon education. As was seen earlier, this serves to homogenize SESs as if their structural differences made no difference, the interests of those vested in them were of no explanatory importance and their cultural goals were hot air and not matters of conviction or tools of persuasion. The changes in question are (1) the emergence of multinational enterprises and their international chains of production and (2) the globalization of educational competition between nations.

The first section dwelt exclusively upon Cycle 1, yet as has already been cautioned it would be invalid to consider that these emergent properties endured unchanged since the Norwegian SES was formed, which is what applying them to the present educational context would imply. However, since this chapter is devoted to the emergent nature of the SESs in two counties, it is suggested that there are two prominent forms of social change to which no SES could remain immune – there or elsewhere. In other words, their external social contexts have changed so radically that it is no longer possible to advance predominantly 'internal' accounts of their SAC responses, even though in Scandinavia, these explanations were never exclusively internalist.

The two novel transformations refer firstly to the internationalization of production. This entails something much more than 'import and export' or even mercantilism. It stands for a variety of types of interdependence, all of which entail a change in the structural, cultural, and agential contexts of SESs. Sometimes this allows that certain facets of production can swing free from national governmental control (as most readily in those countries with a history of colonising others, such as Britain).[30] In others, it is a matter of establishing compatibilities in their supply-chains, ones deemed profitable and sustainable. As far as education is concerned, these constitute both constraints and enablements; certain indigenous skills fall into desuetude (such as coalmining in Great Britain) whilst other new opportunities open-up. In turn, the agential demands upon education, its definition of instruction and forms of certification undergo change although no hidden hand guarantees that they give satisfaction.

The second major change is the globalization of knowledge and refers to the specific transformations occurring towards the end of the 20th century, in which secondary and higher education was annually ranked on so-called League tables across countries. This operated as a straight jacket because not all subjects taught or examined were eligible for inclusion. *Because of this, the procedure worked against specialization and differentiation. Although it had no coercive powers and thus, in theory, could be ignored, it stimulated a worldwide competition for recognition that was an undoubted force for standardization.*

This means that the two changes being signalled here pulled in completely different directions from one another. On the one hand, the multinational corporations represented a pressure for specialization throughout their elongating supply chains, whilst, on the other, Programme for International Student Assessment (PISA) and its parallels worked for a narrowing concentration upon STEM[31] disciplines. Although it is impossible to go into depth, it seems important not to finish without venturing a few hints about how these two factors impacted upon the Norwegian and Danish SESs that had started out with centralized and decentralized structures, respectively.

Multinational production

Throughout the 19th century, Norway and Denmark stood in a similar economic position *vis a vis* other parts of the world with their exports limited to the products of the primary sector, especially fishing, forestry and livestock farming. In their relations with non-Nordic countries, they were almost illustrations of the foundational image of classical economics where two islands exchanged excess apples for the other's superfluous bananas. Yet, by the end of the 20th century, both had become among the best-off countries in the world, or at least within the OECD. Trade had increased, and for Norway, the discovery of North-sea oil (whose extraction began in 1971) provided a huge boost to its economy from the last decades of the 20th century. During this period, the Norwegian Social Democrats held political hegemony and ensured that the periphery (the fisher folk and 'little people') also benefitted from the new influx of wealth, which would have been hard to resist given the highly centralized nature of their Trade Unions. Yet this was also the case in Denmark, where the Social Democratic Party formed the government from 1924 until the 1980s. Nevertheless, it has been argued that stronger economic pressures were exerted by the conservatives and liberals pressing for market-led policies there, pre-dating multinational production as such but preparing the ground.[32] How these forms of morphogenesis impacted on the two SESs would repay intensive study.

For Norway, it began to justify greater *specialization* in the vocationalism of upper secondary education through the expansion of course options. Since these were generally terminal and, thus, entailed no demand for upward linkages, little stood in the way of their steady proliferation even though specialization certainly did not feature on the party-political agenda. By the 20th century, the number of these courses had risen considerably. Denmark's extended range and desire for a larger role in international trade meant both countries embraced ICT which became indispensable for the logistics and coordination involved in multi-national production.

The intervention of the two World Wars had been damaging for both counties, given German occupation. Norway suffered particularly because of heavy fighting in the North, destruction of buildings, including schools and ruining of the transport infrastructure as well as demolishing many electric power stations – all of which accompanied the German withdrawal. By 1945, it was estimated that industrial production had been reduced to half its pre-war level.[33] The King and government went into exile in London in 1940 and from there promulgated the Lex Thagaard to stabilize the monetary system, incur a budgetary deficit in order to promote new investment and shorten the time of rationing. Wage agreements were delegated to negotiations between the Trade Union Federation and the Employers' Association. Although none of these measures were specifically educational, they not only protected Constitutional continuity but enabled the government to exert considerable power over the economy and, thus, indirectly over education.

Denmark too struggled with economic recovery and especially with re-establishing the trade and production links it had established pre-war. In both countries, Marshall Aid was important in kick-restarting production (and avoiding austerity), although Norway was somewhat reluctant about succumbing to American capitalism. Joining NATO in 1949, in conjunction with the Soviet coup in Czechoslovakia overcame resistance. For Denmark and Norway, the increased demand for their exports took up the story of growing multinational production, although for both the orientation switched from collaboration with Germany and central Europe towards the Anglo-Saxon world. The educational effects were immediate: English replaced German as the second language taught in schools and, in turn, enhanced publishing, international academic research and conferences. Since being other than monolingual was minimal in the Anglo-Saxon world, this does seem one of the factors that resulted in the celebration of the 'Nordic Model' with scant regard to the differences between Scandinavian countries. Finally, when Denmark entered the EU in 1973, whilst Norway would countenance only European Economic Area (EEA) status, the former opened itself to the full force of both the influences of international economic and educational competition, in which Norway participated as a member of the OECD but had the structural bulwark of its centralized structure for resisting the full brunt of this new cultural influence. It compromised by extending the range of vocational qualifications whilst ensuring that they dovetailed neatly with other types of schooling.[34]

International competition

In 1997, the OECD began the PISA, open to every country in the world and gaining 79 participating nations in 2018. Of the three stated aims, the creation of new knowledge, changes in national assessment policies and exerting external influence over national educational policy, it was hard to see how such standardized testing could stimulate new knowledge amongst 15-year-olds.[35] However, there are no doubts about achievement of the second and third objectives, but considerable variation in their reception. It should be remembered that Norwegian teachers had strongly resisted according 'grades' to pupils' work in 1939 and only reluctantly acceded to this practice at post-primary level, but successfully defeated its generalization throughout the SES.

Some argued that these large-scale international assessments made comparisons of international SESs an unprecedented innovation.[36] This is pure empiricism. What can the score results of 5,000 pupils on, say 'Literacy', reveal about the multifaceted SESs anywhere, however many correlations or regression coefficients are produced? Where is the causal connection? This type of procedure rates alongside the well-known correlation between the incidence of storks and birth rates in Scandinavia on which many of us were raised! Nevertheless, PISA supporters pressed on to insist a real connection existed between educational outcomes and this aspect of public policy.[37] Some countries protested but in Germany, where each Lande had significant autonomy, poor PISA results did lead to an agreement to introduce shared national standards and a new structure to police their observation. In sum, PISA resulted in a general acceptance of the OEDC – a non-elected body and not until then renowned for its expertise in matters educational. Numerous critiques followed; statistical, methodological, suspicions of the best students being selected for entry and non-response from PISA to the critiques of distinguished scholars. Nevertheless, international competition had embedded itself sufficiently to bring most nations to heel because this was not simply a matter of prestige but had a material impact upon the recruitment of overseas students, wherever 'abroad' was to them.

However, this effect went considerably further where material gains and losses were much higher and the numbers of students considerably greater. Its 'success' stimulated imitation at the level of universities and their league tables. These popped up unsought in our computer inboxes, and usually they had no 'unsubscribe' feature. Basically, they crunch-up a range of factors that can include some metric of 'student satisfaction'. Yet, what is a 'good' or an 'excellent' University? Having spent our adult lives in them, we can recognize a good department, a stimulating course or an outstanding team of professors. But these are qualitative judgements (probably without consensus). Yet what is a 'good' University, for it is certainly not the arithmetic mean, mode or median of the factors included? If it pretends to objectivity, then it should be composed of factors such as accommodation, sporting, and arts facilities – even parking spaces and cost-benefit analysis is not amiss if overseas students are charged double the tuition fees paid by indigenous students as in Britain. The story of League Tables became even more ludicrous when some newer institutions protested it was unfair to rank them alongside medieval foundations or the attractions of Silicon Valley. The solution was simple: another League Table for those founded less than

15 years ago, etc. This the reader might fairly complain is merely an educational version of commodification and would they be wrong?

Conclusion

Why have these two factors been introduced at the end? Because it is unlikely that either will go away and, therefore, it is important to consider – even speculatively – their possible impacts upon the SESs of Norway and Denmark as they had emerged and developed. After all, this could signal the start of a new morphogenetic cycle.

Earlier, it was suggested that these two 'new' influences from outside education pulled in two different directions. Thus, it is ventured that where multinational production is concerned, the concentration on PISA among 15-year-olds upon Science, Mathematics and Literacy (Reading) will tendentially narrow their enthusiasm for more specialized options as they move upwards educationally – and eventually occupationally – because there is a symbolic message conveyed that STEM disciplines are what count. This seems likely to affect both countries, though Denmark's SES may bear more of the brunt because the Norwegian central authorities earlier cut back seriously on the proliferation of vocationally specialized Secondary courses and had explicitly systematized them – as was again to be the policy of the central authority for education.

Yet, as multinational production spreads, there will be more demand for specialist just-in-time manufacturing, assembly and design of 'components' and the related logistics. In other words, Norden will only be an attractive commercial collaborator if it can readily meet these specifications. The implication is that educational differentiation would diminish accordingly and again in both countries. The consequence could be that for all their differences as SESs, sustained for over a century, the possibility of their convergence in a new morphogenetic cycle now requires close examination and consideration. One alternative could be that a revivified and digitalized version of Real schooling and training could emerge to satisfy the global Market, but it would do little to improve positioning on PISA, etc., without concentrating resources and rewards on academic secondary schooling with all its inegalitarian implications. And that would possibly spell the end of the 'Nordic Model'.

Notes

1. Although Archer had insisted that Structure, Agency, and Culture were indispensable to any satisfactory explanation in the social sciences from the start of her work and was one of the main reasons for finding such affinity with Critical Realism, it was only in 2013 that she coined the acronym SAC. Archer, ed, 2013, 'Social Morphogenesis and the Prospects of Morphogenic Society', in *Social Morphogenesis*, Dordrecht: Springer, Ch. 1, 1–21.

2. This does not make SESs dependent on political autocracy because, alternatively, consistent pressure upon the political centre on the part of multiple (though not consensual) collective agents can successfully promote an SES. Such different social origins mark them in different ways.
3. A. Aulard, 1911, *Napoléon I*er*et le monopole universitaire*. Paris: Armand Colin, p. 242.
4. By Archer, who reads none of main Scandinavian languages and has to rely on literature in English and French. Also, this was written during the first COVID-19 lockdown with all University Libraries and Inter-Library Loan closed in Great Britain. Skinningsrud is the co-author conversant with her own country's history.
5. See U. Blossing, G. Imsen and L. Moos, 2014, *The Nordic Education Model*, Dordrecht: Springer.
6. Archer, *Social Origins of Educational Systems*, ibid., p. 54.
7. The emergence of the Danish system is sketched in SOES. pp. 165–169; 190–195; 423–472; 775–790.
8. S. Eisenstadt, 2002, 'Multiple Modernities', in Shmuel Eisenstadt, ed, *Multiple Modernities*, New Brunswick; Transaction, pp. 1–30.
9. U. Blossing, G. Imsen and L. Moos, 2014, *The Nordic Education Model*, ibid., Ch. 7, p. 117.
10. Ibid., p. 118.
11. See Archer, ed, *Social Morphogenesis*, 2013; *Late Modernity: Trajectories Towards Morphogenic Society*, 2014; *Generative Mechanisms Transforming the Social Order*, 2015; *Morphogenesis and the Crisis of Normativity*, 2016; *Morphogenesis and Human Flourishing*, 2017. All Dordrecht: Springer.
12. Olav Hove, 1967, The System of Education in Norway, *Paedagogica Europaea*, 3, 192–228.
13. Tone Skinningsrud and Randi Skjelmo, 2016, 'Regional Differentiation and National Uniformity: Norwegian Elementary School Legislation in the Eighteenth and Early Nineteenth Century', *Nordic Journal of Educational History*, 3 (1), 27–45. http://ojs.ub.umu.se/index.php/njedh
14. Christian Larsen, 2010, 'A History of Primary and Lower Secondary Schools in Denmark – Brief Summary. In Christian Larsen', ed. *Realskolen gennem 200 aar*, Vol 2. Denmark: Danmarks Privatskoleforening, p. 435–442. https://privateskoler.dk/wp-content/uploads/2021/04/Realskolen_gennem_200_aar_-_Bind_2.pdf.
15. Christian Larsen, 2018, 'Danish Secondary Schools 1880-1950: National Legislative Framework and Local Implementation', *Nordic Journal of Studies in Education Policy*, 4 (1), 3–23.
16. In 1886, these free schools, together with folk high schools, were organized in the Danish Free Schools Association (*Den danske friskoleforening*). Its purpose was to protect parental rights to establish schools based on their own conceptions of a good education. In 1996, the association included Catholic Schools, Waldorf schools, as well as non-Christian religious schools, and it had altogether 257 member schools. Since 1899, the Free schools have received state funding. Another association that organises private schools in Denmark is the Danish Private Schools Association (*Danmarks privatskoleforening*) for private secondary schools (Real Schools). In 1996, the Private Schools Association had 118 members. See the folder by Thorstein Balle and Margaretha Balle-Pedersen, eds, 1996, *Den danske friskole – en del av den grundtvig-koldske skoletradisjon [The Danish Free School – part of the Grundtvigian-Koldian school tradition]*, Denmark: Dansk Friskoleforening. https://www.friskolerne.dk/fileadmin/filer/Dansk_Friskoleforening/Billeder_og_video/Friskolernes_Hus/Udgivelser/Shop/Den_Danske_Friskole.pdf

17. Harry Haue, 2010, 'Dannelse og almendannelse – realskolens dannelseskoncept', in Christian Larsen, ed, *Realskolen gennem 200 aar*, Vol 2, Denmark: Danmarks Privatskoleforening, p. 71. https://privateskoler.dk/wp-content/uploads/2021/04/Realskolen_gennem_200_aar_-_Bind_2.pdf.
18. Harry Haue, 2010. 'Dannelse og almendannelse – realskolens dannelseskoncept', in Christian Larsen, ed, *Realskolen gennem 200 aar*, Vol 2, Denmark: Danmarks Privatskoleforening, p. 71. https://privateskoler.dk/wp-content/uploads/2021/04/Realskolen_gennem_200_aar_-_Bind_2.pdf.
19. Harry Haue, 2010. 'Dannelse og almendannelse – realskolens dannelseskoncept', in Christian Larsen, ed, *Realskolen gennem 200 aar*, Vol 2, Denmark: Danmarks Privatskoleforening, p. 70. https://privateskoler.dk/wp-content/uploads/2021/04/Realskolen_gennem_200_aar_-_Bind_2.pdf.
    Despite Madvig's negative response, in 1871, Danish Learned Schools were made to include a science track equivalent to the track for classical languages and literature.
20. See *Social Origins of Educational Systems*, ibid., p. 120f.
21. Willis Dixon, 1958, *Education in Denmark*, London: Harrap, p. 97.
22. One illustration of this point is the fact that Real Schools had twice as many pupils in 1901 as in 1891.
23. Archer, *Social Origins*, ibid., p. 167.
24. Olav Hove, 1967, 'The System of Education in Norway', *Paedagogica Europaea*, 3, 192–228. https://www-jstor-org.mime.uit.no/stable/1502320?origin=crossref&seq=1#metadata_info_tab_contents.
25. For example, Napoleon's public assertion that 'to instruct is secondary, the main thing is to train and to do so according to the pattern which suits the State'. L. Liard, 1888, *Enseignement supérieur en France*, 2 Vols, Paris: Armand Colin et Cie, éditeurs, p. 68.
26. Critical Realism was subject to both incomprehension and critique when Bhaskar first spelt out the causal powers of absences in *Dialectic: The Pulse of Freedom* (1993), maintaining their influence was variable but could be as important as those of presences. Although grossly oversimplifying, at rock-bottom we are quite comfortable with the concept that absences do indeed exercise and generate causal effects in everyday cases such as a medical diagnosis pointing to 'vitamin deficiency', a railway engineer explaining that the track has buckled on an exceptionally hot day because insufficient space had been left between its sections to allow for expansion, or sociologists who attribute underachievement at school to varieties of dysfunctional families.
27. Ove Korsgaard and Susanne Wiborg, 2006, 'Grundtvig – The Key to Danish Education?', *Scandinavian Journal of Educational Research*, 50 (3), 361–382.
28. As Hilson puts it, 'Thus the beginnings of the Welfare State were linked not to the political compromises of the1930s, but to the emergence of a predominantly agrarian middle class in the late nineteenth century'. Mary Hilson, *The Nordic Model; Scandinavia Since 1945*, 2008, London, Reaktion Books. Many readers might wish to question this use of 'middle class', given their relations to production were not those of the industrial context normal for employing it.
29. The Canning School was fascinating but we could not ascertain its date of foundation (tinned sardines seem to have a long history), but it is merely part of a long list of vocational Schools and courses preparing for specific occupations.
30. Archer, 2015, 'Structures, Processes and Agents of Educational Changes', *Pontifical Academy of Sciences, Vatican City* and in H. Battro, A. M. Lena, M. Sanchez-Sorondo and J von Braun, eds, 2017, *Children and Sustainable Development*, Cham: Springer.

31. STEM stands for Science, Technology, Engineering and Mathematics.
32. Susanne Wiborg, 2013, 'Neo-liberalism and Universal State Education: The Cases of Denmark, Norway and Sweden 1980–2011', *Comparative Education*, 49 (4), 407–423.
33. Odd Aukrust and Petter Jacob Bjerve, *Hva krigen koster Norge*, cited by Hilson, ibid., p. 62.
34. Utdanningsdirektoratet, 4 February 2020.
35. It transpired that the pupils were not the intended 'creators', but rather that this Big Data could facilitate the comparative statistical analysis of educational performance indicators.
36. N. Mons, 2008, 'Evaluation des politiques éducatives et comparasions internationales', *Revue Fran*çaise de pédagogie, 164, 223–243.
37. J. Barroso and L. M. de Carvalho, 2008, 'Pisa: Un instrument de regulation pour relier des mondes', *Revue français de pédagogie*, 164, 5–13.

3 A letter by the Sámi Lutheran missionary Thomas von Westen

A critical realist perspective on contextualization

Randi Skjelmo

University of Tromsø

> Therefore, as I now am, in the name of Jesus, on my journey to Finmark, to comply with God's grace what the great Shepherd and You His Faithful Servants have commanded me to, I will now humbly leave a report on the godly institutions of the High Collegium as of this present time.[1]

These lines were written on 21 June 1718, by Thomas von Westen (1682–1727), during a northbound voyage in Norway (Willumsen and Skjelmo 2017). Thomas von Westen, who was head of all missionary work among the Sámi in Norway at the time, wrote this letter when he was travelling in Denmark–Norway from Trondheim to Finnmark, a journey that in missionary history literature is mentioned as the second of three (Hammond 1787; Steen 1954). The letter consists of 25 handwritten pages addressed to the Missionary Collegium in Copenhagen whose members were von Westen's superiors. The document was recently found in the National Archives of Denmark, and it is of great interest for several reasons. Letters and reports from Thomas von Westen to the Missionary Collegium were thought to have been lost in two fires in Copenhagen in 1728 and 1795, during which the archival buildings were damaged. After the dissolution of the union between Denmark and Norway in 1814, archival material connected to Norway was handed over to the National Archive in Oslo. In that process, this letter from Thomas von Westen must have been overlooked, and so it remained in Denmark. Although the Norwegian historian Hans Hammond knew about it (referring to it in his mission history, published in 1787), he did not pay much attention to it, compared to other sources. The mission historian Adolf Steen does not mention the letter at all; perhaps, having done his studies in Norwegian archives, he never knew of its existence.

This chapter will focus on the contextualization of this document, as it was written during an interesting period in Danish–Norwegian mission history: the period between 1714 and 1727. In 1714, the Missionary Collegium

DOI: 10.4324/9781003163527-4

was established by the Danish-Norwegian king, Frederik IV, to contribute to the mission in the colony of Tranquebar in East India. In Tranquebar, missionary work was initiated 1705 and the first missionaries arrived from Copenhagen in Denmark-Norway. This is said to be both the first Lutheran mission in the world and the first protestant mission in India. Education became an important part of the work and the missionaries themselves were educated from Halle in Germany and were German. The activities in Tranquebar have been investigated through colonial history, missionary history, trade history, church history and national history (Brimnes 1999; 2017; Bugge 2005; Glebe-Møller 2005, 127–144; Grindler-Hansen 2009, 61–89; Jeyaraj 2005, 86–103; Nørgaard 2005, 41–85; Pedersen 1951; von Sicard 2005, 104–126). Among recent works are also ethnographic and anthropological studies (Fihl 1989; 2009; Jørgensen 2014).

When the Missionary Collegium was established after a British model in Copenhagen in 1714, the intention was to continue missionary work in Tranquebar.[2] They also included the indigenous people in Norway, the Sámi in their work. Missionary and educational activities among the Sámi people in Norway are also well documented. The work included both children, adolescents and adults of both sexes (Skjelmo 2013; 2015, 81–96; 2017, 83–103; Skjelmo and Willumsen 2017a; 2017b; 2017c; Willumsen and Skjelmo 2017). The Sámi languages also played an important role in the education and mission activities.

Motivated by an interest in the early organization of education in Northern Europe, the purpose of studying this letter is to obtain a better understanding of von Westen's work promoting education.

Theoretical framework

The theoretical framework is the *morphogenetic approach*, which gives a methodology for contextualizing the document. Margaret Archer developed the morphogenetic approach in the course of explaining the social origins and effects of educational systems. Tone Skinningsrud later expanded Archer's theory through her work on the educational system in a Nordic country, Norway. While Archer and Skinningsrud both focused on 'the long lines' through the centuries, this chapter will concentrate on a limited period, using the same methodology to contextualize a primary source.

The concept of *morphogenesis* indicates that society has no preferred form but instead is shaped and reshaped by the interplay between structure and agency (Archer 2007, 319). The term was first used by Walter Buckley (1967, 58) to refer to 'those processes which tend to elaborate or change a system's given form, structure or state'. Morphogenesis, in this sense, is contrasted to *morphostasis*, which refers to those processes in a complex system that tends to preserve the above, unchanged. Archer termed this *analytical dualism*, distinct from metaphysical dualism in that all social properties are activity-dependent in both their origins and their effects. In this way of thinking, the element of *time* is fundamental to the analyses. The premise that structure and agency operate over different periods is founded upon two simple propositions. The first is that structure necessarily pre-dates the action(s), which transform it. The second is that structural elaboration necessarily post-dates those actions, as represented in the basic morphogenetic diagram below.

T1 Structural Conditioning
―――――――――――――――――――

    T2   Social Interaction   T3
    ―――――――――――――――――――

                           Structural Elaboration T4

Although the three lines are continuous, the analytical element consists of breaking up the continuous flow into intervals determined by the problem. Given any problem and accompanying periodization, Archer says, the projection of the lines backwards and forwards would connect with the anterior and posterior analytical circles (2007, 319). She emphasizes this as the bedrock of an understanding of systemic properties – of structuring over time – which enables explanations of specific forms of structural elaboration to be advanced and, thus, provides a tool for substantive investigations. The morphogenetic diagram is used in this chapter to provide a framework for von Westen's letter.

The outline of the chapter is as follows: the first research question is related to the latest interval of the diagram – the elaboration – by the question: What was achieved during Thomas von Westen's missionary work? The final point in the interval – T4 – corresponds to the time of von Westen's death in April 1727. This question will be answered by referring to Hans Hammond's and Adolf Steen's books on mission work among the Sámi population in Norway and Randi Skjelmo's article from 2013 on educating teachers for Northern Norway, specifically with regards to the institutions in Trondheim from 1717 to 1732. The second question is connected to the first interval of the diagram: which conditions made von Westen's achievements possible? The starting point – T1 – corresponds to the date when the Missionary Collegium was established: December 1714. This question will be answered with references to the different instructions and decrees for the work given by the Danish–Norwegian king and the Missionary Collegium. The letter will be placed structurally in the middle level of the diagram, and the analysis will focus on the interaction between Thomas von Westen and the Missionary Collegium. The letter provides information about von Westen's previous work, his preparations and events that had occurred up to the point the letter was written. In addition, it contains information about his plans and expectations regarding his work and that of his assistants and supporters.

Thomas von Westen – A missionary pioneer

Thomas von Westen was born in Trondheim, Norway, in 1682, and brought up in a pharmacist family – his father Arnoldus von Westen owned and ran the *Løveapoteket* (Flood and Brendel 1957, 245–252). von Westen was educated at the cathedral school, and presumably, at the age of 15, he went to Copenhagen in Denmark where, perhaps inspired by his father, he studied medical training before switching to theology. He returned to Norway and worked as a private teacher for the Jacob Dass family in Helgeland,[3] preparing the two sons for advanced studies. To practice as a private teacher was a common way for newly graduated university students to earn their living. One could obtain a university degree in theology after only one to two years of studying, and if the candidate was considered too young for ordination, teaching was regarded as a good temporary occupation. Thomas von Westen accompanied Jacob Dass' two sons to the University of Copenhagen, where he continued his studies, this time in Oriental and European languages. Perhaps he wanted an academic career, as he was later engaged as 'Professor Linguarum & Eloqventiæ' in Russia; two letters of appointment, written in German, were fully rendered by Hammond (1787, 45–48). The tsar, Peter I (1672–1725), wanted to attract intellectuals, and Thomas von Westen must have been seen as such. Nevertheless, he was not allowed to leave for Russia – while on the one hand, his burden of debt was so high that he was threatened by debtors' prison, on the other, he was so intelligent and well-educated that the king wanted his capabilities to remain within the kingdom (Hammond 1787, 45–51). von Westen was appointed as a librarian at the Royal Library in Copenhagen in 1706, with the prospect of becoming a minister.

A few years later, after his marriage to the wealthy Anna Pedersdatter (1655–1746), von Westen left Denmark for a position as vicar in Veøy, on the western coast of Norway. He was now 27. His wife (now 54) and her daughter, Else Sophie, followed him to Norway. Thomas von Westen may have contributed to the theological discussions between the Orthodox and the Pietist Christians, which took place in the Lutheran part of Europe and caused many conflicts. In addition, probably influenced by Pietism, he became a member of 'The Seven Stars' [*Syvstjernen*], a union of seven clergymen who communicated with the authorities in Copenhagen and proposed stronger church discipline.

Within the Pietistic movement, missionary work held a prominent position. The Danish–Norwegian king had initiated missionary work in the colony of Tranquebar in East India by sending German missionaries from the city of Halle, in 1705. The relationship between the missionaries and the colonial priesthood was not friendly; however, and there were also conflicts between the missionaries and the Danish colonial commander. To attend to missionary affairs, the king established the Missionary Collegium in Copenhagen, in December 1714 (Hammond 1787, 148–157). In 1716, Thomas von Westen was engaged by the Collegium to lead the mission among the Sámi in Norway, which was based in the country's northernmost cathedral city, Trondheim. In addition to becoming a lecturer at Trondheim's cathedral school and a notary public, von Westen became the leader of the mission among the Sámi for eleven years until he died in 1727.

In 1717, von Westen moved to Trondheim from his vicarage at Veøy, where he bought a house and settled in with his wife and her daughter. During his work as head of the mission in Norway, he travelled from Trondheim to Northern Norway three times. The first journey took place the same year he started his position as head of missionary work in Norway. From June to November 1716, he went to Finnmark, where he successfully installed the first two missionaries and recruited one teacher and two students to the seminary in Trondheim. The second journey to Finnmark lasted from June 1718 until April the following year. In July 1719, von Westen travelled to Copenhagen, where he informed the Collegium and the king about the mission among the Sámi in Norway. He returned to Trondheim in December 1720. His final journey was to Nordlandene and lasted from June 1722 until May 1723. At the age of 45, Thomas von Westen died from illness in his home in Trondheim. His wife Anna, who had supported his mission work financially and practically for years, now found herself in a difficult situation, with barely enough money left to cover von Westen's funeral expenses. She moved to Meldal, where her daughter Else Sophie now resided with her husband, and Anna lived with them until she died in 1746, at the age of 91 (Steen 1954, 197).

What was achieved during Thomas von Westen's missionary work?

The next part of the article aims to answer the first question: What was achieved during von Westen's missionary work? This question is related to the final interval in Archer's morphogenetic approach: a structural elaboration. von Westen's superiors were the members of the Mission Collegium in Copenhagen. The driving motivation behind the founding of the Missionary Collegium was the escalation of the troubles related to the mission in Tranquebar. During serious conflicts between the German missionaries and the Danish commander for the East India Company, one of the two missionaries had been imprisoned; after his release, both missionaries returned from India to Europe. In keeping with the official name of the Collegium – *Collegium de cursu Evangelii promovendo* – mission work among the Sámi population in Norway was an objective of the Collegium from the very beginning (Koch and Kornerup 1951, 52f). The Missionary Collegium published an informational pamphlet in Danish and German and sent it to the regional governors [*stiftsamtmenn*] and bishops in Denmark and Norway along with a request for advice regarding the preliminary phase (Hammond 1787, 49–157). The pamphlet was also translated into Latin and sent to the

British Society for Promoting Christian Knowledge, in London, both to request advice and to thank them for supporting the mission in East India. The British Society had provided the Pietistic missionaries from Halle with a printing press and paper to assist with their efforts to translate bibles into the vernacular in Tranquebar, as publishing books and dictionaries were seen to be an important aim of mission work.

As the members of the Missionary Collegium were not familiar with the conditions in Finnmark, they solicited advice from Norwegian authorities. The co-rector at the cathedral school in Trondheim, Hans Skanke (1679–1739), suggested to send a trustworthy man to Finnmark to make a plan for the missionary work there and for a school in Trondheim, where he recommended that they appoint a principled man as a teacher [*lektor*]. And Skanke himself was willing to be the director. In addition, the Seven Stars provided advice, including the suggestion not to send the least-able vicars to Finnmark. In addition, to complement the gifted vicars they hoped the Collegium would send, they requested well-educated catechists. The Seven Stars also mentioned the lack of schoolmasters and the lack of literacy in Finnmark and stated that the Sámi should not bear the economic cost of their education, as that would decrease their interest. Further, the group felt that the education of the young Sámi should be done in such a way that at least one in every family could guide the rest of the family. Finally, they emphasized a need for psalms and prayers to be translated into the Sámi language. Thomas von Westen, as both a member of the Seven Stars and the vicar in Veøy, had probably undertaken the correspondence on behalf of the group, but another member – Eiler Hagerup (1685–1743) – went to Copenhagen to present their view in person (Lysaker 2009a). Hagerup later became bishop in Trondheim and the leader of the missionary work in Northern Norway after von Westen's death. In addition to these connections between Norway and the Collegium in Copenhagen, the regional governor of Nordlandene, Owe Schieldrup, also became an adviser for the Missionary Collegium. As such, the mission in Norway was deeply rooted among the secular authorities, perhaps to avoid problems like those in Tranquebar. It is also obvious that the authorities considered searching for knowledge about regional and local conditions as well as learning from missions in other countries, i.e., Britain, as important parts of their planning of the Sámi mission. The Sámi themselves should not pay for the education. And one in each family could inform the others after being educated. In this respect, the authorities were ahead of their times by including 'home-schooling' in their plans.

Organizing the mission

An important part of von Westen's work centred around organizing the mission. As early as April 1715, the Royal instruction for the missionary work among the Sámi in Norway was ready to be implemented (Steen 1954, 372).

During von Westen's leadership, 13 missionary districts were established in the areas where Sámi were living, from Varanger in the eastern part of Finnmark and southwards to Trøndelag. The work targeted both the resident farmers and anglers and the reindeer nomads. Each district would have their missionary, most of whom were ordained priests. They were to serve the Sámi with the 'word of God' and teach in the Sámi language. The first and second districts were established in Finnmark during von Westen's first journey in 1716. The county of Finnmark was divided into two parts, with the eastern section including Varanger, Tana and Laksefjord, and the western part including Alta, Ingøy, Hammerfest and Loppa (Steen 1954, 387–391). The two districts were sparsely populated and required the missionaries to travel enormous distances. During the second journey (1718–1719), Porsanger and Laksefjord became Finnmark's third district, with Skjervøy and Kvænangen becoming district four, district five encompassing Karlsøy, Lyngen and Ullsfjord (near today's city of Tromsø), and Senja and Vesterålen constituting district six. When we read the names of the missionaries, we can see that Kjeld Stub went south with Thomas von Westen in 1718, two years after he became the first missionary in East Finnmark, to become a missionary in Senja and Vesterålen. Jens Kildal became the first missionary in Lødingen, Saltdalen and Gildeskål, in 1721. Subsequently, these three districts received one missionary each. Rana and Vefsn constituted districts 10 and 11, both situated in today's Nordland County. Overhalla and Snåsa in Trøndelag became districts 12 and 13. All the districts belonged to the Nidaros bishopric in Trondheim, where the Danish-born Orthodox Lutheran Christian Peder Krog (1654–1731) was the bishop.

Educational institutions and teaching staff

Another important aspect of Thomas von Westen's work was related to education. He established 37 schools within the missionary districts – the first schools in Northern Norway – throughout the three decades prior to 1739, 1740 and 1741, when public elementary education in Denmark and Norway was instituted via royal rules and regulations. von Westen also engaged teaching staff at these schools and he made instructions for them. von Westen must have been well known to the members of the Missionary Collegium through his studies and engagement in Copenhagen. He had probably been handpicked for the work of leading and organizing the mission effort among Norway's Sámi people because of his perceived ability to meet the extensive demands of the position, and his knowledge of languages and culture. His familiarity with the city of Trondheim and the cathedral school from his early life would have been viewed favourably, as well. Under von Westen's leadership, two seminars were established in Trondheim: the Seminarium Scholasticum and the Seminarium Domesticum (Skjelmo 2013). The Seminarium Scholasticum was connected to the cathedral school, and the seminarists were recruited from among the pupils there. The Missionary Collegium took the initiative to establish this institution. Its purpose was to educate missionaries, catechists and schoolmasters for the Sámi population in Norway, and to act as a preparatory school for the University in Copenhagen. The second of these seminars, Seminarium Domesticum, had a two-year program that prepared students for assistant catechist and assistant schoolmaster positions. It was established as a private institution in von Westen's house, and he not only selected the seminarists and the educators himself but also ran the seminar at his own expense with financial support from his wife. The two institutions complemented each other and represented two different educational paths.

We do not know whether there had been discussions between von Westen and the members of the Missionary Collegium about where the educators should be educated. Hammond maintained in 1787 that the island of Tromsø would have been more suitable than Trondheim, given Tromsø's ruralness and its proximity to the Sámi population. Hammond was also of the opinion that the vicar in Tromsø from 1720 onwards – the Norwegian-born Henning Junghans (1680–1753) – would have been a desirable co-operator for von Westen and the Collegium. After all, it was von Westen who had recommended Junghans for the vicar position in Tromsø, and Junghans had acted as a deputy for von Westen's journey to Copenhagen from 1720 to 1721 (Sandmo, Bertelsen and Høgsæt 1994, 333; Steen 1954, 187). And they may have had shared interests and ideas.

Above, we focused on von Westen's organization of the missionary districts, his establishment of schools within the districts and the two institutions in Trondheim for training and qualifying staff. All of this was realized during his time tenure as head of the mission among the Sámi people, from 1716 to 1727. The schools he established were the first institutions of this kind in the northern part of Norway. Now there was a need for educated staff. Thomas von Westen saw the importance of recruiting staff of different categories together to complement each other. He also saw the importance of educating the Sámi themselves to become educators, both because of their mother tongue in the different Sámi dialects and their cultural knowledge and skills. There have been discussions about whether Tromsø would have been a better location for the new seminaries because of the nearness to the Sámi population. But in Tromsø, no educational institutions existed, as opposed to Trondheim where the bishop had his residence and where a cathedral school with long traditions was established. The cathedral school also qualified for university studies, so there already existed a relationship between education at the two different levels, cathedral schools and university level.

We will now turn our attention to the next question: Which conditions made von Westen's achievements possible? This question is related to the first interval of Archer's morphogenetic approach, *structural conditioning*.

Which conditions made von Westen's achievements possible?

The instructions were given to the Missionary Collegium in Copenhagen by King Fredrik IV, regarding Christian education among the Sámi, as mentioned above.[4] In the winter of 1716, when Thomas von Westen was recruited as the mission leader in Norway, there were already institutions in Trondheim that could support von Westen's work, such as the cathedral school with its headmaster and the cathedral with its bishop. These were important assets, as this was during the Great Nordic War, with its substantial state expenses creating serious financial challenges. The plan for educating missionaries was to start in Norway at the already existing cathedral school in Trondheim and be completed at the University of Copenhagen. Further, part of the school in Trondheim was to be transformed into a new kind of institution: the Seminarium Scholasticum. Two weeks after this set of instructions, a royal decree was sent to the University of Copenhagen regarding Seminarium Scholasticum students.[5] In addition, students who were bound either for mission work in East India or in Norway were to be given priority with regards to lodging and board while at the university. When von Westen had to give up his living at Møre, he was given the title *vicarius*, to be a kind of representative in Norway for the Missionary Collegium. Through his teaching position at the cathedral school and his position as notary public, von Westen was connected both to the school and to the church.

On the journey to Finnmark in June 1716, von Westen travelled with the first two Finnmark missionaries, both ordained ministers. He recruited one teacher, the Norwegian Isaac Olsen (ca. 1680–1730), who had been living in Finnmark for about 15 years and spoke the Sámi language. Two young Sámi were recruited for studies in Trondheim. In February 1717, the Missionary Collegium gave their instructions to von Westen concerning the Seminarium Scholasticum.[6]

A well-known and oft-used source of knowledge is von Westen's report from 1717, where he reported his activities to the Collegium in Copenhagen and gave his advice regarding the mission plans (in Broch Utne and Solberg 1938); it is obvious, upon review of the Collegium's instructions for von Westen, that his recommendations were noted. In March of 1718, the Missionary Collegium provided new instructions regarding the missionary work,[7] and in May of 1718, two missionaries – Rasmus Rachlöw and Elias Heltberg—were sent to Finnmark. They had come from Copenhagen to Trondheim, where they had been prepared for the work by von Westen and Isaac Olsen. For assistance and support, especially with the Sámi language and culture, the two Sámi students who had been sent to the Seminarium Domesticum went with them. In addition, two missionaries, Christopher Norman and Morten Lund, were sent out from Trondheim during the spring of 1718. Thus, the answer to the question posed at the beginning of this section is that the king and the Missionary Collegium took their responsibility for the mission by giving instructions and making decrees, which were based on recommendations provided by their advisers.

The letter by Thomas von Westen as a source of knowledge

We will now turn our attention to von Westen's letter, which is placed in the middle of Archer's diagram, with a focus on the interaction between von Westen and the Missionary Collegium. In the Danish National Archive in Copenhagen, the letter is placed with documents belonging to the Missionary Collegium's archive, which contains documents related to the mission in East India, Norway and Greenland. In the minutes, we can see that cases from the three different mission fields were on the agenda in the same collegial meetings. In the Norwegian National Archive in Oslo, there is a letter by von Westen dated 1722 that was fully rendered by the Norwegian historian Hammond (1787, 680–701), who explained that he did so because a letter written by von Westen was quite rare, and so little from his hand was preserved. In Hammond's 951-page book – which was based on analyses of some of von Westen's private letters to close friends and documents from archives in Copenhagen, as well as on what he had been told about his step-grandfather – the letter dated 21 June 1718 is mentioned only four times (311, 315, 582–583, 647). If Hammond had had a complete copy of the actual letter, perhaps he did not see it as sufficiently important to render. Alternatively, Hammond has been criticized for painting an idealized picture of von Westen – perhaps the content of this letter did not quite map onto the story he wanted to tell. This makes the letter even more interesting. It is obvious that also important problems with the mission's establishment in Norway are announced for von Westen's principals. The content of the letter cannot be said to render an undisputed story. It addressed various problems the mission encountered but also how they could be resolved.

The letter is fully transcribed and represents a new and important source of knowledge about what von Westen had achieved in Trondheim before he wrote it, what he expected to find when he arrived at Finnmark and, finally, his plans. When von Westen wrote the letter, he had recently left Trondheim and was windbound in the coastal town of Refsnes; we can see from both the point-by-point composition style and the formulations that the 25 pages were written over a few days. He had with him what he calls his 'protocol', which must have been a kind of almanack and diary. He refers to this protocol for details about specific times and incidents. He also refers with precision to concrete formulations in the instructions and decrees from both the king and Collegium, so these documents must have been with him on the voyage.

The time preceding von Westen's departure from Trondheim had been a busy one. Just before leaving, he had finished the balancing of accounts and sent the vouchers to Secretary Christian Wendt in the Missionary Collegium in Copenhagen. Working together with co-rector Skanke at the cathedral school, Thomas von Westen had also completed the intake of seminarists for the next scholastic year. However, recruiting students from the cathedral school to the Seminarium Scholasticum was a challenging process; we can see from the letter that von Westen was thinking about this, suggesting that an alternative Seminarium be organized outside Trondheim in case the logistics at the cathedral school fell short of his intentions. In addition, he wrote about his friends and how they would help and support the mission: for example, his friend Hans Hagerup was going to build a house in Trondheim for the students. He also mentions the names of actual students, some of whom were the sons of his friends. The letter is especially detailed regarding the recruitment of missionaries, catechists, schoolmasters and their helpers, his plans (including recruiting new students) and his ideas for developing the education of missionaries, catechists and schoolmasters upon his return.

Through his writing, von Westen emerges as a highly educated, cultured scientist and scholar. He notes that he has heard about the plans for a mission in Greenland, and he recommends specific titles of books in the Royal Library he believes will be helpful. We also see that to broaden his knowledge about the Sámi people – and support his efforts to recruit them – he conducted anthropological field research and sought out books on and translations of the Sámi language. In this letter, we also observe von Westen the educator, when he tells of teaching at the cathedral school and states that the number of students increased once he arrived in Trondheim and took over the teaching, and when he describes how he planned to teach at the seminar in Sámi, upon his return from Finnmark.

Education was an important part of the missionary work initiated both among the Sámi, the inhabitants of Tranquebar and among the Inuit people in Greenland. We can see how Thomas von Westen paid attention to this part of his work. There was a comprehensive need for schools and different kind of educational institutions. Educators needed to be educated and he gave his advice based on the institutions that already existed, the cathedral school in Trondheim and the University in the capital, Copenhagen. He knew about the lack of missionaries. The first of them, who went to Tranquebar, were Germans, educated from Halle in Germany. Thomas von Westen knew there existed a decree in Copenhagen where gifted destitute students could have access to free option and accommodation at the University. The University now expanded this decree to include coming missionaries to Norway, Tranquebar and Greenland resolved by the King and the Collegium. So, in addition to the relationship between the Cathedral school in Trondheim and the University of Copenhagen, a relationship between Seminarium Scholasticum and the University was established.

The schools among the Sámi in Norway and the institutions for educating staff were established more than two decades before the rest of Denmark–Norway see the origin of an elementary school system. Thus, the Sámi population far north were the first inhabitants inside the kingdom to have an education given by the national authorities.

It is also obvious that the language and culture played important roles in these new institutions. Thomas von Westen himself wrote to his principals in 1718 that when he arrived from his second journey he planned to do his teaching in the Sámi language. Due to his comprehensive language skills, he most likely knew the differences among the Sámi dialects, such as North Sámi, Lule Sámi and South Sámi. He wanted the teaching to be done in the pupils and students' own language. Up to now, Isaac Olsen had done the teaching in Sámi at the seminaries in Trondheim. Olsen was an important helper for von Westen. In addition, to teach, he also translated written texts as psalms, prayers and part of the Bible into Sámi. He later became the teacher of Knud Leem, and he was the person who educated Leem in the Sámi language. Leem should later become the first professor in Norway, five decades before the country had its university, and he became a professor in the Sámi language. From the way the education of staff was arranged, we see that cultural knowledge played an important role as well as language knowledge and skills. Staff with different education and knowledge should complement each other, for example, schoolmasters and schoolmaster assistants. Local language skills and cultural skills were important. The content of the education was obviously of the religious kind. But which is seen from the notes left by Isaac Olsen, he had a more comprehensive content in his teaching. We find texts including arithmetic narratives, moral stories, riddles and jokes. Another thing worth remembering; when children have learned to read, their reading competence can be used on other types of texts. Of special interest here is, that in Norway it was a minority, the Sámi, who first got education given by the authorities. Developing a person's ability to read contributes towards power and emancipation. Such a fact could be compared with the origin of the school system in other countries with one or several indigenous people; for example, First Nations, Intuits, Innus and Metises in Canada, Maoris and Aborigines in New Zealand and Australia.

Conclusions

For this chapter, Archer's morphogenetic approach was used to contextualize Thomas von Westen's letter dated 21 June 1718. The first question posed was: What was achieved during Thomas von Westen's missionary work? We saw that the northern part of Norway became divided into 13 mission districts, and 37 schools were established within these districts. We also saw that he engaged missionaries, catechists, schoolmasters and schoolmaster assistants and set up work instructions for them. Finally, we learned that an important part of his work centred on two institutions in Trondheim – the Seminarium Scholasticum and the Seminarium Domesticum – established to educate the staff for the mission. The ideas were rooted in the Halle pietism, so it was German educational ideas and practice which were transferred, via Copenhagen and Trondheim to the northern part of Norway. The international orientation was supplemented by searching for advice and support from Britain. And the first, organized education for both boys and girls was given to an indigenous group, the Sámi.

The second question addressed by this chapter was: Which conditions made von Westen's achievements possible? We saw that the Danish–Norwegian king, Fredrik IV, and the Mission Collegium in Copenhagen initiated the work, provided decrees and gave instructions that were built on the recommendations and advice that they had requested. The mission among the Sámi in Norway was also rooted among the secular authorities as well as among clerical authorities. The economic support came from the King and the Collegium. But von Westen's wife Anna also gave her support, financially and practically. Her husband could never have worked so intensely and with such dedication without her support. His private seminary in Trondheim, Seminarium Domesticum, was completely dependent on her money, her work and her care for the young Sámi students coming to Trondheim.

The final question in this chapter focused on the interaction between Thomas von Westen and the Missionary Collegium. We see von Westen in action as a scientist, educator and organizer. He referred to his 'protocol' for specific details, and the instructions from the king and the Collegium when reporting about his work and making arguments to support his decisions. On his journey to Finnmark, 'to comply with God's grace what the great Shepard and (You) His Faithful Servants' had commanded of him, he sent his report. The connection between the opportunities provided by the Danish–Norwegian king, Frederik IV, and the Missionary Collegium in Copenhagen on the one hand, and von Westen's work on the other, becomes visible.

One next step could be to take as a new starting point the missionary districts and education as new structures, to analyse how the mission was continued after von Westen's death in 1727 and maybe ask how education among the Sámi could have been elaborated if von Westen's view had been followed after his death. Another step could be to study the period before the Missionary Collegium was established and examine the conditions which led to the formation of this new organization in 1714.

Acknowledgement

I want to thank the Foundation for Danish–Norwegian Cooperation for supporting my archive studies in Copenhagen during my stay at Schæffergården.

Notes

1. Thomas von Westens Indberetning, 21/6 1718 angaaende Missionærfeltenes Tilstand i Finmarken. Lnr F 310, Diverse dokumenter Missionskollegiet vedk., legg III Sager Missionen i Finmarken og Nordlandene vedk. 1718–1803 (234 Missionskollegiets arkiv, Rigsarkivet København).

2. SPCK, Society for Promoting Christian Knowledge.
3. Jacob Dass was a younger brother of the famous poet and vicar at Alstadhaug, Petter Dass (1647–1707).
4. The instruction is dated 19 April 1715.
5. The royal decree is dated 3 May 1715.
6. The Instruction is dated 13 February 1717 (Steen 1954, 376–378).
7. The Instruction is dated 19 March 1718 (Hammond 1787, 300–311).

References

Archer, Margaret. 2007. *Dictionary of critical realism*, Merwyn Hartwig (ed.). London and New York: Routledge.
Buckley, Walter. 1967. *Sociology and modern systems theory*. New Jersey: Prentice Hall.
Brimnes, Niels. 1999. *Constructing the colonial encounter. Right and left hand castes in early colonial South India*. Richmond: Curzon.
Brimnes, Niels (ed.). 2017. *Indien: Tranquebar, serampore og nicobarerne*, Volume 3, *i* Danmark og kolonierne. Copenhagen: Gads Forlag.
Broch Utne, Martha and O. Solberg (eds.). 1938. "Topographia ecclesiastica, 2. DEL: FINMARCKIA 1717." In *Nordnorske samlinger I. finnmark omkring 1700. aktstykker og oversikter*. Oslo: Etnografisk Museum.
Bugge, Knud Eyvin et.al. (eds.). 2005. *Det begyndte i københavn: Knudepunkter i 300 års indisk-danske relationer i mission [It started in Copenhagen: Nodes in 300 years old Indian- Danish mission relations]*. Odense: Syddansk Universitetsforlag.
Fihl, Esther. 1989. *Tropekolonien tranquebar [The tropical colony tranquebar]*. Copenhagen: Gad.
Fihl, Esther. 2009. Shipwrecked on the coromandel: The first Indo–Danish contact, 1620. In *Review of Development and Change*, 14 (1 & 2), 19–41. Tropical Tranquebar.
Flood, Ingeborg and Leif A. Brendel. 1957. *Norges apotek og deres innehavere. Bind V [Norwegian Pharmacies and their Owners, Volume V]*. Oslo: Foreningen, 245–252.
Jørgensen, Helle. 2014. *Whose history? Transnational cultural heritage of a former Danish trading colony in South India*. New Delhi: Orient Blackswan.
Glebe-Møller, Jens. 2005. «Nådens rige forutsætter magtens rige. Den danske debat om hedningemissionens teologiske legitimitet» [The Danish debate on the theological legitimacy of missionary work]. In Knud Eyvin Bugge et al., (eds.). *Det begyndte i København: knudepunkter i indisk-danske relationer i mission*. Odene: Syddansk Universitetsforlag, 127–144.
Grindler-Hansen, Keld. 2009. The schools of Tranquebar: An educational field of cultural encounters and conflicts. In *Review of Development and Change*, 14 (1 & 2), 61–89.
Hammond, Hans. 1787. Den Nordiske Missions-Historie i Nordlandene, Finmarken og Trundhiems Amt til Lappers og Finners Omvendelse, fra første begyndelse indtil hen udi året 1727. *[The Nordic mission history in Norlandene, Finmarken and Trundhiems counties among the Sámi, from the beginning up to 1727]*. Kiøbenhavn: Gyldendalske Forlag.
Jeyaraj, Daniel. 2005. *Kolonialisme og mission i forholdet til hinduerne. [Colonialism and Mission among the Hindus]*. 86–103.

Koch, Hal and Bjørn Kornerup (eds.). 1951 *Den danske kirkes historie V. [Danish church history]*. København: Nordiske Forlag.

Lysaker, Trygve. 2009a. "Eiler Hagerup: utdypning–1". In *Norsk biografisk leksikon*. Norway: Aschehoug. http://nbl.snl.no/Eiler_Hagerup/utdypning_%E2%80%93_1 (accessed 27 October 2017).

Lysaker, Trygve. 2009b. "Peder Krog: utdypning." In *Norsk biografisk leksikon* (13 February 2009). http://nbl.snl.no/Peder_Krog/utdypning (accessed 27 October 2018).

Nørgaard, Anders. 2005. *«Missionens forhold til danskerne» [The Relationship between the mission and the danes]*. 41–85.

Pedersen, Johannes. 1951. *Den danske kirkes historie: Pietismens tid 1699–1746 [Pietism 1699–1746]*. In Hal Koch and Bjørn Kornerup (eds.). Copenhagen: Gyldendalske Boghandel.

Sandmo, Anne-Karine, Reidar Bertelsen, and Ragnhild Høgsæt. 1994. *Tromsø gjennom 10000 år. Fra boplass-til by-opp til 1794 [Tromsø through 10,000 Years]*. Tromsø: Tromsø kommune.

Skjelmo, Randi. 2013. "Utdanning av lærere for det nordlige Norge: De tidlige institusjoner i Trondheim 1717–1732" [Teacher education for Northern Norway: The early institutions in Trondheim 1717–1732]. *Sjuttonhundratal*, 10, 39–63.

Skjelmo, Randi. 2015. "Utdanning av lærere for det nordlige Norge før 1826", [Teacher Education for Northern Norway before 1826]. In *Daniel Sjögren og Johannes Westberg (red.) Norrlandsfrågan: Erfarenheter av utbildning, undervisning och fostran i nationalstatens periferi*. Umeå: Kungl. Skytteanska samfundets handlingar, 81–96.

Skjelmo, Randi. 2017. «Fire tekststykker knyttet til samemisjonæren Thomas von Westen 1717 – 1723» [Four texts related to the Sámi Missionary Thomas von Westen 1717–1723]. In *Sjuttonhundratal: Nordic yearbook for eighteenth-century studies*, 14, 83–103.

Skjelmo, Randi Hege and Liv Helene Willumsen. 2017a. "Isaac Olsen - lærer og forkynner". [Isaac Olsen – Teacher and preacher]. *Heimen - Lokal og Regional Historie*, 54 (1), 62–85.

Skjelmo, Randi Hege and Liv Helene Willumsen. 2017b. "Preludium til misjonen i Finnmark" [Prelude to the Mission in Finnmark]. *Teologisk Tidsskrift*, 6 (4), 301–32.

Skjelmo, Randi Hege and Liv Helene Willumsen. 2017c. *Thomas von Westens liv og virke. [Thomas von Westen's life and work]*. Oslo: Vidarforlaget AS.

Steen, Adolf. 1954. *Samenes kristning og Finnemisjonen til 1888. [The Christening of the Sámi and Mission among them up to 1888]*. Oslo: Egedeinstituttet.

von Sicard, Sigvard. 2005. *Ziegenbalg og muslimerne [Ziegenbalg and the Muslims]*. Odense: Syddansk Universitetsforlag, 104–126.

Willumsen, Liv Helene and Randi Skjelmo, 2017. *A letter by the Sámi missionary Thomas von Westen dated 1718*. Norway: The Royal Norwegian Society of Sciences and Letters, 1–.

4 Vindicating Archer's concepts of educational systems – centralized and decentralized – as exemplars of critical realist theorizing

Tone Skinningsrud

Introduction: Critical realist concept formation

Concept formation, or conceptual abstraction, is a crucial stage in social research informed by critical realism (Danermark et al. 2002; Sayer 1998; 1999; 2000). Criteria for the formation of concepts are generally neglected in the mainstream literature on research methods, whilst critical realism considers conceptual abstraction a crucial stage in the research process (Sayer 2000, 27). The formation and choice of concepts are tied up with ontological questions, such as 'what kinds of things exist'? Such questions are seldom discussed explicitly in mainstream research but is considered a fundamental premise by critical realism.

In the literature on critical realist research methods, Berth Danermark et al. (2002) emphasize that conceptual abstractions aim to identify the necessary constituent properties of the object under study. This means finding the generative mechanisms inherent in the object's internal structure. Thus, 'structural analysis' is a particularly important kind of abstraction in research informed by critical realism (Danermark et al. 2002, chapter 3). Likewise, Andrew Sayer, in his book on realist research methods (Sayer 1999, 45), sees conceptualization as the most crucial moment in the research process and the conceptualizations of necessary relationships as 'absolutely critical' (Sayer 1998, 132). Moreover, only careful descriptions of the object and the relationships [structures] in virtue of which they act can help us to identify mechanisms (Sayer 1998, 132). Sayer discusses good and bad abstractions. Good, or rational, abstractions are those which isolate necessary relationships, that is, structures that constitutes the identity of objects in such a way that 'a particular object could not be what it is unless it had that particular power, that way of acting' (Sayer 1998, 125). Sayer underlines that 'Theories make their strongest claims at the abstract level, about necessary and internal relations, about causal powers which exist in virtue of the nature of particular things' (Sayer 1998, 127).

The emphasis in critical realist methodology on the identification of structures and mechanisms is justified at the meta-theoretical level by the concept of 'natural kinds'.[1] Roy Bhaskar (2008) in 'A realist theory of science' argues

DOI: 10.4324/9781003163527-5

that research in the natural sciences consists in identifying 'persistent things' that possess causal powers and tendencies in virtue of their structure (RTS, 171). An important step in identifying 'persistent things' is to work out *real definitions* of them, which entails defining them by referring to something about their nature that explains how they behave.[2] A *real definition* of the thing in question will refer to the powers that cause its tendential behaviour. Thus, real definitions are knowledge of 'natural kinds' (ibid.).

Ruth Groff (2013), in discussing the ontology of natural kinds, uses the term 'social kinds', thereby underlining that 'social kinds' are analogues to 'natural kinds', and that not all social phenomena are necessarily exemplars of 'social kinds'. Which phenomena are 'social kinds', i.e., identifiable by their internal structure and mechanisms, is a matter for social research to find out. Likewise, Sayer argues that whether a given social phenomenon is 'a social kind', analogues to natural kinds, must be investigated in each specific case (Sayer 2000, 84–85).

When Bhaskar (1979) in 'The possibility of naturalism' transposes the conception of natural kinds to social reality, he clarifies that the 'persisting objects' of social science are not 'things', but 'the sum of relations within which individuals [and groups] stand'. They are '[relatively] enduring relations', which are concept dependent as well as activity dependent (PON, 26, 38). Still, Bhaskar claims, the basic challenge in all scientific investigations, in the natural as well as the social sciences, is to establish real definitions: our problem then is shifted from that of how to establish a non-arbitrary procedure for generating causal hypotheses to that of how to establish a non-arbitrary procedure for generating real definitions (PON, 50).

Establishing real definitions that specify the identity of social entities in terms of their internal structures and inherent mechanisms, therefore, is crucial to know how the entity acts or reacts. Thus, such definitions have explanatory power.

My intention in this chapter is to show that Archer's definition of a state educational system – centralized or decentralized (Archer 1984; 1995; [1979] 2013) – is a real definition of such systems in the abovementioned sense of 'referring to something about their nature that explains how they behave, i.e. their structures and mechanisms that tendentially produce certain types of change'. In virtue of being a real definition, Archer's conceptualization of the educational system has explanatory power due to its identification of mechanisms that 'tendentially produce certain types of change'. In identifying structures and mechanisms, it differs from other definitions of educational centralization and decentralization in current use. I will provide examples of recent analyses of educational development in Norway that will demonstrate the greater explanatory power of Archer's concepts.

In the following, I will first give a short presentation of Archer's definition and theory of educational systems – centralized and decentralized – focusing on their explanatory power through their identification of mechanisms. Secondly, I will present some other definitions of educational centralization and decentralization, prevalent in the current research literature, which generally conceive of centralization and decentralization as the redistribution of decision-making authority and of decentralization, specifically, as delegation. Connected to this, I will also briefly discuss the current definition of centralization/decentralization as strategies of governance and as degrees of school autonomy. I will then show how these other conceptions of educational centralization and decentralization have been applied in recent analyses of Norwegian education and compare them with an analysis using Archer's concepts. I will demonstrate how Archer's concepts enable explanations that account for a broader range of phenomena and, therefore, have greater explanatory power than the conceptions of centralization and decentralization in current use.

Archer's concepts of educational systems – Centralized and decentralized

Archer's definition of state educational systems is cited in numerous studies, even those that do not use her morphogenetic approach and theories. The reason for its relatively frequent use is perhaps that she seems to be the only one who has worked out a definition of the educational system. However, the term 'educational system' is also used by many who do not define it at all, as though it was self-explanatory and of not much consequence.[3] They do not see it as a theoretical concept, which captures an emergent level of social reality; a structure with causal powers *sui generis* rather than some patterns of behaviour.

Archer's definition of a state educational system, as 'a nationwide and differentiated collection of institutions devoted to formal education, whose overall control and supervision is at least partly governmental, and whose components and processes are related to one another' (Archer [1979] 2013, 54), identifies two major sets of relations which must be present for a state educational system to exist, (a) the connection to the state and (b) the systemic form. The connection to the state entails at least some state control and supervision but also that central political decision-making affects the system. The system formation means that all the elements and processes in the system are related to one another and that changes in one element lead to changes throughout the system. Archer's definition sees state educational systems as a set of structures, which means that the constituent elements are internally related.[4]

Thus, the system is not just the sum of all educational provisions within a delimited area, say a country or a nation, at a specific point in time, but is the interconnections between various elements. Though the form of state educational systems varies among countries, their commonality is that they are structured totalities connected with the state, but also connected with a multiplicity of other social institutions. They are multi-integrated. Archer's definition also implies that educational systems as structured entities did not always exist. They emerged at specific times in history – in most European countries at various times during the 19th century. Before that, educational provisions of different kinds operated independently of each other. They did not form a system of interrelated elements.

State educational systems, as defined by Archer, have some universal structures and mechanisms:

Unification, meaning that a central educational administration exerts educational control promoting standardized and uniform provisions. There are two types of unification: intensive and extensive. (a) *Intensive unification* concerns the strength with which the central state controls education to ensure that it is in line with central policies. (b) *Extensive unification* concerns how encompassing central standards and uniformities are, for example, to what extent there are private provisions that are not under state control, and whether there are local programmes and offerings which do not conform to the centrally decided standardized programmes.

Systematization, meaning that different schools and programmes are defined in relation to each other, such as the definition of levels (primary, secondary, and tertiary). Systematization entails the removal of bottlenecks in the system and incorporation of previously isolated units.

Differentiation, meaning that education is a distinct social institution with its own special work operations and role structure, where internal operations are performed with considerable autonomy and little interference from outside.

Specialization, meaning that the system contains various types of schools and provisions with different recruitment bases, internal processes and output competencies (Archer 1984, 72 ff).

When educational systems emerged in European countries during the 19th century, they were two different types, centralized and decentralized systems. In her comparative-historical study, Archer identified and explained the emergence of decentralized systems in England and Denmark and centralized ones in France and Russia (Archer [1979] 2013).

In Archer's definitions, centralization and decentralization are properties of educational systems as totalities. A centralized system is defined as *'one in which one element or subsystem plays a major or dominant role in the operation of the system* [...] *the system is centred around this part. A small change in the leading part will then be reflected throughout the system, causing change'*. Though all state educational systems are integrated with the central state and its administration, only in centralized systems is it the 'leading part'. A decentralized system, on the other hand, has no leading part (Archer 1984, 73–74, my emphasis).

Figure 4.1 below presents a model of Archer's conception of the structural conditioning of educational interaction in centralized systems. Educational demands from various groups (education professionals and external groups) are input to the political centre, the 'leading part' of the system, where decisions are made. In the centralized system, *political manipulation* is the

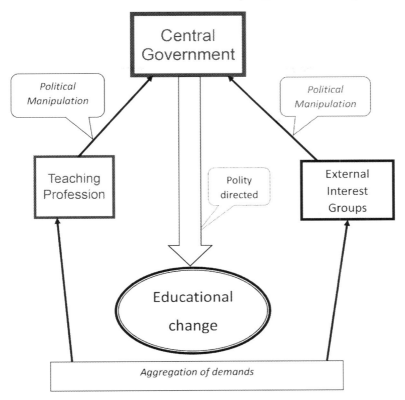

Figure 4.1 Educational interaction in centralized systems.

dominant type of interaction. Policy based on negotiated demands is implemented top-down without significant interference.

In centralized systems, the processes of *unification* and *systematization*, which is the effect of the mechanism inherent in the relationship between education and the state, tend to dominate. The vested interest of the state as 'the leading part' in maintaining educational control predominates in centralized systems, and tendentially, change in such systems will consist in increased unification (every locality offers the same state defined provisions) and systematization, which entails the facilitation of smooth and efficient functioning of the system, as well as the gradual incorporation into the system of previously independent provisions.

Decentralized systems (Figure 4.2) differ from centralized ones in two major ways. Firstly, they have no 'leading element' and secondly, their relations with the environment differ from centralized systems. In decentralized systems, educational demands are transacted directly between external interest groups and educational institutions. Such transactions may take place at various locations in the systems. Interactions in decentralized

58 Tone Skinningsrud

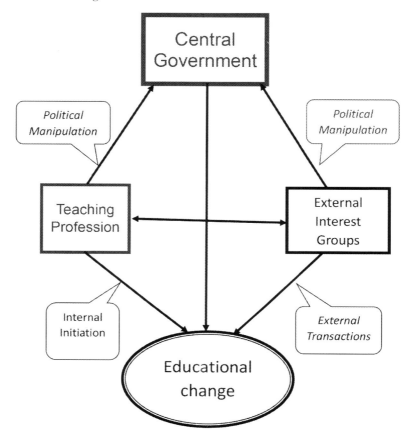

Figure 4.2 Educational interaction in decentralized systems.

systems are more varied than in centralized systems and consist of *external transactions* and *internal initiation* in addition to *political manipulations*. Therefore, change in such systems originates from various sources that may pursue conflicting educational policies. For example, the educational demands from external interest groups may be at odds with the policy of the central state. The dominant processes of change in decentralized systems are *specialization* and *differentiation* (of the system). Increased differentiation entails that the system becomes more autonomous in the sense that there is less outside interference with internal work operations. Thus, the tendential developmental trajectory of decentralized and centralized educational systems differs. In the centralized system, there is a tendency towards increased unification and systematization, which is generated by the structural connection between education and the state. In decentralized systems, specialization and differentiation are more likely to predominate due to the structures connecting education with external interest groups and the incorporated teaching profession.

Centralized and decentralized systems also differ in the kinds of problems they typically encounter. In decentralized systems, the effective implementation of state policy encounters problems since change is transacted in different places in the system independently of state policies. Centralized systems, on the other hand, encounter problems relating to their environment since educational demands are not negotiated directly with providers but are subjected to processes of political compromise between often conflicting demands. Reforms in centralized systems seldom answer to any group's precise educational needs or requirements. Thus, reforms often replace old discontent with new discontent.

Important to note is that both types of systems, in Archer's historical account, emerged as *unintended consequences* of the interaction between groups competing for educational control ('competitive conflict'). They did not come about as the implementation of a specific educational reform intended to implement either educational centralization or decentralization.

Other conceptions of educational centralization and decentralization

Archer conceptualizes educational centralization and decentralization as properties of structured entities with emergent causal powers, i.e., as systems. The systems emerged at specific times in history as unintended consequences of interaction. But once they had emerged, they exercised causal powers influencing processes in the system and their further structural elaboration in terms of unification, systematization, differentiation and specialization (Archer [1979] 2013).

Since Archer's early contribution in defining the system, accounting for how they emerged, identifying their mechanisms, describing the difference between centralized and decentralized systems, and how they tendentially are structurally elaborated, numerous empirical and theoretical studies addressing educational centralization and decentralization have been published. However, these more recent studies, which will be examined below, employ quite different definitions of educational centralization and decentralization and generally do not account for the system as a theoretical concept referring to an emergent level of social reality with distinct causal powers.

The focus of attention in more recent research has been on educational decentralization, which is often defined as shifting the locus of decision-making from the centre to the periphery. The major models of educational decentralization that have been discussed are: (i) *deconcentration,* which involves the *transfer of tasks,* but not authority, to other units in the organization; (ii) *delegation,* which involves the *transfer of decision-making authority* from higher to lower hierarchical units, allowing the withdrawal of authority at the discretion of the delegating unit; and (iii) *devolution,* which refers to the *transfer of authority to an autonomous unit* that can act independently, or without first asking permission (Zajda 2006, 12). Each of these models may include several domains of decision-making, i.e., finance, human resources and curriculum (Hanson 2006, 11; Zajda 2006, 11). These models, or definitions, do not consider educational decentralization as a type of system, but rather as a type of action, as governance strategies (Karlsen 2000). Emphasizing that decentralization is a kind of action (decentralizing), some authors underline that it is not a 'fixed state' but a dynamic process (Bray 2013).

In the 1980s and 1990s, the reform policy of educational decentralization was spread on a global scale when international funding bodies made it a precondition for financial assistance, the so-called structural adjustment policy (SAP) (World Bank, 1998, quoted in Zajda 2006, 6).[5] The conditionalities for educational aid, shared by the World Bank (WB) and the International Monetary Fund (IMF), which also informed advice provided by the Organization of Economic Co-operation and Development (OECD) to national governments, included decentralization, privatization and community financing of education. Studies of educational centralization and decentralization connected with the implementation of the decentralization policy promoted by these international agencies generally chose to define decentralization as the *delegation* of decision-making authority (Hanson 2006, 10–11; Lauglo 1995; Zajda 2006, 11).[6]

In justifying their definition of decentralization, these studies consider which kinds of decentralization models can realistically be implemented (Hanson 2006) and which models are durable (Hanson 2006), adapting their choice of definition to what is politically feasible. The focus on policy implementation is also reflected in the attention paid to what kinds of conditions facilitate or hinder the implementation of decentralization (Bjork 2006, 2). Causes of decentralization are sought in the ideas and rationales of policy-makers justifying decentralization policies (Lauglo 1995; Weiler 1990). Studies investigating the effects of decentralization focus mainly on students' achievements (Hanushek, Link, and Wossmann 2013; Haug 2009; Wöbmann et al. 2007). Some have noted as a paradox that decentralization policy, which aims to shift decision-making authority from higher to lower levels, is invariably initiated from the top (Bray 2013; Karlsen 2000).

Discussions about which models that are feasible and likely to succeed actualize the question about the limits to educational decentralization. It is claimed that the challenge for policymakers is to find the right balance between centralization and decentralization, by which the authors mean between state involvement and local decision-making. Whilst some have argued that devolution, i.e., total autonomy for local schools, premised on the wholesale privatization of educational provisions, is the only durable model of decentralization, Hanson claims that '[i]n reality, almost all decisions (e.g., finance, personnel, curriculum) retain degrees of centralization or decentralization – the issue is finding the appropriate balance' (Hanson 2006, 11).

He denies that there is 'such a thing as a decentralized system', meaning systems with no state involvement. Likewise, Zajda (2006, 11) claims that 'there is no total political and administrative decentralization, since all policy decisions concerning finance, personnel and staffing retain various degrees of centralization and decentralization. Hence, the real policy issue is one of finding the right balance'. Based on an assessment of what is realistically obtainable, these authors choose to define decentralization as the delegation of decision-making authority, rather than devolution, since they admit that total local autonomy is unobtainable.

Still, some researchers convinced that the market model for educational provisions is the best, underline that school autonomy should be a vital concern for decentralization policy. They consider competition among educational providers and informed choice among 'consumers' as likely to improve student achievement because competition and choice 'provide incentives for everyone to improve the learning environment'. Decentralization in the sense of considerable school autonomy is a precondition for market mechanisms to be effective (Wöbmann et al. 2007, 16–17).[7]

The most prevalent definition of decentralization in current research that practically covers the globe is delegation, in the sense of transfer of decision-making authority from the central to the local level. This definition is not of an entity with internal structures, but of a category of action, associated with the implementation of reform-policies. Since the analyses that define educational decentralization as delegation normally do not define or conceptualize the educational system, although sometimes using the term in a loose sense, little information is supplied of what the educational system consists of, apart from it having a vertical structure of decision-making. Hanson (2006, 11) and Zajda (2006, 11) imagine centralized systems as totally state dominated entities and decentralized systems as all together free from state control and intervention. On this account decentralized systems do not exist and are not likely to ever become a reality. But delegation of decision-making, providing considerable school autonomy, is possible.

Research on educational change in Norway during recent decades has raised the question whether Norwegian education is centralized or decentralized. Generally, these studies have adopted the definition of decentralization from mainstream international research, seeing it as delegation of decision-making, following the trend of neglecting to consider the broader system, with its structures and mechanisms.

The Norwegian scene – Recent analyses of centralization and decentralization

Analyses of educational centralization and decentralization in Norway having adopted the current mainstream definition and seeing it as the redistribution of decision-making authority have come up with contradictory results. Some of them conclude that Norwegian education has been and continues to be centralized (Aasen 1999; Karseth, Møller, and Aasen 2013), others see it as increasingly more decentralized (Arnesen and Lundahl 2006; Haug 2009; Helgøy and Homme 2007; Volckmar and Wiborg 2014). Haug's study, which has applied the OECD indicator for 'school autonomy' on the Norwegian case, comparing it with Australia, Canada, Finland, and Sweden, concluded that Norwegian education is undoubtedly decentralized.[8]

A major part of the research concerning centralization and decentralization of Norwegian education has been descriptive and not explanatory. Exceptions are Haug's study (2009) investigating the effect of decentralization on school performance, and Arnesen and Lundahl (2006), who are concerned about the future of the egalitarian Nordic Model, asking whether decentralization as part of a neo-liberal policy will lead to greater inequalities in Norwegian education. Others have addressed to what extent Norwegian education has become decentralized and market-oriented (Volckmar and Wiborg 2014) and whether recent reforms, heralded as decentralizing reforms, have, in fact, led to decentralization and not its opposite (Aasen 1999; Karlsen 2000; Karseth, Møller, and Aasen 2013).[9]

All the mentioned authors follow the mainstream by defining decentralization as the delegation of authority from the centre to more peripheral locations in the decision-making hierarchy. Some focus specifically on the freedom for teachers to choose methods of instruction, i.e., whether teaching methods are prescribed in the National Curriculum (centralization) or left to be decided by the teachers (decentralization) (Karseth, Møller, and Aasen 2013). All of them lack a definition of the educational system. Karlsen (2000) explicitly defines centralization and decentralization as strategies of governance.

Research addressing whether Norwegian education is centralized or decentralized by using the definition established in the international literature, started with an OECD report claiming that the Norwegian system during the 1980s had been subjected to a 'forceful effort towards decentralization' (OECD, The Norwegian Ministry of Church and Education, and the Norwegian Ministry of Culture and Science 1989, 175).[10] Pointing to the 1986 reform of the funding system from earmarked to block grant funding, and the 1987 curriculum reform, which made it statutory for schools to work out their own local versions of the National Curriculum, the report found it necessary to remind the Norwegian authorities to uphold important state functions, to reinforce state supervision of the system and evaluate its output (OECD, The Norwegian Ministry of Church and Education, and the Norwegian Ministry of Culture and Science 1989, 165).

In apparent contradiction to the 1989 OECD-report's assessment of Norwegian education as excessively *decentralized* during the 1980s, Aasen (1999, 38) claims that the Norwegian system in the 1980s was 'strongly centralized' but in the early 1990s was transformed to a 'decentralized and deregulated system'. He traces this transformation to the introduction of Management by Objectives (MbO), which entailed the state setting objectives to be achieved by local schools. MbO allowed some local freedom by delegating decision-making to teachers regarding their teaching practice and methods of instruction; however, it also meant increased central control through the reporting of results to central authorities (Aasen 1999, 38). Aasen, therefore, concludes that the deregulation introduced by MbO was only apparent. In fact, it served to legitimate 'a new control system, which revitalized a strong state' (Aasen 1999, 56). Reinforced by a new more detailed and prescriptive National Curriculum in the 1997 Act, the local freedom for teachers effected by MbO in the early 1990s was annulled, and Norwegian education, at the turn of the millennium, was as centralized as it had been in the 1980s (Aasen 1999, 47).

Also, evaluations of the most recent educational reform, the Knowledge Promotion Reform from 2006, conclude that Norwegian education is centralized. Despite being launched as a decentralizing reform in the government White Paper, Culture for learning (*Kultur for læring*) (Meld. S. 30 (2003-2004)), the outcome was the opposite, namely strengthened state control, i.e., centralization. The evaluators assert that 'we have hardly ever had a larger and stronger central administration of basic education' (Møller et al. 2013, 14). The Knowledge Promotion Reform introduced a competency based National Curriculum intended to allow greater local freedom, curricular adaptations to local conditions and innovative teaching practices. But it also introduced basic skills (reading, writing, numeracy, digital and oral skills) as integrated elements in all school subjects. The curriculum framework for basic skills not only provided a detailed description of five levels of attainment, but also the appropriate learning activities for the different levels. The evaluators considered this to be a constraint on the freedom of teachers and an infringement of their professional autonomy[11] (Karseth and Engelsen 2013, 53).

The OECD-report, Aasen's account and the evaluation of the Knowledge Promotion Reform all see decentralization as delegation, i.e., the transfer of decision-making power. They use the term 'educational system' when claiming that the delegation of authority is 'a systemic change' (Møller et al. 2013, 30). What they see as a decentralizing 'systemic change' is a change in the political 'steering system' and a redistribution of power, without providing further details about how power is redistributed (Karseth, Møller, and Aasen 2013, 14). However, they conclude that the Norwegian system is centralized despite the political authorities' claim of having implemented a decentralizing reform.

Whilst the abovementioned analyses emphasize the centralized nature of Norwegian education during the period 1980–2013, several other authors have claimed the opposite, that this was the period during which decentralization took place. Arnesen and Lundahl (2006, 290) claim that during the 1980s, and the 1990s in particular, 'a radical transformation of educational governance took place [in all the Nordic countries] including decentralization, deregulation and marketization'. Stating that the change has been 'quite dramatic in some respects', they refer to statistics published by the

European Commission, which show that the Nordic countries have devolved responsibilities to schools and municipalities to a greater extent than other European countries. Since decentralization normally leads to greater differences between schools, Arnesen and Lundahl underline that the picture is complex, considering that the Nordic countries, contrary to expectations, also show the smallest variance between schools in student performance, for example, in mathematics.

Likewise, Helgøy and Homme (2007, 233, 235) claim that Norwegian education has become decentralized, although 'reluctantly' so, and market mechanisms have been implemented only to a 'limited degree'. Volckmar and Wiborg (2014) also claim that during the 1990s, Norwegian education became moderately decentralized. In their assessment, it was the reorganization which followed the 1992 Norwegian Municipality Act, which abolished the 'long-lived [Norwegian] tradition of centralized state control of education' (ibid., 128). Agreeing that Norwegian education is moderately decentralized they point to the transfer of decision-making authority in public sector education from the central level to the municipalities and individual schools, which happened without substantial growth in private provisions (Volckmar and Wiborg 2014, 128–129). Despite their shared definition of decentralization, Arnesen and Lundahl (2006) and Helgøy and Homme (2007) draw opposite conclusions regarding educational centralization and decentralization in Norway.

Among those who have analysed centralization and decentralization in Norwegian educational system, several have pointed out that delegating and retracting decision-making authority is often carried out at the same time in different domains as well as granted and withdrawn in rapid succession withing the same domain. This makes it difficult to assess whether a given reform leads to centralization or decentralization. Also, researchers point out that certain aspects of reforms are highlighted as decentralizing by the government whilst the centralization of decision-making in other domains are not communicated to the public (Aasen 1999, 56; Helgøy 2003, 62; Karlsen 2000; Volckmar and Wiborg 2014, 125).

The contradictory conclusions in the various studies of centralization and decentralization in Norwegian education reflect that none of the studies define what they mean by an educational system, what it consists of and how it operates. Since they have no clear conception of the system, they cannot establish a prior state of the system, before the decentralizing policy is implemented. Researchers explicitly or tacitly assume that education becomes centralized when decision-making is shifted upwards and decentralized when shifted downwards. Analyses restricted to the identification of delegation of decision-making without considering the broader picture of how the state exerts influence and control, for example, through centralized exams and national testing regimes, tend to adopt politicians' conceptions of their own reforms. The lack of ambition to explain anything, except for school achievement, and be content with descriptions may account for why researchers do not seek concepts that identify mechanisms that can explain a wider range of phenomena.

Is the Norwegian system centralized or decentralized? Applying Archer's concepts

How would the Norwegian educational system be conceptualized using Archer's definitions of centralized and decentralized systems and based on investigations of recent processes of change? In the following, I will identify processes of unification (intensive and extensive), specialization and differentiation in the Norwegian system since the early 1990s. I will also describe some of the discontent generated by one of the reforms, the 1994 reform of upper secondary education. This will show that unification has increased while specialization and differentiation have decreased, and, moreover, that the process of unification tends to generate recurrent discontent, all of which indicate that the Norwegian system is centralized.

Archer's theory of centralized and decentralized educational systems includes a broader range of phenomena than just shifts in the locus of decision-making, autonomy for teachers in choice of methods of instruction and school autonomy in financial, curricular, and other matters. It entails investigating intensive and extensive unification, which has to do with the impact of state policy and standardization of courses; systematization, which concerns the coherence and inclusiveness of the system; differentiation, which is about the autonomy of institutional operations and the political influence of the profession, and specialization, which concerns the heterogeneity of provisions.

Unification and systematization are the results of mechanisms inherent in the relationship between the system and the state. The state authorities and the central administration tend to prefer nationally uniform provisions (unification) and smoothly functioning systems without bottlenecks (systematization). Differentiation and specialization, on the other hand, predominate in decentralized systems, are the result of the relationship between the system and the teaching profession and with external groups. The teaching profession will tendentially pursue their interests and values and strive to increase autonomy for the system (differentiation), whilst external interest groups will, when possible, transact specialized provisions that are tailormade for their educational needs (specialization). If the processes of unification and systematization dominate in a system, and processes of specialization and differentiation/autonomy are in decline, it is likely that the system is centralized, i.e., the state is the leading part in the system.

Increased intensive unification and reduced differentiation

In Norway, since the beginning of the 1990s, the processes of intensive unification (increased impact of state policy) and reduced differentiation (reduced professional autonomy) have predominated. The educational policy of the state has increased its impact at the expense of the teaching profession, whose insertion in the policy process has been reduced and whose autonomy has been curtailed.[12] Several state interventions have resulted in reduced autonomy for the teaching profession: (a) introduction of a new rationale in public administration including education, MbO,[13] (b) a reorganization of the municipalities and (c) reforms of upper secondary vocational education – in particular, the 1994 reform (Reform 94) of upper secondary education.

I will focus on the interventions mentioned above because they concern two processes, the processes of unification and of differentiation. Several other interventions could be mentioned that affect teacher autonomy (differentiation). It is generally acknowledged that in recent years, Norwegian teachers have become subjected to more external control and demands for accountability and transparency in their work, such as the introduction of a national quality assessment system, in 2004, including a national testing regime with results published in so-called league tables, the introduction of mandatory teacher-parents conferences, individual student assessments and an upgrading of the National Curriculum to become a legally binding contract between the pupils/parents and the school (Helgøy and Homme 2007; Mausethagen 2013, 424).

a The 1990 White Paper 'Om organisering og styring i utdanningssektoren'[14] (St. meld. 37 (1990–1991)) introduced MbO as the principle of management in the education sector. Educational objectives were to be clearly formulated and communicated by state authorities and followed up by the systematic gathering of information about obtained results. Arguably, this represented increased state control of teachers' professional work, although some have seen it as a decentralizing move in providing more freedom for the teaching profession (Aasen 1999). Some have admitted that its effects are ambiguous in both providing certain local freedoms, but at the same time introducing tighter state control (Aasen 1999; Karlsen 2000).

   The same White Paper also announced another curtailment of professional autonomy, notably by reducing the influence of the profession on state-education policy and administration by eradicating several National Advisory Councils. Each council had consisted of professional educators from different levels in the educational system providing policy advice to the authorities. The government argued that these councils had become a 'state in the state' and increasingly advocated their own educational policies. Abolishing the councils would ensure that official state policy was more clearly communicated without dissenting voices from the teaching profession.

b Likewise, the 1992 municipal reform, which was introduced as a decentralizing reform by allowing municipalities to choose how to organize their services, reduced the influence of the teaching profession. Existing politically elected school boards and top administrative officials for education recruited from the profession were made optional. Most municipalities opted for no school boards and no professional educator as the top official for education. This change in the local hierarchy of decision-making was inspired by a globally circulated script on 'flatter organizations with fewer hierarchical levels'. Furthermore, the removal of professional teachers from the municipal administration of schools was supported by the New Public Management (NPM) principle that leadership is a profession by itself and requires no detailed knowledge of concrete work operations in the organization (Helgøy 2003, 63). A process, by political scientists called 'de-sectorization' of education, took place in that educational policy issues at the local level no longer were handled by a dedicated leader recruited from the profession, but by leaders from other 'sectors' or from newly created 'merged sectors' (Helgøy 2003, 64). As a result, the professional community of educators at the local level was fractured and disintegrated and educational expertise became subordinate to political and administrative decision-making (Helgøy 2003, 66). The municipal reform had the dual effect of increasing the impact of state policy and reducing the influence of the profession at the local level. The side-stepping of professional educators from local leadership spelled increased intensive unification and reduced institutional differentiation.

c Reduced influence for the profession and increased influence for the administration on educational operations was also the result of the 1994-reform of upper secondary education, which includes initial vocational education. A new practice was introduced in the authorization of vocational specializations, approval of apprenticeship enterprises, handling of apprenticeship contracts, etc. These authorizations were previously performed jointly by representatives of the national employers' association (The Confederation of Norwegian Enterprise; NHO) and the confederation of trade unions (The Norwegian Confederation of Trade Unions; LO). But after Reform 94, the authorizations were partly transferred to the central state administration and partly to regional administrative authorities (Høst and Hovdhaugen 2013). Thus, decision-making on vocational education was no longer deliberated by representatives of employers and labour organizations but handled by administrators at various levels, informed by national policies.

The introduction of MbO and the abolishment of National Advisory Councils in 1991, the reform of the municipalities in 1992 and Reform 94 of upper secondary education increased the intensive unification of the system: state policy was implemented more effectively. At the same time, the teaching profession was subjected to more control by the introduction of MbO. It was also deprived much of its influence on policy both at the central and local level, at the central level by the eradication of the National

Councils, at the local level as an effect of the 1992 municipal reform. The national employer and labour organizations representing industry also lost influence over initial vocational education.

Increased extensive unification and reduced specialization

In addition to changes in the authorizations connected with vocational education, the 1994 reform of upper secondary education also reduced the range of course options for basic vocational education. The total number of first year options was in 1994 reduced from over 100 to 13. Consequently, the content of each course became more general and less specialized. The 13 new courses were nationally uniform, identical in each locality, whilst the over 100 courses they replaced had covered several vocational specialisms originating in local contexts. Thus, the system went through a process of increased extensive unification at the expense of specialization. All local course offerings at the upper secondary level had now become standardized national courses.

Extensive unification in vocational upper secondary education was intensified by the 2006 Knowledge Promotion Reform. This reform reduced the number of vocational options in the second year from 86 to 52, reducing specialization and increasing the general content of each course. This was justified by a series of arguments in the government White Paper 'Kultur for læring'[15] (St. Meld. Nr. 30, 2003-2004, 67): fewer course options would be easier to plan and implement, pupils could postpone their final choice of specialization, they could attend a course closer to home, and the mismatch between demand and supply of apprenticeship places, which were often in short supply, would be reduced because the pupils would have general qualification and be qualified for several specialized apprenticeships and vocations. Reform 94 had initiated reduced specialization and national standardization of vocational education, a trend that was continued by the 2006 Knowledge Promotion Reform.

Discontent generated by standardization (unification)

Centralized and decentralized educational systems tendentially encounter different problems in their functioning. The centralized system encounters tension in relating to its environment since educational reforms are often the result of compromise between different and even contradictory demands. Therefore, reforms do not fully accommodate specific educational demands. The decentralized system, on the other hand, encounters problems in implementing state policy, since changes which are transacted at various locations in the system may conflict with the general policy decided at the political centre.

In Norway, the increasing standardization and reduced specialization of the upper secondary programmes in vocational education introduced by Reform 94 resulted in protests from various industries, which wanted to retain specialized courses particularly fitted to their needs. In 2012, the Federation of Norwegian Construction Industries (BNL) demanded that important decisions concerning vocational education, such as the curriculum, quality criteria and the model for alternation between school-based and work-based learning should be made by joint committees representing employer and labour organizations instead of administrative officials. They specifically suggested a new model for alternation between school-based and work-based learning, contesting the 2 + 2 model (2 years of school-based education + 2 years apprenticeships), which had been introduced by Reform 94 (Høst and Hovdhaugen 2013, 77).

These demands were addressed by two government White papers 'Utdanning for velferd'[16] (Meld. St 13 (2011–2012)) and 'På rett vei'[17] (Meld. St 20 (2012–2013)), which suggested a new model for the combination of school-based and work-based learning with more frequent alternations between the school and the workplace. Two state funded pilot projects were carried out 2013–2017 and 2014–2018.

An evaluation study of the pilot projects covering six different geographical regions of Norway and a selection of vocational tracks: motor vehicle maintenance, health and caring occupations, building and construction and retail, service and tourism concludes that 'the new alternation model represents a common solution applied to very different problems in vocational education, in different industries and in various regions' (Bjørnset et al. 2018, 6). The evaluators point out major differences between the education and training traditions in the various industries participating in the pilot. The construction industry had a long history of apprenticeships as a way of recruiting new workers. They had initiated the new alternation model themselves, based on their long experience. Likewise, the programme for repair of light vehicles educating car mechanics was established in an industry with long apprenticeship traditions. The health and caring vocations, on the other hand, had no established tradition for apprenticeships, which was the result of political decision-making, prepared by the two government White Papers. Likewise, 'retail, service and tourism' was a new apprenticeship programme with no tradition. Retail, where most of the apprenticeship places in the project were located, had no traditions for apprenticeships (Bjørnset et al. 2018, 24).

Public and private sector work places also differed greatly in how they dealt with apprentices. Whilst most private apprenticeship enterprises offered their apprentices a job when they had finished their Journeyman Certificate, public sector institutions receiving health and caring apprentices did not regard them as a way of recruiting new personnel. The public institutions had not themselves initiated apprenticeships in their organization, and they did not participate in recruiting and selecting them. The whole apprenticeship arrangement was based on decisions made by politicians (Bjørnset et al. 2018, 23).

Clearly, state authorities, by piloting a new alternation model, had designed a uniform solution to problems that varied among industries and vocations as well as between regions. The tendency of the state-education-mechanism to produce uniform provisions (unification) is here manifested in the introduction of a new uniformity (the alternation model) that does not fit all, trying to solve problems created by the old uniformity (the 2 + 2 model), which also did not fit all.

Educational change in Norway after 1990 analysed with Archer's concepts unification, differentiation and specialization, demonstrates that the processes and structural elaborations of the system have been dominated by increasing unification, reduced specialization and reduced differentiation (autonomy for the profession). Uniformity and national standardization have increased, while the autonomy of the system, including professional autonomy and influence on policy, has been reduced. Also, examples of discontent generated by the uniformity of provisions and lack of responsiveness to demands for specialized programmes follow the pattern that new reforms tend to replace old discontent with new discontent. We can, therefore, infer that the Norwegian system operates as a centralized system, according to Archer's real definition.

Comparing the different analyses

A striking feature of the Norwegian studies that use 'delegation' as their definition of decentralization is the contradictory results of their analyses. One reason why the researchers arrive at opposite conclusions, despite using the same concepts, seems to be variations in which domains of decision-making are included in their analyses. Some researchers focus on the delegation of decision-making to teachers, on whether teaching methods are prescribed in the National Curriculum (centralization) or left to be decided by the teachers themselves (decentralization). Other studies are less precise about the domains in which the locus of decision-making is shifted, whether it is economic, curricular or decisions on human resources. None of the studies consider the introduction of new types of accountability introduced by the state, such as national tests and league tables, which affect local practices. These inaccuracies and omissions result in contradictory assessments of local independence and unimpeded decision-making.

The claim about 'moderate decentralization', seen as a definitive break with state control in the early 1990s (Volckmar and Wiborg 2014), is justified with reference to the decentralizing reform of the municipalities, which shifted administrative responsibility to individual schools. Another effect of this reform, which was to decrease professional autonomy, in the sense of teachers' influence on local educational decision-making, is not considered in Volckmar's and Wiborg's analysis.

The conclusions that Norwegian education is *strongly decentralized* rely on statistical data from the EU (Arnesen and Lundahl 2006) and the OECD

(Haug 2009) concerning 'school autonomy'. Based on EU-data, Arnesen and Lundahl (2006, 290) make the strong claim that the Nordic countries 'stand out' in the European context by having devolved responsibilities to municipalities and schools to a greater extent than other European countries.

In addition to the uncertainty generated by the inclusion of different domains of decision-making, there is also a tendency to infer that shifting decision-making from the centre to the periphery results in a decentralized system without defining the educational system and therefore without an assessment of its previous state. Also, since decisions to delegate authority are often retracted, and opposite moves are carried out at the same time in different domains, it becomes difficult to assess whether a given reform increases centralization or decentralization. This 'dynamic' has led some to define centralization and decentralization as strategies of governance, i.e., as categories of action rather than as structures (Karlsen 2000). The notion of action is underlying the concept of 'delegation', and the implicit ontological assumption of the whole tradition of seeing educational decentralization as delegation, seems in fact to be an 'ontology of praxis'. This means seeing educational systems as merely 'the repertoire of repetitive or routinized practices surrounding education' (Archer 1995, 107) and not as a social form, i.e., as an emergent structure with its own distinct mechanisms and causal powers.

Consequently, entirely missing in the conception of decentralization as delegation is an understanding of the tendencies towards change inherent in the educational system, in virtue of its structures and mechanisms. The existence of mechanisms entails that the 'dynamics' of the system consists of more than the implementation of reforms and other piecemeal changes decided at the centre. For example, educational demands from external groups are 'processed' in the system, in a different way in centralized and decentralized systems. Thus, the 'dynamics' of the system includes more than the implementation of reforms.

Conclusion

In Archer's theory of educational systems, internal processes are generated by educational demands. The prominent characteristics of decentralized educational systems, structures, and processes are specialization and differentiation (relative autonomy of the system). Specialization results from the successful transactions of educational change by external groups, i.e., new tailormade provisions are established. Differentiation results from multiple integration, which means that the system must deal with educational demands from a variety of different groups and must, therefore, develop provisions that reconcile various demands.

More recent studies of educational decentralization, on the other hand, show only moderate interest in how state educational policy is generated, except for Weiler (1990) who claims that a policy of decentralization may increase the legitimacy of the state and has been shown to transport educational conflict away from the centre. That is why decentralization remains on the political agenda despite documented difficulties in implementing it. However, generally, in current research, the generation of decentralization policies is given less attention than policy implementation. Researchers have, however, noted as a paradox that decentralization policy during recent decades is invariably initiated from the top and even resisted by the periphery, which is supposed to benefit from it.

The current alternatives to Archer's concepts of centralized and decentralized educational systems, which reduce the system to the redistribution of authority, strategies of governance or to one indicator measuring 'school autonomy', lack a conception of social structure as an emergent ontological level with causal powers *sui generis*. These other definitions have no conception of mechanisms which tendentially generate certain types of change in the system, and are, in this sense, not 'dynamic' but 'static', which paradoxically is a criticism levelled against the conception of a system.

Much current research using the concepts of educational centralization and decentralization is evaluation research commissioned by policymakers, national and international. The indicators of school autonomy developed by supra-national bodies like the EU (Eurydice) and OECD (the PISA-test) are increasingly and unquestioningly used in national research, categorizing, for example, the Norwegian educational system as decentralized. In this way, important premises in knowledge production are supplied by agencies with their own political agenda. The close relationship between researchers and policymakers also seem to influence research questions, which are often purely descriptive with no explanatory ambitions. However, we must not forget the one explanatory hypothesis that is underlying the international policies of decentralization and research associated with it, which is that it leads to higher school achievement. It has, however, been difficult to find evidence for decentralization (delegation/school autonomy) boosting achievement.

What are the dangers associated with the uncritical adoption of concepts and indicators endorsed by international agencies in this area of research? Bhaskar points out that social scientific terms often are refined versions of everyday language and ideological conceptions. 'Social scientific theory [...] is produced, at least in part, by the transformation of [such proto-scientific ideas]' (PON, 48). The first step in the transformation of proto-theories to scientific theories will, thus, be an attempt at a real definition (PON, 49). It seems that few efforts have been made by educational researchers to refine policy-makers' conceptions of educational centralization and decentralization and develop concepts with greater explanatory power. Archer's real definitions of centralized and decentralized educational systems on the other hand, which explain a wide range of phenomena, are derived from her comprehensive comparative-historical studies of European education. This testifies to Bhaskar's claim that real definitions 'are not plucked a priori out of hats, spun out of thought alone. Rather they are produced *a posteriori*, in the irreducibly empirical process of science' (PON, 43).

Notes

1. Discussions about essentialism, natural (social) kinds and causality in contemporary philosophical debates and the standpoint of critical realism in relation to other contemporary philosophies on these issues are presented in Ruth Groff (2013).
2. Bhaskar uses the example of copper, pointing out that the electronic structure of copper can explain its dispositional properties, among which are the tendency to conduct electricity (RTS, 171).
3. This widespread neglect of the educational system as a social structure embodying causal mechanisms has been ignored, even by the prominent educational sociologists Basil Bernstein and Pierre Bourdieu (Archer 1983), and this neglect prevails in current mainstream educational research.
4. Internal relations are relations of natural necessity, where one element cannot be what it is without its connection to the other elements in the relation.
5. Between 1992 and 1997, 12% of all educational projects funded by the World Bank involved 'decentralization'. In 2006, more than 40 governments were receiving support from international agencies to decentralize education (Bjork 2006, 1).
6. Christopher Bjork (2006) from the UNESCO-UNEVOC International Centre for Education in Bonn presents case studies of educational decentralization from ten countries in the Asia-Pacific region: China, Macau, Singapore, Japan, Korea, Indonesia, Malaysia, India, Pakistan, and Sri Lanka. Joseph Zajda (2006) presents case studies from Canada, the UK, Mexico, Columbia, Chile, Thailand, Indonesia, Kerala (India) and regions of Latin America, Europe, and Africa.
7. An indicator of decentralization, seen as the amount of decision-making delegated to the school level measuring so-called 'school autonomy' has been developed by the OECD. In connection with the international achievement test Program for International Student Assessment (PISA), principals of participating schools are asked to indicate which operations of their schools are decided locally, by them. These include the hiring and firing of teachers, decisions on teacher salaries and salary increases, formulation of school budgets and budget allocations, practices regarding student discipline, assessment of students, admission, choice of textbooks, course content and the kinds of courses offered (Haug 2009, 112). The EU has also developed indicators for 'school autonomy', which are published in European Commission (2014).
8. The data collected in the PISA survey revealed major differences in the within country/between school variance of school autonomy. The variance between schools were higher in Norway and Canada than in the other countries on a composite variable called Autemploy, which includes the right to hire and fire teachers, establish teachers' salaries, and determine salary increases. Haug finds this difference between schools surprising considering the long history of state involvement in Norwegian education (Haug 2009, 84).
9. Susanne Wiborg has, in another article, suggested explanations of why privatization of education was boosted in Sweden in the early 1990s and not in Denmark and Norway (Wiborg 2013).
10. During the 1960s and 1970s, in Norwegian public debate, 'educational centralization' referred to the closing down of small rural schools, which entailed transferring/transporting pupils to more centrally located schools. This

policy was initiated by the Labour government and was justified as an intervention intended to improve the quality of education for pupils in rural areas (Solstad 1978). 'Educational centralization' in the Norwegian political debate still carries overtones from this period and is associated with the closing down of small rural schools.
11. https://www.udir.no/contentassets/fd2d6bfbf2364e1c98b73e030119bd38/framework_for_basic_skills.pdf
12. These two aspects of teacher autonomy, (a) individual autonomy in choice of pedagogy and (b) collective autonomy in having influence on educational policy formation and the policy process (insertion), are also observed by Helgøy and Homme (2007).
13. Management by objectives (MbO) is sometimes denoted as Management by objectives and results (MbOR), which is more accurate, since the principle entails measurements of obtained results. The notation MbO is used here because it is more commonly used in Norwegian documents.
14. English: On organizing and governing the education sector.
15. English translation: A culture for learning.
16. English translation: Education for welfare.
17. English translation: On the right track.

References

Aasen, P. 1999. "Det Sosialdemokratiske Prosjektet. Utdanningsreformer i Sverige og Norge i etterkrigstiden [The Social-Democratic Project. Educational Reforms in Sweden and Norway After the Second World War]." In *Både – og. 90-tallets Utdanningsreformer i Historisk Perspektiv*, edited by A. O. Telhaug and P. Aasen, 13–64. Oslo: Cappelen Akademisk Forlag.

Archer, M. S. 1983. "Process without System." *European Journal of Sociology* 24: 196–221.

Archer, M. S. 1984. *Social Origins of Educational Systems*. University Edition. London: Sage.

Archer, M. S. 1995. *Realist Social Theory: The Morphogenetic Approach*. Cambridge: Cambridge University Press.

Archer, M. S. [1979] 2013. *Social Origins of Educational Systems*. London: Routledge.

Arnesen, A.-L., and L. Lundahl. 2006. "Still Social and Democratic? Inclusive Education Policies in the Nordic Welfare States." *Scandinavian Journal of Educational Research* 50 (3): 285–300.

Bhaskar, R. [1979] 1998. *The Possibility of Naturalism. A Philosophical Critique of the Contemporary Human Sciences*. London: Routledge. (PON).

Bhaskar, R. 2008. *A Realist Theory of Science (with a New Introduction)*. London: Routledge. (RTS).

Bjork, C. 2006. "Introduction." In *Educational Decentralization: Asian Experiences and Conceptual Contributions*, edited by C. Bjork, 1–7. Dordrecht: Springer.

Bjørnset, M., H. Høst, T. Nyen, K. Reegård, and A. Hagen Tønder. 2018. Evaluering av Vekslingsmodeller i Fag-og Yrkesopplæringen [Evaluation of Alternation Models in Vocational Education and Training]. Sluttrapport. Oslo: Fafo-rapport 2018: 42 & NIFU-rapport 2018: 13.

Bray, M. 2013. "Control of Education: Issues and Tensions in Centralization and Decentralization." In *Comparative Education: The Dialectic of the Global and the*

Local, edited by R. F. Arnove, C. A. Torres, and S. Franz, 188–207. New York: Rowman & Littlefield.
Danermark, B., M. Ekström, L. Jakobsen, and J. Ch. Karlson. 2002. *Explaining Society. Critical Realism in the Social Sciences*. London: Routledge.
European Commission. 2014. *Key Data on Education in Europe*. Brussels: European Commission. Eurostat. Eurydice.
Groff, R. 2013. *Ontology Revisited. Metaphysics in Social and Political Theory*. London: Routledge.
Hanson, E. M. 2006. "Strategies of Educational Decentralization: Key Questions and Core Issues." In *Educational Decentralization. Asian Experiences and Conceptual Contributions*, edited by C. Bjork, 9–25. Dordrecht: Springer. Education in the Asia-Pacific Region Series. Asia-Pacific Educational Research Association.
Hanushek, E. A., S. Link, and L. Wossmann. 2013. "Does School Autonomy Make Sense Everywhere? Panel Estimates from PISA." *Journal of Development Economics* 104 (C): 212–232.
Haug, B. 2009. "Educational Decentralization and Student Achievement. A Comparative Study Utilizing Data from PISA to Investigate a Potential Relationship Between School Autonomy and Student Performance in Australia, Canada, Finland, Norway and Sweden." Master Thesis, Faculty of Education, University of Oslo. https://www.duo.uio.no/bitstream/handle/10852/ 31127/ MasterxThesisxBeritxHaugxPFI.pdf
Helgøy, I. 2003. "Fra Skole til Tjenesteleverandør? Endringsprosesser i Norsk Grunnskole [From School to Service-Provider? Processes of Change in Norwegian Basic Education]." *Norsk Statsvitenskapelig Tidsskrift* 19 (1): 55–79
Helgøy, I., and A. Homme. 2007. "Toward a New Professionalism in School? A Comparative Study of Teacher Autonomy in Norway and Sweden." *European Educational Research Journal* 6 (3): 232–249.
Høst, H., and E. Hovdhaugen. 2013. "Ny Struktur – Tradisjonelle Mønstre. Kunnskapsløftets Endringer i Historisk Perspektiv [New Structure – Traditional Patterns. The Changes of the Knowledge Promotion Reform in Historical Perspective]." In *Reformtakter. Om Fornyelse og Stabilitet i Grunnopplæringen*, edited by B. Karseth, 61–81. Oslo: Universitetsforlaget.
Karlsen, G. E. 2000. "Decentralized Centralism: Framework for a Better Understanding of Governance in the Field of Education." *Journal of Education Policy* 15 (5): 525–538.
Karseth, B., and B. U. Engelsen. 2013. "Læreplanen for Kunnskapsløftet: Velkjente Tråkk og Nye Spor [The Curriculum of the Knowledge Promotion Reform – Familiar and New Tracks]." In *Reformtakter. Om Fornyelse og Stabilitet i Grunnopplæringen [Reform-Rythms. On Renewal and Stability in Basic Education]*, edited by B. Karseth, J. Møller, and P. Aasen, 43–60. Oslo: Universitetsforlaget.
Karseth, B., J. Møller, and P. Aasen. 2013. "Opptakten." In *Reformtakter. Om Fornyelse og Stabilitet i Grunnopplæringen [Reform-Rythms. On Renewal and Stability in Basic Education]*, 13–20. Oslo: Universitetsforlaget.
Lauglo, J. 1995. "Forms of Decentralisation and Their Implications for Education." *Comparative Education* 31 (1): 5–30.
Mausethagen, S. 2013. "Accountable for What and to Whom? Changing Representations and New Legitimation Discourses among Teachers under Increased External Control." *Journal of Educational Change* 14: 423–444.

Møller, J., T. S. Prøitz, E. Rye, and P. Aasen. 2013. "Kunnskapsløftet som styringsreform." In *Reformtakter. Om Fornyelse og Stabilitet i Grunnopplæringen [Reform-Rythms. On Renewal and Stability in Basic Education]*, edited by B. Karseth, l. Møller, and P. Aasen, 23–41. Oslo: Universitetsforlaget.

OECD, The Norwegian Ministry of Church and Education, and The Norwegian Ministry of Culture and Science. 1989. *OECD-vurdering av Norsk Utdanningspolitikk. Norsk Rapport til OECD. Ekspertvurdering fra OECD. [OECD-evaluation of Norwegian Educational Policy. Norwegian National Report to the OECD and Expert-evaluation of the Norwegian report by the OECD]*. Oslo: Aschehoug & Co (William Nygaard).

Sayer, A. 1998. "Abstraction: A Realist Interpretation." In *Critical Realism. Essential Readings*, edited by M. Archer, R. Bhaskar, A. Collier, T. Lawson, and A. Norrie, 120–140. London: Routledge.

Sayer, A. 1999. *Method in Social Science. A Realist Approach*. 2nd Edition. London: Routledge.

Sayer, A. 2000. *Realism and Social Science*. London: SAGE.

Solstad, K. J. 1978. *Riksskole i Utkantstrok [The National School in Peripheral Regions]*. Oslo: Universitetsforlaget.

Volckmar, N., and S. Wiborg. 2014. "A Social Democratic Response to Market-Led Education Policies: Concession or Rejection." In *The Nordic Education Model: 'A School for All' Encounters Neo-Liberal Policy*, edited by U. Blossing, L. Moos, and G. Imsen, 117–131, Policy Implications of Research in Education 1. Dordrecht: Springer.

Weiler, H. N. 1990. "Comparative Perspectives on Educational Decentralization: An Exercise in Contradiction?" *Educational Evaluation and Policy Analysis* 12 (4): 433–448.

White Paper, Kultur for Læring [Culture for Learning] (Meld. S. 30 (2003–2004)).

White Paper, Utdanning for Velferd [Education for Welfare] (Meld. S. 13 (2011–2012)).

White Paper, På Rett Vei [On the Right Track] (Meld. S. 20 (2012–2013)).

Wiborg, S. 2013. "Neo-liberalism and Universal State Education: The Cases of Denmark, Norway and Sweden 1980-2011." *Comparative Education* 49 (4): 407–423.

Wöbmann, L., E. Lüdemann, G. Schütz, and M. R. West. 2007. "School Accountability, Autonomy, Choice and the Level of Student Achievement: International Evidence from PISA 2003." OECD Education Working Papers, No 13. Paris: OECD.

Zajda, J. 2006. "Introduction." In *Decentralisation and Privatisation in Education. The Role of the State*, edited by J. Zajda, 3–27. Dordrecht: Springer.

Part II
The spatial context of educational mechanisms

5 Towards a critical realist ontology for spatial education analysis

Unn-Doris K. Bæck

Introduction

Dropout from upper secondary education[1] stands out as one of the main challenges for the Norwegian education system. Politicians, educational authorities, newspaper editors and commentators, as well as 'ordinary people', have cried out about a lost generation of youngsters, who due to lack of educational qualifications will enter adulthood with a serious disadvantage, making them more prone to unemployment and to becoming future passive receivers of social benefits. Numerous measures meant to counteract the high dropout rates have been instigated by educational authorities at different levels, most of them with minor success. Within the research communities, the focus has been on the usual suspects, with explanations related to individual or family characteristics, such as socio-economic status (SES), parents' educational level, gender or ethnicity (see, e.g., Byrhagen, Falch, and Strøm 2006; Lie et al. 2009). The problem of early school leaving is worse in vocational education and training (VET), and there is also a relevant geographical factor, as a main dividing line between those who drop out and those who complete their education, tends to differentiate between students from rural versus students from urban regions. Boys from low SES backgrounds residing in rural areas and attending a VET program are those most prone to drop out of school without completing. Furthermore, other forms of differences in educational achievement between those from rural and urban settings have also been documented throughout the education system, such as in national tests in reading, English and mathematics and in final exams at the end of compulsory schooling.

In this chapter, the main focus is on the spatial factor, and on how explorations of spatial differences in education can be understood through employing insights from critical realism (CR). There are several justifications for this focus. Firstly, there is evidence that place matters in educational outcomes in the sense that rural students are underperforming compared to their urban counterparts, even after controlling for variables such as grade levels and social background (Bæck 2015; Byrhagen et al. 2006; Hargreaves, Kvalsund, & Galton 2009). Research by among others Green and Corbett (2013)

DOI: 10.4324/9781003163527-7

shows that this is also an international phenomenon. Secondly, despite the existence of research documenting the rural-urban divide when it comes to educational attainment, the focus on this problem in mainstream education research and among educational authorities and policy makers is minor. Location is often disregarded as a valid factor for understanding attainment differences, and the urban setting is presupposed in educational debates and analyses (Bæck 2015; Butler and Hamnett 2007; Hargreaves et al. 2009). Thirdly, the tendency to employ explanations focusing primarily on individual characteristics in research on attainment differences brings with it a danger of over-emphasizing the individual as the primary analytic entity. In consequence, effects that can better be understood at the level of schools, classrooms, local communities, regions or nations are sometimes overlooked or misinterpreted (Bæck 2015). Fourthly, this research field is lacking in theoretical discussions and advances, as is also pointed out by Corbett (2015), who calls for a stronger engagement of the conceptual tools of sociology and contemporary social theory in scholarship on rural education (see also Kvalsund & Hargreaves [2009] on this subject). Through focusing on spatial differences in early school leaving and educational attainment, this chapter addresses all four concerns, but its main contribution is related to the two latter elements. Insights from CR are used to explore and map out a theoretical basis for a spatial analysis of this topic, one that goes beyond the atheoretical and individually centred approaches that have dominated the research field thus far and that takes into consideration the actor-structure interplay in order to understand individual action and how societal structures work as causal factors in this regard. In line with this, in order to investigate why young people's educational behaviour varies according to *where* it takes place, the chapter focuses primarily on the material and structural conditions under which young people act and conduct their choices.

In the next sections, some of the main features of CR will be introduced. This is followed by an outline of generative mechanisms, which serves as the most significant analytical link for understanding spatial differences in education in this chapter. Several generative mechanisms are put forward as especially relevant for the problem at hand.

Critical realism: The empirical, the actual and the real

The starting point for the discussion proposed in this chapter is a desire to understand why young people from different geographical contexts act differently when it comes to dropping out of or completing upper secondary education and why their educational outcomes are significantly different from each other. In other words, the goal is to *explain* something, and what is ultimately sought to be explained is *individual action*. However, it is not individual action per se, or the actors' individual stories about or explanations or interpretations of their own actions that are at the centre of the

Towards a critical realist ontology 81

analysis proposed here – although these are certainly important. Instead, the aim is to investigate how structures and mechanisms emanating at meso or macro levels, impact upon the choices made at the micro level. For this purpose, CR can be fruitful, as it puts forward a dynamic understanding of how different levels interact with each other, creating upward and downward causation that may induce processes of change or reproduction.

The relationship between structure and agency is fundamental for theoretical understandings of individual action, and a preliminary CR framework for understanding this relationship was presented in Bhaskar's transformational model of social activity (Bhaskar 1998), and later developed in Archer's morphogenetic approach (Archer 1995). Here, the actor is regarded as intentional and active, and therefore as capable of making decisions. At the same time, decisions are made in contexts or settings where structural and institutional conditions must be taken into consideration, arguing that even micro-level analyses need to have a macro-level foundation. The relationship between individual agency/action and the social and material structures contextualizing the individual is, therefore, central for understanding how young people's decision-making processes are related to education when viewed through a CR lens. How are such decision-making processes constituted and how are they affected by space?

A central assumption in CR is that there is a real world out there that impinges upon actors at a number of different levels – and even though we cannot prove or disprove its existence, we behave as if it is real. The levels interact with each other and influence each other, implying the existence of dynamic relationships that can induce change in contexts for action. While acknowledging the existence of a material world, individual action and social structure are seen as emerging from, but not reducible to, the material world. Both the natural and social worlds have an objective reality, but the social world is overlaid with human constructs and conceptions that obscure the underlying mechanisms (Fox 2013). There is a deep structure to the social world that forms the causal mechanisms behind social processes. Structures are seen as a precondition for intentional individual action and must, therefore, exist prior to such action. Societal structures are not created through simultaneous individual behaviour and also cannot be reduced to such behaviour. In this sense, structures, therefore, have independent existence as emergent properties and powers.

According to Bhaskar (1975), the world should not be conflated with our experience of it, and in this sense, it is misleading to speak of the 'empirical world'. As pointed out by Sayer (2000), CR should, therefore, not be confused with empirical realism, or empiricism, which identifies the real with the empirical, that is, with what we can experience – 'as if the world just happened to correspond to the range of our senses and to be identical to what we experience' (Sayer 2000, 11). Instead, a central feature of CR ontology is the distinction between the real, the actual and the empirical – the three levels into which reality is stratified. The first level is the *empirical*, defined as the domain of experience, that is, events as we experience them, and for a researcher this is the level where objects or events can be measured empirically (Fletcher 2017). In my study, this is the level where the young informants experience being a student in upper secondary education and share their experiences with me as a researcher. As stated by Fletcher (2017), the events at this level are always mediated through the filter of human experience and interpretation.

At the middle level, the *actual*, there is no filter of human experience. Events occur whether or not we experience or interpret them, and these occurrences are often different from what is observed at the empirical level (Danermark et al. 2002 as cited in Fletcher 2017). For my study, this level will consist of educational landscapes and opportunity structures that the young people relate to (more on this later).

Finally, the last level, the real, is the realm of objects, their structures and powers. They can be physical (like minerals) or social (like bureaucracies) (Sayer 2000). These objects have certain structures and causal powers, that is, capacities to behave in particular ways and causal liabilities or passive powers, that is, specific susceptibilities to certain kinds of change. A primary goal of CR is the aspiration to explain social events through reference to these causal mechanisms and the effects they can have throughout the three strata of reality (Fletcher 2017). The real is whatever exists, be it natural or social, regardless of whether it is or is not an empirical object for us, and whether we happen to have an adequate understanding of its nature. Bhaskar (1986, 5) states: 'This layer of reality already exists and is in action even if we are not informed of it and in most cases, it is independent of the scientist and his scientific activities' – it is *intransitive*, in Bhaskar's terminology. According to Sayer (2000), the belief that there is a world existing independently of our knowledge of it is a defining feature of CR.

We may be able to observe the real or the actual, for example, the real as the social structure of an organization, as well as what happens when they act (actual events), but some structures may not be observable. As stated by Sayer (2000), observability may make us more confident about what we think exists, but existence itself is not dependent on it. Critical realists, therefore, cannot rely on a criterion of observability in order to determine what exists. Instead, realists accept a causal criterion (Collier 1994 as referenced in Sayer 2000). Sayer (2000, 12) states: '... a plausible case for the existence of unobservable entities can be made by reference to observable effects which can only be explained as the products of such entities'.

Generative mechanisms

Central for understanding the relationship between structure and agency and how phenomena can be explained in CR is the concept of generative mechanisms – the *modum operandi* of the domain of the real. Bhaskar states that a generative mechanism is 'nothing more than a way of acting of a

Towards a critical realist ontology 83

thing' (Bhaskar 1975) and 'a causal structure that explains a phenomenon' (Bhaskar 1998). According to Archer (2015), generative mechanisms explain *how* a given correlation works, rather than merely *that* such an association is statistically significant, thereby providing the real basis of causal laws. As already mentioned, the real exists regardless of our knowledge of it; for example, causal laws exist regardless of the presence or absence of statistical associations with outcomes at the level of events (Archer 2015). Generative mechanisms can be understood as the process, or factor, in a system that produces a result and is, therefore, responsible for the action, or reaction or outcome of a natural or social phenomenon (Wight 2015). In this sense, mechanisms provide the explanation for a phenomenon. According to Wight (2015), mechanisms are not statements about experiences (the domain of the empirical) or events (the domain of the actual), but are claims about the way things act in the world independent of their being experienced.

Even though the notion of 'mechanism' can bring with it associations of determinism, this is not how mechanisms are understood in CR. Social systems are considered open systems, that is, systems that allow interactions between the different elements of the system and the system's surroundings, as opposed to closed systems that are completely isolated from their surroundings, for example, laboratory closure in natural science. According to Wight (2015), mechanisms cannot be deterministic since they operate in a social world characterized by contingency and flux and where multiple mechanisms are constantly interacting. He emphasizes that the outcome of a particular process, therefore, cannot be determined a priori by knowing the type of mechanism that is at work, implying that we cannot talk about *laws* relating to these mechanisms. Instead, the outcomes must be understood as *tendencies* generated by mechanisms operative within open systems.

Even though generative mechanisms possess the powers to produce outcomes, powers may still exist unexercised; they can be either activated or remain dormant (Sayer 2000). According to Wight (2015), mechanisms are, therefore, best understood as 'potentialities' that sometimes may need a trigger, or to reach a tipping point, before becoming operative. The implication of this is that the future should be understood as essentially open. Sayer (2000, 12) expresses it in the following way: 'What has happened or been known to have happened does not exhaust what could happen or have happened'. According to Sayer, the nature of the real elements that are present at a given time, constrains and enables what can happen, but does not predetermine what will happen. 'Realist ontology therefore makes it possible to understand how we could be or become many things which currently we are not: the unemployed could become employed, the ignorant could become knowledgeable, and so on' (Sayer 2000, 12). According to Wight (2015), this is crucial for how researchers should approach the question of mechanisms in empirical analyses. 'Given that all social systems are open', he says, 'and that a range of interacting mechanisms will typically constitute them, what we mean when we identify one mechanism among many, is to imply that this mechanism is important in some way. This requires that explanation via mechanisms must specify the powers and propensities of that particular mechanism and identify the causal tendencies produced by it, as well as specifying when those tendencies might and might not be manifest' (Wight 2015, 61).

We now turn to the empirical problem that is the basis for this chapter, spatial differences in education outcomes, exemplified by early school leaving from upper secondary education. The aim is to discuss how this can be analysed in terms of the CR approach of the real, the actual and the empirical, and how an analysis of geographical education differences can benefit from the open systems-approach inherent in the CR ontology. The main questions in such an analysis are how we can identify, describe and explain the generative mechanisms that produce the observable outcome, students dropping out of school without formal qualifications. How does reality materialize for the students in a way that encourages so many of them to leave school? And, on the other hand, what preconditions need to be in place for the students to stay in school instead of leaving without formal qualifications? How can different levels of influence interact in such a way that change can be induced?

Young students' experiences of the transition to upper secondary education – description of the empirical

The analysis in this chapter is based on a study of upper secondary school students in the northern part of Norway. The rationale for the study was to investigate processes behind early school leaving in upper secondary education in the north of Norway, which is a major problem, especially in many rural places where as few as 30% of the students finish within standardized study time. The main research questions had to do with whether spatial factors were relevant for how students reflected on their educational plans and choices and for their experiences in school. Qualitative interviews – 54 in number – were conducted among students in seven upper secondary schools in a county in Northern Norway. The students were interviewed during their last semester of their first year in upper secondary school. The majority of the students were in VET, and two-thirds of them were girls. Four of the schools were located in what we may call rural settings, while the other three were located in two different towns in the county. While all of the schools recruited students from both rural and urban areas, the student body of the four schools in rural locations consisted primarily of rural students, with just the occasional student from one of the more urban places in the county.

Common for the majority of the students interviewed, irrespective of geographical background, was their upholding of the existing knowledge paradigm, which explained the students' emphasis on education as an obvious, and in a way inescapable, part of the life phase they found themselves in. Continuing from lower secondary to upper secondary education was considered self-evident, and variations in how the youngsters reflected upon educational choices became more visible only when they were asked to talk about their plans after upper secondary education.

When the students were asked questions about making their way through the education system, the data revealed variations in terms of which factors they addressed, and this was connected to the spatial reality to which they related (see Bæck 2019 for more on this study). During the interviews, three main topics connected to their experiences of being an upper secondary school student stood out as particularly essential for the rural students. These were issues connected to moving away from home, issues connected to estrangement from place and 'costs' related to loss of social networks. These topics concern the domain of experience at the empirical level, that is, the outcomes of the generative mechanisms we aim to reveal through the analysis.

The transition to upper secondary education implies several different transitional experiences for the young. It has to do with the transition between two different parts of the educational system, between lower and upper secondary school, which involves new ways of working and new demands and expectations. Some of the students we interviewed talked about how they experienced the school subjects as more challenging and the teachers' demands higher, compared to what they had experienced in lower secondary school. Spatial transitions are also a part of the picture, as starting upper secondary education entails a geographical move from one physical school building to another, having to get acquainted with new school grounds, halls and corridors. Transitioning to a new school also means moving to new social environments and getting to know new classmates, new teachers and being integrated into new school classes.

During the interviews, it became clear that some of these transitions provided different challenges for the students depending on whether they resided in rural or urban areas. Since not all municipalities have an upper secondary school and since not all study tracks are represented in all schools, the physical transition of changing schools would often entail a greater spatial movement for the rural than for the urban students. Rural students commuted long distances on a daily basis to go to school or they moved away from home to live in school dormitories, bedsitters or with relatives. Such spatial movement and physical transition would affect the social aspects of transitioning to new school environments. The rural students often started their new school without an established social network of friends to lean on, which was described as challenging. One of the rural students, for example, had moved to town to go to school and didn't know anyone else in the class, so her transition to upper secondary school was hard since she struggled with establishing social relations, which, the student said, also made it difficult for her to relate to the subjects and to be active in class. For many of the rural students, the biggest challenge was related to going from living at home to living by themselves as 15–16-year olds. Without the immediate support of parents and family, they had to get used to new and higher educational demands and get acquainted with new classmates, while at the same time fending for themselves when it comes to getting up in the morning, shopping, cooking and cleaning, finances etc. Many of the students experienced that they struggled more with the subjects than they had done previously, which could also be the case for the students who lived at home during upper secondary education. However, moving away from home, living by oneself and being exposed to new social situations were described as energy consuming and reduced their motivation for school-work.

For VET students, the years in upper secondary education often entail several moves over a four-year period. The different VET subjects and programs are divided between different schools, and changing tracks means changing schools. Also, the VET-students are dependent on apprenticeship positions in order to complete their education, which also means having to relocate. Adding to this that the average VET-student enters upper secondary education with lower grades from lower secondary education compared to the average student opting for the academic study programs, this group of students is put in a more vulnerable position when it comes to ability to complete their education.

Moving away from home also affected the students in other ways. The rural students would travel home almost every weekend and every school holiday. The new life situation of living in one place and being at home during weekends and holidays would affect their opportunities to take part in social interaction and be included in social networks, both in their home-places and in the new place of residence. The changing social circumstances and the loss of valuable social networks also affected access to part-time employment, in both places. For many of the rural students, securing a part-time job was a necessity in order to finance the bedsitter or the dormitory. Not being able to do so would put a strain on the parents' ability to pay, to the point that some of the rural students talked about giving up upper secondary education and moving back home.

In an analysis rooted in a critical realist approach, we are interested in the explanations behind the situation described above; why did the rural youngsters we interviewed experience more hardship in the transition from lower to upper secondary education, than their urban counterparts, potentially making it harder for them to complete upper secondary education?

Opportunity structures and educational landscapes at the level of the actual

In order to understand the experiences young people in the study expressed during the interviews, the context in which they undertake their deliberations is crucial. The context is made up of occurrences or events at the actual level, and as already stated, these events occur whether we experience or interpret them or not. Contexts make up structural and cultural conditions for individuals' actions and choices, and essential elements when we discuss young people's educational orientations are the spatial patterning of the educational system and of work opportunities. The term 'opportunity structure' is a way of pinpointing the existence of conditions and barriers that affect students' motivations and choices. As outlined elsewhere (Bæck 2019), different geographical locations constitute different opportunity structures, providing options and barriers that directly and indirectly promote or hinder opportunities for individuals, which may again affect students' motivations and choices. The local presence of particular educational institutions is part of the opportunity structure that forms young people's perceptions of possible and probable educational routes, which may in turn affect individual school choices made and subsequent motivation within school. According to Million et al. (2017), the spatial organization of educational institutions implies shaping places as educational landscapes. They show that spatial proximity of educational institutions has positive effects on the successful outcome of people's educational biographies. Over the years, the spatial organization of educational institutions in Norway has changed dramatically. The spatially dispersed organization of schools that was the preferred approach for many years, where smaller schools would be established as close to the students' homes as possible, has been substituted by spatial concentration of institutions in what may be considered more centrally located settings. Schools in smaller communities have been closed down and the students have been moved to larger schools in municipal centres. This has been taking place at all levels of education. In upper secondary education, it has led to considerable spatial variations when it comes to the structure of available courses and apprenticeships, restricting the opportunities for young people residing in rural communities, creating logistical barriers and making weekly commuting a necessity for many students from the age of 15–16. Also important for the shaping of educational landscapes are factors such as resources allocated to education, differences in access to learning resources and differences in teacher recruitment and retention. These are factors that are crucial for the quality of the education offered and that may also vary according to place. In this way, the organizational structure of upper secondary schooling constitutes a spatially differentiated objective reality for young people. Many rural youngsters relate to an educational system that offers them limited options where they live, making certain educational routes hard to realise and making them more susceptible to dropping out of school (Bæck 2019).

Identification of possible mechanisms

In accordance with a CR ontology, it is at the level of the real that we can identify generative mechanisms that can explain rural students' educational experiences; the challenges related to moving away from home, the danger of dropping out and the problems with coping with school. The opportunity structures and educational landscapes at the level of the actual can be traced back to three mechanisms that are at play: the centralized education system, the efforts in national education policy made towards decentralization, and international educational trends as they are made visible through local politics and priorities.

The centralized education system

According to Skinningsrud (2012, 2014), who has thoroughly described and analysed the historical emergence of the state education system in Norway, it is highly centralized. This is confirmed by a number of other researchers who claim that the Norwegian education system shows the dominant characteristics of being a centralized education system, for example, through detailed and binding governmental framework plans, rigid administrative regulations, control systems, evaluations and sanctioning systems and also since the education system is governed by one law and one national curriculum (Aasen 1999, 2013; Karseth, Møller, and Aasen 2013; Møller et al. 2013; Skinningsrud 2012, 2014; Telhaug, Mediås, and Aasen 2006).

Archer (2013, 174–176) uses two pairs of characteristics to discuss the difference between centralized versus decentralized education systems: unification plus systematization and differentiation plus specialization. Unification and systematization concern structural features of the education system as a consequence of how education is related to the state. This refers to what extent educational establishments, activities and personnel are developed under a central, national educational framework of administration, including national standardization of educational inputs, processes and outputs and whether the education system is systematized through interconnected elements within a unified whole. When it comes to differentiation and specialization, this relates to the education system's responsiveness to society's components. Differentiation refers to how education is differentiated from other social institutions (Archer 2013, 179), which is the result of the multiplicity of goals imposed on education by various influential parties and pressures of powerful interest groups associated with different social institutions. Specialization refers to the development of internal educational specialization within the education system, that is, an internal differentiation of the system itself, such as specialization in intake, processes and outputs (Archer 2013, 181). How much specialization develops depends partly upon the range, variety and complementarity of the services demanded from it, and partly on the relative power of those voicing the demands.

According to Skinningsrud (2019), the developmental trajectories when it comes to these two pairs of characteristics differ between decentralized and centralized educational systems. While a centralized system shows increased unification and systematization, generated by the structural connection between education and the state, a decentralized system is characterized by specialization and differentiation, due to the structures connecting education with external interest groups and the incorporated teaching profession. She claims, that increased differentiation means that the system becomes more autonomous in the sense that there is less governmental interference with internal work operations. Skinningsrud characterizes the Norwegian educational system as centralized, and using Norway as an example, Nordkvelle and Nyhus (2017) reinforce the point that in a centralized system, the teaching professions will have limited autonomy when it comes to designing learning environments, changing examinations or curricula etc. Another example from the Norwegian context is parents' position in school. In a decentralized system, parents could be a potential interest group, however, as shown elsewhere (Bæck 2022), in reality parents have limited opportunities to negotiate, demand or influence what goes on in school within Norway's centralized system.

Efforts to decentralize

Efforts to decentralize the Norwegian education system can also be seen as a generative mechanism in this study, in the sense that this has affected the local presence of educational institutions and, thus, the opportunity structures that form young people's perceptions of possible and probable educational routes. Nordkvelle and Nyhus (2017) describe how efforts to decentralize the Norwegian education system, especially after 1970, initially entailed aspects such as involving local schools, politicians and communities in the governance of education, or rooting the curriculum closer to the local environment in order to increase the relevance of the school to local conditions. However, from 1984, a deregulation of budget and other financial arrangements prompted the municipalities to develop their own aims and ideas for how they should develop the local school (Nordkvelle and Nyhus 2017, 224). The new financing model for the municipalities meant that the ministry went from earmarking money for certain missions to transferring a lump sum of money to the municipalities, leaving it up to the municipalities to prioritize between different sectors, According to Nordkvelle and Nyhus (2017), this gave the municipalities a much larger space for their own priorities. However, with a scarcity of public funding, the education sector had to compete with other public administrative and service tasks and sectors for which the municipalities were responsible, and at the local level the authorities were forced to make priorities and balance considerations that had to do with local politics. Solstad and Andrews (2020) point out that prior to the reform, the municipalities had no economic incentive to close down or amalgamate schools since the money came as earmarked grants. After the reform, on the other hand, the closure of a large number of small schools in peripheral (rural) areas (Knutas 2017) led to a widespread centralization of school provision. According to Solstad and Andrews, the municipalities had the financial motive to save money by closing schools, and they had the power to do so, even if the national policy still was to keep a relatively centralized school structure throughout the country. The same is shown by Nordkvelle and Nyhus (2017) who point out that while the previous arrangement had secured for small schools a solid financing in remote regions, the new system weakened their position significantly. Karlsen (2006, 2014) claim that with the decentralization of responsibilities from state to municipalities, local authorities became left to their own devices to solve disparities between a decreasing population and a shrinking economy. The same tendencies are still ongoing to this day, and in the northernmost county in Norway, the number of schools have decreased significantly since the reform was implemented, making it a significant generative mechanism for young people's educational orientations and experiences, especially in rural areas.

According to Skinningsrud (2014), despite efforts to award more responsibility and autonomy for school contents etc. to the local school, municipal or county level, such decentralization efforts have not led to changes when it comes to power distribution, and real democratization has, therefore, not taken place. Nordkvelle and Nyhus (2017) have also questioned the same lack of transfer of authority in relation to restricting greater decentralization. The role of the state has, thus, remained prominent, with decentralized approaches being dependent upon reduced forms of governmental control. Therefore, processes of centralizing, decentralizing and *recentralizing* have represented the key dynamic for the governance of the educational system for many years.

Neo-liberal education policy

Traditionally, education policies were under the firm control of the nation state (Fulge, Bieber, and Martens 2016). At present, on the other hand, international initiatives are important triggers for reformulation of education policies, shaping national debates and educational landscapes. A third generative mechanism worth mentioning is, therefore, neo-liberal education policy, as described by Pring (2015), with its focus on managerialism, performance indicators, audits, inputs related to outputs, target-settings and efficiency gains. As Pring (2015, 21) puts it, this is an educational system where teachers 'deliver' the goods to the 'consumers' according to agreed 'targets'. The period of decentralization described in the previous paragraph was, according to Telhaug et al. (2006), followed by what they call the era of globalization and neo-liberalism, starting around 1990. The background for this new era was a need for better control systems for the education sector, among other things to get a clearer overview of resource use and quality measures employed. Nordkvelle and Nyhus (2017) point out that increased accountability together with a 'global perspective' on education gradually replaced a national-cultural perspective. They, along with other researchers, for example, Karlsen (2014), have connected this development to the strong influences emanating from international organizations such as EU, UN, WTO, OECD and, in particular, to the PISA-activities of the OECD. Nordkvelle and Nyhus (2017, 229) state that the traditional values stressing the school's responsibility for the overall education of the students have gradually been displaced by a technical-economic or cognitive-instrumental rationale, where controlling the output through testing and grading plays an important part.

This development affects the opportunity structures and educational landscapes of young people in several ways. It has an effect on the content of the education provided, resulting in a standardization that is particularly relevant for the spatial perspective proposed here. The national core curriculum in Norway allows for taking local circumstances into consideration and for incorporating local contents in the teaching. However, the *incentives* to do so are missing. The school owners, the municipalities, do not have any obligation to develop and implement locally relevant contents, and in already overloaded schedules these are in danger of being deprioritized. Among other things, as a result of the neo-liberal education policy and educational managerialism described above, teachers work days are more than ever filled with numerous tasks in addition to their actual teaching; more and more administrative tasks, assessment work, following up students with special education needs, as well as their parents and so forth. All these tasks compete with more 'voluntary tasks', such as developing and implementing local contents, which often lose out and become deprioritized. In this way, teachers' space for manoeuvring in accordance with local needs may be affected by influence from neo-liberal education policy and the managerialism that follows. There are also other processes pulling in the same direction: the main assessments that are being made of the students, such as the national tests and final exams, are highly standardized. They are nationally provided and identical for all students. As schools spend time preparing the students for the tests, these forms of assessments compete for time that could have been spent on developing and implementing local contents in the teaching. Rural schools that make an effort when it comes to developing and implementing local curricula will not be rewarded for this, as long as it is performance on the centralized tests that are the goal. Such international initiatives may, therefore, have consequences for the spatial aspects of education, leading to a more limited concept of quality in education, where high quality means high PISA-scores.

As mentioned above, the opportunity structures and educational landscapes young people relate to can be traced back to how the education system is set up according to national education policy. As described here, neo-liberal education policy, a centralized education system, but also decentralization reforms affecting the education sector, are generative mechanisms explaining the orientations and actions behind young people's educational trajectories. Together they are responsible for the outcome.

However, as mentioned in the introduction, the powers of generative mechanisms do not necessarily become activated. The generative mechanisms outlined above represent potentialities that may or may not be triggered into becoming operative, and in the next section, we will explore space as a precondition for the activation of these generative mechanisms, in order to explain how the mechanisms may lead to certain outcomes in certain geographical locations and not in others.

Context and space as conditions for activation of potential powers

Above I have sought to identify, describe and explain the generative mechanisms that produce the observable outcome of early school leaving. Figure 5.1 sums up and illustrates the relationship between the different levels of reality and its constituent elements identified in the analysis. The powers and liabilities of the mechanisms have been specified, but we also need to take into consideration conditions that enable or restrict their operation. As stated above, CR upholds that what has been known to happen does not exhaust what could have happened (Sayer 2000), thus the future remains open. There are multiple possible futures, and the actual is only a part of the real world, which also consists of non-actualized possibilities and unexercised powers of the already existing structures and mechanisms (Patomäki 2006). Causal powers inherent in social structures and in social processes are understood as *potential* powers, and as pointed out by Sayer (2000),

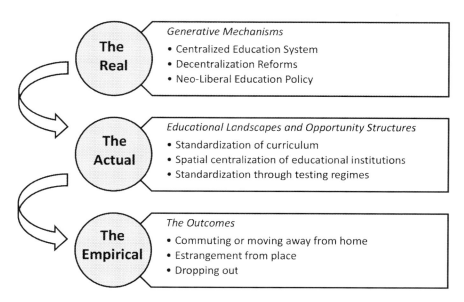

Figure 5.1 Overview of the spatial education analysis.

Towards a critical realist ontology 93

whether or not they are ever exercised depends on the presence of certain conditions or on actors' interpretations of situations, or of both. If they *are* exercised or activated, the outcome will also depend on different conditions, and the results can be unacknowledged or unintended. Thus, context, where space is concerned, represents a condition for the activation of potential powers and, therefore, as a mediating factor for the outcome of generative mechanisms. With context representing an enabling or constraining condition, the generative mechanisms play out in different ways at the empirical level. Events take place within geo-historical contexts, implying that the mechanisms deriving from the structures present are space and time specific. As pointed out by Sayer (2000), the same mechanism can produce different outcomes according to context, or more precisely, according to its spatio-temporal relations with other elements, having their own causal powers and liabilities, which may trigger, block or modify its action. Sayer emphasizes that given the variety and changeability of the contexts of social life, this absence of regular associations between 'causes' and 'effects' should be expected. The conditional nature of causation intrinsic to CR ontology implies that specifying enabling or restricting conditions under which the mechanisms operate become necessary. A mechanisms-based approach, therefore, has to consider the contexts in which the mechanisms function.

For example, the funding system for the education, described above, that leaves it to the municipalities to prioritize between the different forms of instruction and certification and between different municipal sectors may affect different contexts differently. Economic considerations may force smaller, less prosperous municipalities to initiate spatial concentration of educational institutions through school closures and amalgamations. In small, rural communities with geographically dispersed populations, these are reoccurring themes when economic prioritizations are to be made. At the secondary school level, we can find the same dynamic and a school structure geared towards fewer, bigger and more specialized schools, with the result that students have to attend school far away from their homes and engage in long-distance commuting or move away from home at a very early age. Again, this is especially true for those who reside in smaller, rural communities. A decentralized governance structure, therefore, has in many cases resulted in the increased spatial centralization of educational institutions.

Final remarks

In the analysis presented in this chapter, the primary analytical focus has been at the structural level, showing how the education system is set up to deliver education policy in terms of governance, organization and funding, and the relevance of space when it comes to the outcomes produced. Such outcomes can be, for example, students' educational experiences and orientations, student outcomes, equity and quality, or preparing students for the future. In a CR understanding of geographical education differences, the domain of the real with the generative mechanisms put forward above is regarded as the causal agent of early school leaving – and not the individual student. Cultural and structural mechanisms condition the actions of agents, and these mechanisms, which are part of the domain of the real, are also always historically and spatially situated and conditioned. Space and context may work as constraining or enabling factors for the generative mechanisms at play, and, as outlined, what happens when these mechanisms are activated is part of the domain of the actual. In this chapter, I have argued that generative mechanisms create spatially specific opportunity structures that produce spatial differences in educational trajectories and outcomes. Then, how agents respond to the constraining or enabling structural and cultural contexts they have 'inherited' (Westaway, Kaiser, and Graven 2019) is part of the domain of the empirical, here shown through students' experiences and reflections when it comes to education. Part of the opportunity structure and agents' interpretations of opportunity structure is the 'learning to leave' paradigm that has been pointed out by Corbett (2007), where the educational system prepares students for life outside the rural communities, effectively de-qualifying them for life within rural communities.

In this chapter, several mechanisms particularly essential to explaining and understanding the spatial differences in young people's educational orientations and experiences have been identified. Space provides context for the operation of generative mechanisms and is as such crucial for understanding their manifestations and outcomes. Through the above analysis, I have specified the powers and propensities of the generative mechanisms and identified the causal tendencies produced by them, as well as detailing when those tendencies might be and might not be manifested and the conditions that enable or restrict their operation. The ontological stance of CR implies that mutual relations between micro and macro levels are emphasized – in both macro and micro oriented analyses. In order to understand spatial inequalities in education, we need to establish knowledge about the structures and mechanisms that are significant for how the education system functions at the macro level and the effect they have on individual actors' educational decisions. These things can play out differently in different settings, and we have to take into account the mutual interaction between individual, intentional actors and relevant societal structures and institutions, as well as material, physical structure and conditions. Analyses based on a critical realist methodology makes it very clear that societal structures and mechanisms are phenomena that are time and space specific. As shown above, generative mechanisms produce opportunity structures and educational landscapes or educational spaces, with centralization, decentralization and standardization, materialized in many forms, as key elements. The emphasis on the conditional nature of causal powers as potential powers is a reminder that all social analyses need to take space and time into consideration, and a CR ontology is a promising foundation for doing so.

Note

1. A comprehensive upper secondary system combines academic education and vocational training, offering students three general academic programmes and nine vocational programmes. After two years of vocational studies, or after completing the four-year vocational studies programme, students can enter university if they complete a supplementary year. Vocational education and training (VET) has a strong tradition in Norway and 50% of the students choose VET. Choice of study program varies somewhat from county to county and in the two northernmost counties, the majority of the students are in VET (52% in Troms and 60% in Finnmark). The completion rates in upper secondary education in Norway are below OECD average, and the biggest challenge facing the system is dropout. For the northernmost counties, the dropout rates are alarmingly high.

References

Aasen, P. 1999. "Det sosialdemokratiske prosjektet." [The social-democratic project]. In *Både – og. 90-tallets Utdanningsreformer i Historisk Perspektiv [Education Reforms in the 1990ies in a Historic Perspective]*, edited by A. O. Telhaug, and P. Aasen, 13–64. Oslo, Norway: Cappelen Akademisk Forlag.

Aasen, P. 2013. "Accountability under ambiguity. Dilemmas and contradictions in education." In *Teacher Education Research between National Identity and Global Trends*, edited by A.-L. Østern, K. Smith, T. Ryhaug, T. Krüger, and M. B. Postholm, 77–92. Trondheim, Norway: Akademika.

Archer, M. S. 1995. *Realist Social Theory: The Morphogenetic Approach*. Cambridge, UK: Cambridge University Press.

Archer, M. S. 2015. "Introduction: Other conceptions of generative mechanisms and ours." In *Generative Mechanisms Transforming the Social Order. Social Morphogenesis*, edited by M. S. Archer, 1–24. New York: Springer International Publishing. https://doi.org/10.1007/978-3-319-13773-5_1

Bæck, U.-D. K. 2015. "Rural Location and Academic Success. Remarks on Research, Contextualisation and Methodology." *Scandinavian Journal of Educational Research* 59: 1–14. doi:10.1080/00313831.2015.1024163

Bæck, U.-D. K. 2019. "Spatial Maneuvering in Education. Educational Experiences and Local Opportunity Structures among Rural Youth in Norway." *Nordic Journal of Comparative and International Education* 33: 61–74. doi: http://doi.org/10.7577/njcie.3274

Bæck, U.-D. K. 2022. "Understanding the Space for Parental Voices in School Governance – Perspectives from Norway." In *School Governance in Global Contexts: Trends, Challenges and Practices*, edited by Nicholas S. K. Pang, and Philip W. K. Chan. London: Routledge.

Bhaskar, R. 1975. *A Realist Theory of Science*. Leeds: Leeds Books.

Bhaskar, R. 1986. *Scientific Realism and Human Emancipation*. London: Verso.

Bhaskar, R. 1998. *The Possibility of Naturalism: A Philosophical Critique of the Contemporary Human Sciences*. London: Routledge.

Butler, T., and C. Hamnett. 2007. "The Geography of Education: Introduction." *Urban Studies* 44 (7): 1161–1174. doi: doi.org/10.1080/00420980701329174

Byrhagen, K. N., T. Falch, and B. Strøm. 2006. *Frafall i Videregående Opplæring: Betydningen av Grunnskolekarakterer, Studieretninger og Fylke. [Dropout from*

Upper Secondary Education: The Significance of Grades, Study Programs and Counties]. Trondheim: Senter for økonomisk forskning.
Collier, A. 1994. *Critical Realism: An Introduction to Roy Bhaskar's Philosophy*. London: Verso.
Corbett, M. 2007. *Learning to Leave: The Irony of Schooling in a Coastal Community*. Black Point, NS: Fernwood Publishing.
Corbett, M. 2015. "Rural Education: Some Sociological Provocations for the Field." *Australian and International Journal of Rural Education* 25 (3): 9–25.
Danermark, B., M. Ekström, L. Jakobsen, and J. C. Karlsson. 2001. *Explaining Society: An Introduction to Critical Realism in the Social Sciences*. London: Routledge. https://doi.org/10.4324/9780203996249
Fletcher, A. J. 2017. "Applying Critical Realism in Qualitative Research: Methodology Meets Method." *International Journal of Social Research Methodology* 20 (2): 181–194. doi: 10.1080/13645579.2016.1144401
Fox, N. J. 2013. "Comparison of Post-Structuralist, Critical Realist and Neo-Materialist Perspectives." Accessed Jan 14 2021. https://www.academia.edu/5536917/Comparison_of_post_structuralist_critical_realist_and_neo-materialist_perspectives_Table_
Fulge, T., T. Bieber, and K. Martens. 2016. "Rational Intentions and Unintended Consequences: On the Interplay between International and National Actors in Education Policy." In *Handbook of Global Education Policy*, edited by K. Mundy, A. Green, B. Lingard, and A. Verger, 453–469. Hoboken, NJ: John Wiley & Sons. https://doi.org/10.1002/9781118468005.ch25
Green, B., and M. Corbett. 2013. "Rural Education and Literacies: An Introduction." In *Rethinking Rural Literacies: Transnational Perspectives*, edited by B. Green, and M. Corbett, 1–13. New York: Palgrave Macmillan. doi: 10.1057/9781137275493
Hargreaves, L., R. Kvalsund, and M. Galton. 2009. "Reviews of Research on Rural Schools and their Communities in British and Nordic Countries: Analytical Perspectives and Cultural Meaning." *International Journal of Educational Research* 48 (2): 80–88. doi: https://doi.org/10.1016/j.ijer.2009.02.001
Karlsen, G. E. 2006. *Utdanning, Styring og Marked. Norsk Utdanningspolitikk i et Internasjonalt Perspektiv. [Education, Governance and Market. Norwegian Education Policy in an International Perspective]*. Oslo: Universitetsforlaget.
Karlsen, G. E. 2014. "Internasjonale aktører som premissgivere for Norsk utdanningspolitikk med særlig vekt på OECD." [International Actors as Premise Providers for Norwegian Education Policy, with Special Emphasis on OECD]. In *Reformideer i Norsk Skole. Spredning, Oversettelse og Implementering [Reform Ideas in Norwegian School. Dispersion, Translation and Implementation]*, edited by K. A. Rørvik, T. V. Eilertsen, and E. M. Furu, 121–146. Oslo: Cappelen Damm Akademisk.
Karseth, B., J. Møller, and P. Aasen. 2013. "Kapittel 1: Opptakten." [Chapter 1: Introduction]. In *Reformtakter. Om Fornyelse og Stabilitet i Grunnopplæringen [Education Reforms. On Change and Stability in Primary Education]*, edited by B. Karseth, J. Møller, and P. Aasen, 13–20. Oslo: Universitetsforlaget.
Knutas, A. 2017. "Nordic Education Policy in Retreat Neoliberal Economic Rationalization and the Rural School." *Policy Futures in Education* 15 (6): 695–712. doi: https://doi.org/10.1177/1478210317716307
Kvalsund, R., and L. Hargreaves 2009. "Reviews of Research in Rural Schools and their Communities: Analytical Perspectives and a New Agenda." *International Journal of Educational Research* 48 (2): 140–149. https://doi.org/10.1016/j.ijer.2009.02.002

Lie, I., M. Bjerklund, C. Ness, V. Nygaard, and A. E. Rønbeck. 2009. *Bortvalg og Gjennomstrømming i Videregående Skole i Finnmark. Analyser av Årsaker og Gjennomgang av Tiltak. [Dropout and Throughput in Upper Seondary Education in Finnmark. Analyses of Factors and Measures]*. Alta, Norway: Norut.

Million, A., T. Coelen, A. J. Heinrich, C. Loth, and I. Somborski. 2017. "Educational politics and urban design for learning. Local educational landscapes in policy and practice." In *Education, Space and Urban Planning: Education as a Component of the City*, edited by A. Miller, A. J. Heinrich, and T. Coelen, 177–191. New York: Springer. https://doi.org/10.1007/978-3-319-38999-8_17

Møller, J., T. S. Prøitz, E. Rye, and P. Aasen. 2013. "Kapittel 2: Kunnskapsløftet som styringsreform." [Chapter 2: The knowledge promotion reform as governance reform]. In *Reformtakter. Om fornyelse og Stabilitet i Grunnopplæringen [Education Reforms. On Change and Stability in Primary Education]*, edited by B. Karseth, J. Møller, and P. Aasen, 23–42. Oslo, Norway: Universitetsforlaget.

Nordkvelle, Y., and Nyhus, L. 2017. "Management by objectives as an administrative strategy in Norwegian schools: Interpretations and judgements in contrived liberation." In *Administrative Strategies of Our Time*, edited by N. Veggeland, 219–260. New York: Nova Science Publishers.

Patomäki, H. 2006. "Realist Ontology for Futures Studies." *Journal of Critical Realism* 51 (1): 1–31. doi: https://doi.org/10.1558/jocr.v5i1.1

Pring, R. 2015. "The Teacher as High Priest and Usherer in of the Kingdom of God." *Power & Education* 71 (1): 19–28. doi: 10.1177/1757743814567380

Sayer, A. 2000. *Realism and Social Science*. London: Sage.

Skinningsrud, T. 2012. "Fra reformasjonen til mellomkrigstiden. Framveksten av det norske utdanningssystemet." [From the reformation to the interwar period. The emergence of the norwegian educational system]. Doctor Philosophiae dissertation, UiT The Arctic University of Norway, Tromsø, Norway.

Skinningsrud, T. 2014. "Struktur og Prosess i Norsk Utdanning på 1990- og 2000-Tallet - et Makrososiologisk Perspektiv." [Structure and Process in Norwegian Education in the 1990ies and the 2000s - A Macro-Sociological Perspective]. *Norsk pedagogisk tidsskrift [Norwegian Pedagogical Journal]* 98(4): 222–234.

Skinningsrud, T. 2019. "Vindicating Archer's Concepts of Educational Systems – Centralized and Decentralized – as Exemplars of Critical Realist Theorizing." *Journal of Critical Realism* 18 (4): 453–473. doi:10.1080/14767430.2019.1656924

Solstad, K. J., and Andrews, T. 2020. "From Rural to Urban to Rural to Global: 300 Years of Compulsory Schooling in Rural Norway." *Journal of Rural Studies* 74: 294–303. doi:doi.org/10.1016/j.jrurstud.2019.10.034

Telhaug, A. O., Mediås, O. A., and Aasen, P. 2006. "The Nordic Model in Education: Education as Part of the Political System in the Last 50 years." *Scandinavian Journal of Educational Research* 50 (3): 245–283. doi:10.1080/00313830600743274

Westaway, L., Kaiser, G., and Graven, M. 2019. "What Does Social Realism Have to Offer for Research on Teacher Identity in Mathematics Education?" *International Journal of Science and Mathematics Education* 18: 1229–1247. doi: doi.org/10.1007/s10763-019-10021-4

Wight, C. 2015. "Mechanisms and models: Some examples from international relations." In *Generative Mechanisms Transforming the Social Order. Social Morphogenesis*, edited by M. S. Archer, 49–64. New York: Springer International Publishing. https://doi.org/10.1007/978-3-319-13773-5_3

6 Structural constraints on teachers' work

Comparing work experiences in rural and urban settings in Northern Norway

Daniel Andre Voll Rød

Introduction

This chapter compares work experiences among teachers from two different cases of municipalities in Northern Norway in order to understand spatial differences in teachers' work experiences. The comparison is between a case study municipality given the pseudonym *Grønnvik*, which represents a rural context, and Tromsø, which represents an urban context.

Since the turn of the century, the importance of place in education studies has been increasingly recognized, such as in White and Corbett (2014) and Gulson and Symes (2007). However, whereas some research has focused on rural settings and rural versus urban settings, place has often been a variant between urban settings (Bæck 2016; Beach et al. 2019; Hargreaves, Kvalsund, and Galton 2009; Paulgaard 2017). In Northern Norway, the area in Norway with the lowest population density, the students score below average on measurements of educational outcomes than elsewhere in Norway in terms of dropout rates from upper secondary schools (Markussen, Lødding, and Holen 2012; SSB 2019a; Vibe et al. 2012) and in grade ten national tests and exams (Bæck 2019). It has also been generally assumed that larger urban schools are of higher quality than rural schools (Hargreaves, Kvalsund, and Galton 2009). In Troms and Finnmark County, a county with a high percentage of rural settlements, schools contribute less than average to the students' national exam results in grade ten when adjusted for parental background, according to the Norwegian directorate for education and training (Utdanningsdirektoratet 2020). However, this superiority of urban schools over rural schools is contested (Beach et al. 2018; Solstad 2009; Solstad and Thelin 2006).

The two most prominent researchers on rural education in Norway in the 1990s and 2000s were Karl Jan Solstad and Rune Kvalsund. According to Solstad, laws regarding urban and rural education differed in Norway up until 1959, at which point rural and urban schools were subsumed under the same national curriculum plan. This upgrading of rural basic schooling was part of a process that merged vocational and grammar schools into a comprehensive lower secondary education, and eventually, in 1969, the duration

DOI: 10.4324/9781003163527-8

of compulsory schooling was extended from seven to nine years (Solstad and Thelin 2006). Solstad argues that the county and municipality-funding system (*NIS-86*) introduced in 1986 worsened the economic situation for poorer municipalities and counties. Before 1986, municipal school budgets, including primary and lower secondary education, were approved by the state, which earmarked and transferred money to the municipalities based on an approved budget. In 1986, a new system for municipal funding based on local taxes and a block grant transfer from the state was introduced, and the funding of elementary and lower secondary education became a part of the municipality budget. The intention behind this delegation was to give the municipalities greater autonomy and to allow them to move funds from financially well-off sectors to less affluent sectors in accordance with local needs (Solstad 2009; Solstad and Andrews 2020; Solstad and Thelin 2006).

At present, several small and rural municipalities have difficulties in financing the local services they are obliged to provide, which can partly be explained by the demographic differences between rural and urban communities. Rural areas struggle with the depopulation of people of working age and an ageing population, affecting both the taxpayer base and welfare costs. This is the case for such communities all over Norway at present and in the future, as projected by a Statistics Norway population prognosis for 2040 (Leknes et al. 2018; Onsager 2019; Solstad 2009; Stein 2019). There is also higher expenditure in rural communities per capita for legally required tasks such as infrastructure maintenance, education and health services. A specific example is the lack of benefits of scale, leading to a need for more teachers per student due to smaller classes. When resources are scarce due to low tax income and small state transfers, municipalities must prioritize between different public services. This situation has led to poor funding of the educational sector. The 1992 municipality reform provided municipalities with more autonomy over local school structure, but the consequence of the combination of a poor municipality economy and the municipality reform of 1992 was often closing down schools to save money, as teachers' salaries are negotiated centrally. Such municipality economies are themselves the major justification for school closures, with the second being rural demography and depopulation (Nordkvelle and Nyhus 2017; Solstad 2009; Solstad and Andrews 2020; Solstad and Thelin 2006). School closures and other cuts in welfare services, in turn, affect local communities and their attractiveness to potential new inhabitants, and these effects may lead to people moving elsewhere (Autti and Hyry-Beihammer 2014).

Kvalsund provided a methodological critique of previous studies, arguing that much educational research is of a single case in an urban setting, often locked inside the classroom. At the time of writing, he argued a need for contextual detail and new, large multiple case studies (Kvalsund 2009). Since 2009, several researchers have taken up Kvalsund's call. The

Learning Regions Project compared educational attainment levels in two Norwegian counties and developed a methodology for schools and municipalities to improve their attainment levels (Langfeldt 2015). Special journal issues have focussed on the subject of space and place. *Places* need comparative attention in order to improve our understanding of the differences in issues such as student attainment based on location (Reegård, Rogstad, and Hegna 2019). Dropout rates from upper secondary school in Northern Norway can be partly explained by opportunity structures, such as a lack of access to a relevant education in the vicinity of the local labour market (Bæck 2019). Furthermore, rural-urban comparisons show differences not only in local education and employment opportunities but also in local culture and understanding of education (Hegna and Reegård 2019). School closures and consolidations are still often a rural challenge rooted in the contextual conditions at the municipality level (Solstad and Andrews 2020), and municipality administrators often play a surprisingly active role in such processes (Aasland and Søholt 2020).

Why focus on teachers and their work experiences? Teachers and parents are the two most influential external factors for student achievement, which implies that the quality of teaching is important for student results (Kristiansen 2014). According to Stronge, teacher effectiveness and teacher quality had a major impact on student's academic success, and he argued that the quality of teaching was the most important school-related factor in student achievement (Stronge 2010). Similar results have also been reported by others, such as Hattie (2003). The teacher's position is also at the centre of a web of educational relations, as they provide insights on their own challenges, the challenges students are facing and how both relate to the context. Examples of context include the educational system, national guidelines, school leaders, student families and the local community. Teachers are, therefore, uniquely practical when inquiring about influential aspects of school (Barter 2013). Rural schools and teachers also face distinct, geographical challenges. Examples include problems in attracting and retaining qualified teachers in rural areas (Lind and Stjernström 2015; Stelmach 2011) and limited opportunities in rural areas for professional development (Downes and Roberts 2018). Due to the importance of teachers and their position in the educational system, it is crucial to know what kinds of impediments they experience in their work situations across geographical contexts. A further discussion of teachers' work experiences is presented in the theory section.

The research questions are as follows: (1) *Do rural and urban teachers experience different kinds of constraints in their professional work?* (2) *What causes these kinds of differences in work experience?* This chapter utilizes a comparative approach; in this case, two schools in one urban and one rural municipality in Northern Norway. It also contributes to a macro-sociological focus on social structures. The analysis is based on a data set of qualitative interviews and participant observations.

Theoretical framework and previous research

The main theoretical focus of this chapter is the macrostructures related to education, and it draws especially from two contributions from Margaret Archer's authorship. The first contribution is the relationship between structure and agency (Archer 2007, 1995), and the second is the distinction between the decentralized and centralized educational systems (Archer [1979] 2013).

The relationship between structure and agency

The relationship between structure and agency has been thoroughly discussed in Archer's book *Realist Social Theory: The Morphogenetic Approach* (1995). The rationale for using parts of this framework in the analysis is the inclusion of structure, culture and agency. Structure and culture provide limitations and enabling conditions to both individual and group agency. However, structural and cultural enablements and constraints do not determine, but only condition agency. This happens by structural and cultural properties establishing a situational logic for the agents (collectivities of individuals), which guides action. This guidance may or may not be followed, since the agent has a degree of self-determination. In turn, agents act and interact, often guided by a situational logic that comes with their relative position or role in a social structure. Changes and/or reproduction in structure and culture emerge over time due to interaction. Note that several of these cycles of structure-culture conditioning agency, followed by interaction, which lead to change or reproduction in structure-culture that again conditions agency, can happen in parallel and on several levels simultaneously. The results of a cycle on a national level may have implications for later cycles on the national level or cycles on a local level with different agents. Furthermore, this framework including both structure-culture and agency helps to avoid ending up with a deterministic structure-culture without room for agency or a partially decontextualized agent or individual whose agency is not completely limited or benefitted by external influence (Archer 1995).

To further illuminate the relationship between structure and agency, I have chosen to include the three-stage model from *Making our Way through the World* (Archer 2007, 17) to illustrate the individual level as well:

1 Structural and cultural properties objectively shape the situations that agents confront involuntarily, and inter alia possess generative powers of constraint and enablement in relation to ...
2 ... Subjects' own constellations of concerns, as subjectively defined in relation to the three orders of natural reality: nature, practice and the social.
3 Courses of action are produced through the inner reflexive deliberations of subjects who subjectively determine their practical projects in relation to their objective circumstances.

The important point for this chapter is between bullet point one and two, which is the connection between structural (and cultural) properties that constrain the formation and realization not only of collective agents but also the individual subject's own concern. Note that this chapter puts its focus on structural concerns, putting cultural properties in the background for now. In order to take teachers' work experiences and their constraints seriously, one has to include their concerns, as a concern is necessary in order to experience constraints. Individuals have some freedom of choice and may incorporate themselves into collective agents to change their circumstances. I will shortly discuss the teachers' work experience and concerns before discussing some structural properties.

Teachers' work experiences and concerns

Teachers' work experience is a crucial concept in this chapter, justified by the importance of teachers as established in the introduction. Enquiring into teachers' work experiences may provide insights both into teachers' professional identity (Beck 2017; Connelly, Clandinin, and Applebaum 1999), their concerns and reflections (Archer 2007) and insights into the highly structured frameworks of education (Goodson 1999; 1996). Teachers' experience, knowledge and pedagogical thinking are context bound and affected by the environment (Connelly, Clandinin, and Applebaum 1999; Goodson 1996; Karlberg-Granlund 2019), and according to Goodson, teachers' narratives should not be investigated singularly in a vacuum, but rather within a context of history and social construction (Goodson 1999). Context is many-faceted, and this chapter is mostly interested in the structural aspect and especially in the material and external contexts surrounding them (Clarke and O'donoghue 2017). Teachers' work experiences have also been used to investigate rural-urban differences in education elsewhere (Karlberg-Granlund 2019; Preston 2012). Teachers' work experiences are here defined as the teachers' own experiences and reflective knowledge of their work, including their professional concerns and motivations (Archer 2007).

The Norwegian educational system as structured and centralized

An important structural property for analysing spatial differences from the data is the educational system. There is a debate about whether the Norwegian educational system is centralized or decentralized (e.g., Kvalsund 2009; Skinningsrud 2014; Volckmar and Wiborg 2014), and arguments for a decentralized system often refer to the distribution of decision making in the Norwegian educational system (Smith 1989). According to Skinningsrud, most of these studies only discussed certain aspects of the system and did not describe the broader system in its totality, and she proposed drawing upon Margaret Archer's analysis of educational systems in order to overcome these problems (Skinningsrud 2014).

Archer defined the state educational system as 'a nationwide and differentiated collection of institutions devoted to formal education, whose overall control and supervision is at least partly governmental, and whose components and processes are related to one another' (Archer [1979] 2013, 54). According to Archer, a centralized educational system is one that is governed centrally, where a small element or subsystem of the state plays a dominant part. This leading subsystem is often politicians in parliament, who pass legislation and decide on reforms and guidelines from a centre of power. Few channels of real influence exist, as influence and demands for change have to be channelled to the central arenas of political decision making where political negotiations occur. This is different in a decentralized educational system, where the structure and content can be decided more locally, as local interest groups, such as parent groups and local businesses, can influence and demand or transact changes from local educational institutions, such as local school boards (Archer [1979] 2013).

The Norwegian educational system emerged as a centralized system in Archer's terms between 1896 and 1940, and in Norway, elected members of Parliament discuss and pass educational legislation, which is national in scope (Skinningsrud 2013). Professional and external interest groups exert influence on politicians in parliament on relevant political cases. Most notable among the professional interest groups in a Norwegian context are the teacher unions, which concern themselves with political cases relevant for their member group. This does also include spatial inequalities and rural education to some degree, e.g., Lund and Wedde (2019).

A dominating process in a centralized educational system is a tendency towards extensive and intensive *unification*, leading to uniformity across different geographical contexts, such as through a national curriculum. Another dominating process in a centralized system is a high level of *systematization*, that is, a lack of bottlenecks in the system between primary, secondary and tertiary education (Archer [1979] 2013; Skinningsrud 2013). The latter is very much the case in the Norwegian educational system, where transitions between levels in education are very streamlined. Dominating processes in a decentralized education system include *specialization* and *differentiation*. The parliament decides on a standardized national curriculum with low levels of specialization for students in the 6–16 age group in primary and lower secondary schools (Nordkvelle and Nyhus 2017; Skinningsrud 2014; 2013; Solstad and Thelin 2006). The differentiation, which refers to the autonomy of the Norwegian educational system vis-à-vis other institutions, has traditionally been relatively strong. However, in recent years, the introduction of various measures of accountability and management by objectives has reduced the autonomy of teachers and of the system as a totality vis-à-vis other public institutions. Furthermore, the number of vocational tracks was lowered in the 1990s and 2000s through the R94 and LK06 reforms, increasing unification and systematization and lowering differentiation and specialization (Skinningsrud 2014). The distinction between the two types of educational systems matters for rural education, as different processes dominate them, and local demands and issues are solved centrally through the leading group in the centralized system, whereas it is solved more locally through, for example, a school board in a decentralized system.

Another important structural property in the educational system includes resource distribution. According to Archer, access to resources that educational operations depend upon is a key aspect for a dominant group to keep its dominance over the educational system once it has been gained. Resources in this context would include both the financial and human assets upon which educational operations depend and by extension could be transformed into schools and teachers. These resources can be guarded through ideology legitimising the current dominance and/or a series of constraints that prevents other groups from challenging the dominating group (Archer [1979] 2013, 91–98). In Norway, education funding has been decided by the parliament both before and post NIS-86: directly to the schools from the state up to 1986 and through state transfers to local municipalities after 1986.

Methods

The analysis in this chapter was based on data collected in two case studies of municipalities presented later in this section. This work was part of a larger research project, which aimed to shed light on spatial inequalities in education by collecting detailed information about relatively few units, with a diverse set of data collection methods combined for a sociological case study. Since the phenomena in question are both complex and sensitive to context, this is considered a favourable approach (Bartlett and Frances 2017; Bæck 2016; Fangen 2010). The empirical analyses in this chapter were based on 18 qualitative semi-structured interviews with teachers at lower secondary schools residing in both types of municipalities: 12 from a rural municipality and 6 from an urban municipality. The teachers interviewed in the data material for this chapter were recruited based on their availability in between duties during the working day, as well as their willingness to participate. The interviews were conducted with the written consent of the teachers. They were recorded electronically before being transcribed and analysed utilizing NVivo. The interviews provided insights into teachers' concerns, how the teachers experienced their work and what they thought of as causes for experienced constraints in their work operations in the two municipalities.

The author also conducted participant observation in the case municipality of Grønnvik and especially around the municipality centre over a period of three months in the first half of 2018. Not only did the participant observation yield data in and of itself, it also provided a contextual understanding for the interview data and increased the quality of the interviews by enabling the author to raise questions that would not be asked otherwise. The interviews covered a significant portion of the teacher collegium but not all of it. Participant observation was helpful in filling in the gaps and investigating the validity of the interview data. The combination of interviews and observations also allowed avoidance of the possible conflation between self-report and behaviour (Fangen 2010; Jerolmack and Khan 2014). Furthermore, participant observation and the use of former experiences enabled further substantiation of work experiences beyond the interviews. This combination facilitates a higher degree of validity as it makes it possible to crosscheck the data from different methods against each other (Fangen 2010). No participant observation was conducted in Tromsø. However, the analysis also drew on the author's knowledge and experience from the case municipality of Tromsø. The background of the author includes teacher training with work placements and work experience as a teacher in Tromsø. The author also lives in Tromsø, which also made access to contextual information for the interviews easier.

Case municipalities

The rural case municipality, Grønnvik, is one of the largest municipalities in Norway in terms of land area. The local community appreciates its arctic nature with dramatic mountains, rivers, valleys and fjords with a rich flora and fauna. It has a population of approximately 5,000 people, and the municipality centre is a few hours drive away from any significantly larger city. Half of the population resides in or close to the municipality centre, whereas the rest live in smaller communities scattered around it. The largest employer is the public sector and in particular the health sector. The case study municipality has a handful of public elementary schools and only one public lower secondary school. There is also a public upper secondary school and some private schools in the municipality.

Most of the population self-identifies as Norwegian, but a significant portion of the population in this municipality self-identifies as Sami and/or Kven as well. The Sami are an indigenous group primarily situated in the northern parts of Norway, Sweden, Finland and Russia, whereas the Kven are an ethnic minority who emigrated into Norway from the 1700s onwards from Tornedalen in Sweden and Finland. There has also been a history of cultural assimilation in education in Norway: Sami and Kven languages were forbidden in school contexts in 1850–1950, and many students experienced ethnic discrimination (Jensen 2005; Minde 2003; Niemi 2017).

The urban case study municipality was Tromsø. It is the largest city in Northern Norway, but it also contains areas that are of a more rural nature. The great majority of the municipality's more than 70,000 inhabitants reside in the city. The city functions as a regional centre with central institutions like a large hospital, a university and major parts of the county administration. The majority of the population is employed in the public sector, but there is also a significant private sector in the city. There are quite a few public elementary and lower secondary schools in the municipality and also several upper secondary schools and private schools.

Distinguishing between rural and the urban contexts is not straightforward, and the terms themselves are contested (Bæck 2016; Roberts and Green 2013; White and Corbett 2014). The municipal centre of Grønnvik is, according to Statistics Norway, considered a town with a relatively dense population, having many features that are usually related to urban locations (SSB 2019c). However, this vast school district's only public upper secondary school draws its pupils from the entirety of the municipality, including remote villages that are certainly more rural in character. The two municipalities can, therefore, be understood to represent different positions in relation to a rural-urban continuum. For this reason, this chapter does not include a taxonomy of the rural-urban continuum but instead focuses on distinct spatial contexts and proposes *contextualization* as a method to address and understand spatial differences (Bæck 2016).

Categories of experienced constraints in the rural and urban school

In this section, I present some concerns and constraints experienced from teachers' work, emphasising rural-urban differences. The examples are chosen partly because of their prevalence in the data and partly through comparison between the municipalities. I would like to provide two caveats about this selection.

First, the differences presented below are not exhaustive of the differences found between the two municipalities: teachers in Grønnvik claimed there were differences in socioeconomic status between the parents in rural and urban areas, as well as differences in parental expectations and involvement in education. There were also differences in terms of ethnicity: Grønnvik has a history of assimilation of the Sami and the Kven in education. Future job opportunities for the students also worry rural teachers more than urban teachers. One of the differences between the two places includes opportunity structures, such as possibilities for and access to education and work (Bæck 2019). The differences between the respective opportunity structures leads to people moving out of rural districts and into urban areas for work or education and relevant work post-education, which results in rural depopulation (Corbett 2007). 'Knowledge cities' such as Tromsø attract many young people from rural areas who want upper secondary and especially higher education (Stein 2019).

Second, there were also similarities across the two municipalities that deserve mention. All the teachers had similar ideas about certain aspects of the teacher profession. An example was *time pressure* due to an increase in administrative tasks infringing on the time needed to plan for teaching and learning activities. Time pressure has been reported as a problem for teachers on a national basis (Rød and Bæck 2020; Skaalvik and Skaalvik 2017). Another relevant similarity between urban and rural teachers was that differences between teaching in rural and urban spatial settings were hardly addressed during their teacher education. Only one teacher mentioned that she had received training relevant for teaching in rural areas.

Teachers' concerns

The teachers' motivations to become and stay a teacher were diverse: some had experienced very bad or very good teachers themselves; some enjoyed teaching and some came and stayed in the profession for other reasons. However, they all shared an idea of students' well-being and learning as a main concern in their work, as exemplified by the teacher below:

> To work with young people, you will never have a boring day. It is my driving force to work with children and young, and especially the young. I have worked with toddlers, and that was not for me. When you feel that the communication is flowing, and when they are curious, enjoying themselves and learning, that is the driving force.

The quote above was typical across both municipalities: teachers in both contexts wished to deliver high-quality education and held their student's learning and well-being as a main concern.

Lack of economic resources, support functions and cultural institutions

The economic difficulties for schools in Grønnvik are long-lasting, and the municipal board has closed down several smaller schools through rounds of school closures to save money. The teachers in Grønnvik were very concerned about the local economic situation in the municipality. The teachers spoke about the financial difficulties at length, arguing that economic problems cause negligence of basic needs, such as insufficient writing books and computers at school.

> We have had some serious budgeting issues. We have had to put purchases on freeze. The earliest purchase halt we had was in October. We ran out of pencils that year before Christmas. There has not been money for anything for as long as I have been here, but this year has brought some positive news.

The lack of resources was confirmed through observation: the lack of functioning computers and updated textbooks was evident. This lack of resources was also verifiable through the Norwegian municipality economy database, KOSTRA, which showed that the municipality of Grønnvik spent significantly less money, both per student and as a total percentage of the municipal budget than both similar municipalities and the national average over the last five years (SSB 2019b). Due to the severity of cuts in the school budget, which entailed a lack of basic teaching materials, some teachers blamed local politicians for not placing education sufficiently high on their agenda. The economic situation of Tromsø was also mentioned by the teachers who worked there. Their sentiments were different as they disagreed among themselves about the priorities of the municipal board, which had decided to fund prestigious projects and buildings rather than to renovate and build schools and nursing homes. The problems connected with the scarcity of funding for the school was more often addressed by the teachers in Grønnvik.

The lack of access to support functions and cultural institutions was a sub-category of the constraints caused by the economic hardship in the rural municipality. One of the rural teachers, who previously worked in two of the largest municipalities in Northern Norway, had the following to say about the support functions in the urban and rural municipalities:

> City schools have access to a larger range of offerings. One might use the environment in form of cultural offerings, among other things. And other things as well, let us take Tromsø. When I worked there, there were dedicated IT-support groups that helped all schools, and we got the newest, most updated. There was a clear and strong effort. Here, we have one person, a teacher that doubles as an IT adviser, responsible for all the computers and their functioning.

The same teacher also had the following to say about the access to cultural institutions:

> The cultural outbid is much better in the city school like in Bodø, where one worked towards larger theatre plays, and the school was very close to the cultural centre. When it is this close, one gets culture in school. But here, there are no such traditions.

The lack of access to cultural institutions in Grønnvik was partly explained by the teachers as a combination of a lack of local cultural institutions, long travelling distances to larger municipalities and the lack of money. Travelling outside the immediate surroundings of the school incurred travelling costs and time spent away due to long distances. This was in stark contrast to an urban school in which the teacher mentioned above had worked, where the school itself was located in close proximity to the largest cultural institution in the municipality. In short, the teachers in the rural school experienced work constraints caused by austere school budgets to a much greater extent than teachers in urban schools.

Different levels of involvement by the municipal school owners in their schools

The second difference between the work experiences of the teachers in the two case study municipalities concerned the teachers' experiences of the municipalities' involvement as school owners. Both municipalities have a traditional model of governance: *the municipality board* makes decisions within their mandate granted from the Ministry of Education and Research, which the municipality chief executive (Norwegian: *rådmann/kommunedirektør*) has to implement. These decisions are then operationalized and implemented by a designated part of the *municipality administration*, which is tasked with the day-to-day operation of overseeing the schools in the municipality. This is often led by a head of schools (*skolesjef*). Lastly, every school has their own *school leadership group*, headed by the principal at the school (Aasland and Søholt 2020). There is also a newer model, with no administrative level between the municipality chief executive and the school leadership led by the principal, but none of the municipalities studied had such an arrangement (ibid.).

The teachers in the urban municipality of Tromsø experienced a high degree of involvement both from the municipality board and the municipality administration. There were some negative sentiments against the school owner, mostly related to budgeting and decisions that was perceived as detailed management at a distance:

> Our municipality is very hands on. This has increased in later years, where they try to control our occupation in detail. It was not like that when I started off as a teacher, nor when I worked further north in another municipality. There, one was more autonomous, and your competence was considered good enough to make decisions. The municipality of Tromsø has also started to control the principals more.

Another teacher exemplified this by him receiving a personal mobile phone for work from the municipality so that he could be accessed by both students and other teachers:

> Now, everyone is expected to have a work phone. The phones were used so little that they went out of battery after a couple of weeks, untouched. This makes me think about the resource management and prioritisation by the municipality. I would rather have a new computer, which I need.

Whereas the negative sentiments above occupied the teachers in Tromsø, all perceived the municipality board and administration to be very involved in education. For example, the municipality had its own ambitious five-year plan for education, with designated focus areas both at the municipal and school level (Tromsø Kommune 2015). Their school leadership was also stable in terms of staff turnover.

The teachers in Grønnvik painted a different picture. They felt that education was not prioritized by the municipality council, pointing to economic hardship exemplified by multiple school closures and limited school budgets compared with other municipalities. The rural teachers also experienced frequent turnover both in the relevant parts of the municipality administration and the school leadership group. Although some of the staff replacement could be explained by personal circumstances, the high turnover in leadership positions had negative consequences according to one teacher:

> There has been a handful of principals and almost twice the number of inspectors [second-in-command] [the last decade]. Many of my colleagues have stepped into these roles for a year or so to keep the operation running. But something is amiss. I feel that it has been a problem. Things have not been in order from a teacher perspective.

The consequence according to the teacher was a lack of streamlining of issues, such as administrative tasks, which increased the workload. It also affected the work environment, as they experienced that many projects were started, but very few were completed.

Uneven supply of qualified teachers

In general, the use of teachers who are not fully qualified is higher in rural than urban municipalities in Norway (Bakken 2018). In all the Nordic countries, it is generally harder to attract and keep competent teachers in rural areas than in urban areas (Lind and Stjernström 2015). However, the undersupply of qualified teachers typical of rural areas affected Grønnvik only moderately.

Tromsø is host to a university with teacher education, and the municipality contracts a specialized temporary staff recruitment agency for pedagogical staff. The replacement frequency of teacher staff was relatively high but not too high according to the teacher interviews, and it provided the existing teaching staff with new initiatives and didactical updates when new employees came in. The situation in Grønnvik was satisfactory in terms of qualified teachers at the beginning of the school year. Most of the teachers on the staff were qualified teachers, and they had some access to post-education courses as a part of both state and local efforts. The remaining few 'unqualified' ones were close to finishing their teacher training programmes. The situation was also stable in terms of teacher replacement frequency:

> It is very stable here. But new impulses are also good for an organisation. We are getting a high average age on the teacher staff, and we would like some newly educated teachers so we could learn from them.

The data demonstrated a similar situation in terms of access to qualified teachers in both municipalities, with some differences in replacement frequency. There was, however, some difference between the two. Whereas the results indicated enough qualified teachers being available when school started, they also demonstrated that the rural municipality experienced recruitment problems if sick leave or leave of absence among teachers occurred during the school year. This was further exacerbated when epidemics hit the local community: the author even participated as a substitute teacher in an instance when half the staff and students were absent during the yearly common flu season.

Analysis: Structural causes of experienced constraints

A concern is needed in order to experience something as a constrain: a concern or a project is not constrained before there is an incongruence between structural or cultural properties and said concern or project (Archer 2007). This does not mean that a concern predates a structural constrain: structures predates agency as the latter is involuntarily and sometimes unknowingly placed in the former (Archer 1995). The teachers in both municipalities reported that one of their main concerns was to deliver high-quality teaching and to ensure their students' well-being. However, the constraints experienced and outlined above landed the teachers in a situation where their concern about providing high-quality education for their students was jeopardized. I will now discuss some of the structural causes behind these constraints experienced on teachers' concerns.

A major cause of such constraints among teachers in the rural school was the meagre school budget, which led to purchase stoppages, a lack of funding for excursions, too few computers and a general lack of teaching materials. The austere school budget in Grønnvik reflected the general economic situation of the municipality. The funding system for municipal services in Norway is decided by the Norwegian Parliament and managed by The Ministry of Local Government. As such, it is a centrally decided funding mechanism in a centralized educational system (Archer [1979] 2013; Skinningsrud 2014; 2013). After 1986, local municipality budgets consisted of local taxes (mainly property taxes) and state transfers, as described in the introduction and in Solstad (2009); Solstad and Andrews (2020) and Solstad and Thelin (2006). A national arrangement, such as the block grant funding system, does not provide the same economic conditions in all localities; state transfers do not appear to compensate sufficiently for the low levels of local income from taxation and higher welfare costs, which results from the typical demographic profile of small rural communities. The combination of the current municipality funding system – NIS-86 – and the rural demographic profile defined by an ageing population and the out migration of working-age residents has led several rural municipalities into economic hardship. This situation results in harsh prioritization between health and education, the two largest expenditures. This has led to several rural municipalities experiencing a lack of resources in both health and education, as demonstrated in the lack of resources in education in the rural case study of Grønnvik compared with Tromsø (Solstad 2009; Solstad and Andrews 2020; Solstad and Thelin 2006). The local politicians in Grønnvik, who in accordance with NIS-86 and the Municipal Act of 1992 were supposed to exert local autonomy in prioritising between different municipal services, instead had to decide how to distribute cuts in funding services. Similar economic conditions were not experienced in the urban municipality of Tromsø.

The economic situation in Grønnvik is also partially behind the teachers' claim regarding differences in access to support services and cultural institutions. The access to services is in some ways a result of the scale and the agglomeration of benefits found in Tromsø vis-à-vis Grønnvik. Grønnvik is not in a position to compensate for the lack of large-scale operation benefits and cannot offer the same access to services as their urban counterparts, such as fulltime positions for IT technicians. The economy is also related to access to cultural institutions but not in the same way, as travelling distance and time spent travelling to relevant institutions both increased travelling costs and takes away time from teachers in Grønnvik. The schools in Tromsø can rely on local offerings and cooperative efforts among schools within the municipality to drive costs down.

The second difference was how the teachers in the two case studies perceived the municipality they were working at. The teachers in Tromsø felt that the municipality board and administration were much more involved than in Grønnvik: school closures and lack of educational material were only two examples of why the teachers in Grønnvik felt that they were given a lower priority. I will propose that this is partially another consequence of the NIS-86 reform together with the 1992 municipality reform. The NIS-86 reform together with the 1992 municipality reform allowed local politicians more autonomy over school funding and local school structure. It also increased local political decision making on education within the framework of the centralized educational system. In the case of Grønnvik, this has been problematic. The economic situation has been poor, which means that several unpopular decisions, such as school closures and workforce cuts, have been made by the municipality board. An underfunded and small municipality administration and its educational administration were then given the thankless job of implementing these decisions in collaboration with the school leadership. It is probable that this led to a situation where the politicians on the local municipality board were put in a difficult situation. Little political and economic elbowroom existed; furthermore, not much political gain could be obtained by prioritising education. As a consequence, the municipality administration and school leadership at different municipal schools were given a difficult job, which resulted in burnouts, sick leave and a high frequency of staff turnovers among school administrators and principals. The situation was quite different in Tromsø. For example, the municipality has its own five-year plan for education. There is probably also more political and economic latitude for change, and the political gain from educational involvement is higher than in Grønnvik. The municipal administration in Tromsø is presumably also better equipped with a larger and more specialized staff due to large-scale operational benefits and, therefore, also more stable, with a lower turnover rate in leadership and administration than in Grønnvik. However, the teachers in Tromsø did not welcome what they considered over-detailed management by the municipality, as they felt it questioned the teachers' own professional judgement.

The third difference in work experiences was the access to qualified teachers between the two municipalities. Whereas this was not the most pronounced problem in the comparison between the two case studies, it remained an issue to some degree in Grønnvik and a rural issue in general. As described in the results, the differences in teacher supply between the two municipalities is not so great at the beginning of every school year but rather in the middle of the year when sick leave and leaves of absence occur with some frequency. Tromsø houses its own university with teacher education and access to a contracted pedagogical temporary staffing agency, which eases the access to qualified substitute teachers considerably. In such cases, Grønnvik loses out as they do not have a pool of available substitute teachers to recruit from for temporary replacements. The rural access to qualified teachers is in some ways a component of two larger issues. The first is a general lack of teachers nationwide, which is projected to grow from about 1000 teachers in 2017 to 4700–5800 teachers in 2040 (Fredriksen 2018). The second problem is the net negative migration of working-age residents from rural areas to urban areas for education and work, with the logical consequence of a lack of access to qualified labour in certain positions for affected municipalities.

Here, Archer's contributions on the relationship between structure and agency and the state educational system can provide crucial insights beyond a description of events that has led to the status quo. Resource distribution is a major structural property in structural relations and educational systems, and it is not only limited to financial assets but also includes both financial and human resources upon which educational operations depend (Archer [1979] 2013). Analysing the three differences above together, it appears that the teachers and their concerns in the rural case municipality of Grønnvik are in a worse situation vis-à-vis Tromsø. They are more constrained not only in (the lack of) economic resources but also regarding the (perceived lack of) involvement from the school owner and access to qualified teachers when such needs appear. The municipality funding system post NIS-86 and the municipality reform of 1992 together with rural demography were found to be major causes of both the lack of economic resources and the perceived lack of involvement from the school owner. Putting rural demography aside, I suggest that the municipality funding system post NIS-86 is not only a result of political decisions made in parliament in a centralized educational system but that it is also a continuation of an educational resource monopoly in the hands of politicians in parliament, although indirectly through the municipalities. Simultaneously, the unified formula-based funding system post NIS-86 was also a push in the direction of *unification*, which is a dominating process in a centralized educational system (Archer [1979] 2013). This push for unification and uniformity creates unequal access to several types of resources based on place and appears to be hostile to a spatially sensitive educational policy as it does not sufficiently consider rural challenges. However, a crucial point is that structural properties can be changed. Individuals reflexively experience the constraints they live under and may decide that they want to change them. In a centralized educational system, educational change occurs on a national level, meaning that individuals must incorporate themselves into pressure groups. For teachers in Norway, this means teacher unions, as introduced in the theory chapter. Some policy implications are presented at the end of the concluding remarks.

Concluding remarks

The main finding in this chapter is that national uniformity or equal treatment of different regions and localities do not necessarily result in a spatially just educational system but, in fact, results in unequal working conditions for teachers in different types of municipalities or communities. The teachers participating in this study all considered it a major concern to deliver high-quality education and ensure the well-being of their students. However, the results and analysis in this chapter reveal that teachers in the rural case municipality of Grønnvik face different and more constraints than teachers in the urban case municipality of Tromsø. These constraints include (1) the lack of economic resources, support functions and cultural institutions, (2) different levels of involvement by the municipal school owners in their schools and (3) an uneven supply of qualified teachers.

The origins of these constraints are structural. The Norwegian educational system is centralized in terms of power distribution, with highly unified funding models, educational laws and curriculum, which aim to provide equal conditions and the same quality of schooling in various parts of the country. Many of the constraints that affect rural teachers more than urban teachers are due to underfunding by the municipal funding system, which does not compensate small rural communities enough for low tax incomes and extra expenditures due to their aging demographic profile and other rural challenges. The municipality funding system after the NIS-86 reform and the 1992 municipality reform in combination with the rural depopulation of working-age residents and the resulting demographic profile are causing the economic differences between the municipalities studied. The same factors are also partly causing the differences of level of involvement of school owners in their schools. In sum, rural municipalities such as

Grønnvik are losing out on education resource distribution both in terms of the financial and human assets necessary for education and the centralized educational system and its tendency towards unification contributes considerably to this phenomenon.

The results and analysis in this chapter are based on qualitative data and are concerned with two case municipalities. However, I suggest that the findings in this chapter may be transferable to other municipalities and rural-urban comparisons. The municipality funding system is applicable to Norway as a whole. Several rural municipalities have a demographic profile similar to Grønnvik, and many urban municipalities may be similar to Tromsø. Whereas this chapter is concerned with a Norwegian context, the results might also be relevant for other countries with similar educational systems.

Some implications

Systemic educational change, including change in the municipality funding system, is locally unattainable in Norway due to the characteristics of a centralized education system, where changes have to go through the national parliament, often raised by external interest groups or professional interest groups like teacher unions (Archer [1979] 2013; Skinningsrud 2014). This chapter reveals that teachers experience worse working conditions in rural and underfunded municipalities. Knowledge about spatial inequalities in education can inform said pressure groups that want to change policies that produce unfair outcomes. Education is currently high on the political agenda as shown, e.g., by the introduction and discussions about new national guidelines and curricula (Ulvestad 2018; Utdanningsdirektoratet 2019), and quality in education is a professed aim by most political parties. In this context, spatial inequalities could potentially receive considerable public attention if raised as an issue, as 18% of the Norwegian population currently live in non-urban settlements (SSB 2019c).

Political pressure in this direction has been exerted at the time of writing. The demographic challenges tied to rural depopulation and the inadequacies of the funding system have led to problematic economic conditions for some municipalities. This has reached the government, which has started a review of the municipality funding system to improve the situation (Regjeringen. no 2020). Here, teacher unions may benefit their members by influencing central politicians. However, more resources for poor municipalities do not necessarily mean more money for education, as the municipalities are free to make these prioritizations themselves. One of the many possible methods of looking into the municipality and school funding system could be examining the possibility for specific rural funds, where affected schools can apply (Lind and Stjernström 2015; Onsager 2019).

Providing better framework conditions may help address the sentiment of teachers in Grønnvik who feel a lack of involvement from their municipality. However, the urban school owner in Tromsø differed from the rural school owner in Grønnvik, as the teachers perceived over-involvement from the municipality in their work operations. The politicization of the educational sector has led to a high degree of involvement from politicians at the national level and in local contexts where the availability of economic resources makes it possible. Some of the teachers perceived such involvement as too specific and detailed. A possible solution could be for teachers and teacher unions to inform school owners (municipalities) and schools that certain local policies put the teachers' own professional judgement into question. Furthermore, removing autonomy from teachers also removes the latitude teachers have to make adaptations for their students in order to deliver high-quality education.

Access to qualified teachers is a general problem for rural municipalities, due to a national lack of teachers and to people of working age migrating out of rural areas. Rural depopulation is a global phenomenon, and educational policy has limited potential to alleviate this problem. However, recruiting students to become teachers may counteract the projected general lack of teachers. Keeping local opportunity structures, such as access to work and education and basic welfare, are tools to keep or increase the attraction of migration and to address the rural depopulation problem (Stein and Buck 2019). Teacher education institutions can also help by offering decentralized study programs. Preparing teachers for a diverse set of spatial contexts throughout their education through relevant curricula and rural teacher placements in campus-based teacher education can also help as it might increase the willingness to teach in rural areas or at least better prepare the ones who wish to do so.

References

Aasland, Aadne, and Susanne Søholt. 2020. "Agents of Centralization? Local School Administrations and Contested School Closures in Norwegian Rural Districts." *Journal of Rural Studies* 80:595–605. doi: https://doi.org/10.1016/j.jrurstud.2020.09.008.

Archer, Margaret S. 1995. *Realist Social Theory: The Morphogenetic Approach*. Cambridge: Cambridge University Press.

Archer, Margaret S. 2007. *Making Our Way through the World: Human Reflexivity and Social Mobility*. Cambridge: Cambridge University Press.

Archer, Margaret S. [1979] 2013. *Social Origins of Educational Systems*. London: Routledge.

Autti, Outi, and Eeva Kaisa Hyry-Beihammer. 2014. "School Closures in Rural Finnish Communities." *Journal of Research in Rural Education* 29 (1):1–17. https://jrre.psu.edu/sites/default/files/2019-08/29-1.pdf

Bakken, Anders. 2018. Ungdata. Nasjonale Resultater 2018 [Youth Data. National Results 2018]. In *NOVA Rapport [Report] 8/18*, edited by Anders Bakken. Oslo: Ungdatasenteret ved Velferdsforskningsinstituttet NOVA, OsloMet – Storbyuniversitetet.

Barter, Barbara. 2013. "Rural Schools and Technology: Connecting for Innovation." *Australian & International Journal of Rural Education* 23 (3):41–55.
Beach, Dennis, Tuuli From, Monica Johansson, and Elisabet Öhrn. 2018. "Educational and Spatial Justice in Rural and Urban Areas in Three Nordic Countries: A Meta-ethnographic Analysis." *Education Inquiry* 9 (1):4–21. doi: https://doi.org/10.1080/20004508.2018.1430423.
Beach, Dennis, Monica Johansson, Elisabet Öhrn, Maria Rönnlund, and Per-Åke Rosvall. 2019. "Rurality and Education Relations: Metro-centricity and Local Values in Rural Communities and Rural Schools." *European Educational Research Journal* 18 (1):19–33. doi: https://doi.org/10.1177/1474904118780420.
Beck, Jamie L. 2017. "The Weight of a Heavy Hour: Understanding Teacher Experiences of Work Intensification." *McGill Journal of Education* 52 (3):617–636. doi: https://doi.org/10.7202/1050906ar.
Bæck, Unn-Doris K. 2016. "Rural Location and Academic Success: Remarks on Research, Contextualisation and Methodology." *Scandinavian Journal of Educational Research* 60:435–448. doi: https://doi.org/10.1080/00313831.2015.1024163.
Bæck, Unn-Doris K. 2019. "Spatial Manoeuvring in Education." *Nordic Journal of Comparative and International Education (NJCIE)* 3 (3). doi: https://doi.org/10.7577/njcie.3274.
Bartlett, Lesley, and Vavrus Frances. 2017. "Comparative Case Studies: An Innovative Approach." *Nordic Journal of Comparative and International Education (NJCIE)* 1 (1). doi: 10.7577/njcie.1929.
Clarke, Simon, and Tom O'donoghue. 2017. "Educational Leadership and Context: A Rendering of an Inseparable Relationship." *British Journal of Educational Studies* 65 (2):167–182. doi: https://doi.org/10.1080/00071005.2016.1199772.
Connelly, Michael, Jean Clandinin, and Sheila Dermer Applebaum. 1999. *Shaping a Professional Identity: Stories of Educational Practice*. New York: Teachers College Press.
Corbett, Michael. 2007. *Learning to Leave: The Irony of Schooling in a Coastal Community*. Halifax: Fernwood Publ.
Downes, Natalie, and Philip Roberts. 2018. "Revisiting the Schoolhouse: A Literature Review on Staffing Rural, Remote and Isolated Schools in Australia 2004-2016." *Australian & International Journal of Rural Education* 28 (1): 31–54.
Fangen, Katrine. 2010. *Deltagende Observasjon [Participant Observation]*. 2nd ed. Bergen: Fagbokforlaget.
Fredriksen, Kristin. 2018. Norge Kan Mangle Opptil 4 700 Grunnskolelærere i 2040 [Norway May Lack up to 4700 Teachers in Basic Education in 2040]. Online article published by SSB [Statistics Norway]. https://www.ssb.no/utdanning/artikler-og-publikasjoner/norge-kan-mangle-opptil-4-700-grunnskolelaerere-i-2040.
Goodson, Ivor. 1996. *Att Stärka Lärarnas Röster: Sex Essäer om Lärarforskning och Lärar-Forskarsamarbete [Strenghtening the Voices of Teachers: Six Essays on Research on Teachers and Cooperation between Teachers and Researchers]*. Vol. 5, Didactica, Stockholm: HLS förlag.
Goodson, Ivor. 1999. Representing Teachers. In *Researching School Experience: Ethnographic Studies of Teaching and Learning*, edited by Martyn Hammersley and Jennifer Nias. London: Falmer Press.

Gulson, Kalervo N., and Colin Symes. 2007. *Spatial Theories of Education*. New York: Routledge.

Hargreaves, Linda, Rune Kvalsund, and Maurice Galton. 2009. "Reviews of Research on Rural Schools and Their Communities in British and Nordic Countries: Analytical Perspectives and Cultural Meaning." *International Journal of Educational Research* 48 (2):80–88. doi: https://doi.org/10.1016/j.ijer.2009.02.001.

Hattie, John. 2003. "Teachers Make a Difference, What is the Research Evidence?" Wellingon, New Zealand: Australian Council for Educational Research. Paper presented at the Building Teacher Quality: What Does the Research Tell Us ACER Research Conference, Melbourne, Australia. October 2003. http://research.acer.edu.au/research_conference_2003/4/.

Hegna, Kristinn, and Kaja Reegård. 2019. "Lokal Yrkesfagskultur og Ulikhet i Fortellinger om Ungdoms Utdanningsvalg – et Stedssensitivt Blikk på Oslo og Rogaland." [Local Vocational Education Culture and Differences in Stories about Young People's Educational Choices – a Place-sensitive View on Oslo and Rogaland]. *Nordic Journal of Comparative and International Education* 3 (3):91–108. doi: https://doi.org/10.7577/njcie.3246.

Jensen, Eivind Bråstad. 2005. *Skoleverket og de Tre Stammers Møte [The Educational System and the Meeting of Three Tribes]*. Tromsø: Eureka Forlag, Høgskolen i Tromsø.

Jerolmack, Colin and Shamus Khan. 2014. "Talk Is Cheap: Ethnography and the Attitudinal Fallacy." *Sociological Methods & Research* 43 (2):178–209. doi: https://doi.org/10.1177/0049124114523396.

Karlberg-Granlund, Gunilla. 2019. "Exploring the Challenge of Working in a Small School and Community: Uncovering Hidden Tensions." *Journal of Rural Studies* 72:293–305. doi: https://doi.org/10.1016/j.jrurstud.2019.10.017.

Kristiansen, Andrew. 2014. "Teachers as Rural Educators." *Alberta Journal of Educational Research* 60 (4):629–642.

Kvalsund, Rune. 2009. "Centralized Decentralization or Decentralized Centralization? A Review of Newer Norwegian Research on Schools and Their Communities." *International Journal of Educational Research* 48 (2):89–99. doi: https://doi.org/10.1016/j.ijer.2009.02.006.

Langfeldt, Gjert. 2015. *Skolens Kvalitet Skapes Lokalt: Presentasjon av Funn fra Forskningsprosjektet "Lærende regioner" [School Quality is Locally Created: Presentation of Findings from the Research Project "Learning Regions"]*. Bergen: Fagbokforlaget.

Leknes, Stefan, Sturla Løkken, Astri Syse, and Marianne Tønnesen. 2018. Befolkningsframskrivingene 2018, Modeller, Forutsetninger og Resultater [Population Projections 2018, Models, Preconditions and Results]. In *Rapporter/Reports 2018/21*. Oslo: Statistisk Sentralbyrå. https://www.ssb.no/befolkning/artikler-og-publikasjoner/_attachment/354129?_ts=1643ab45088.

Lind, Tommy, and Olof Stjernström. 2015. "Organizational Challenges for Schools in Rural Municipalities: Cross-National Comparisons in a Nordic Context." *Journal of Research in Rural Education* 30 (6):1–14.

Lund, Eirik, and Elise Wedde. 2019. *"Inntaksordninger og Stykkprisfinansiering i Videregående Opplæring." [Admission Systems and Per Piece Funding in Upper Secondary Education]*. Utdanningsforbundet ressurshefte 3/2019 [Resource Booklet

3/2019]. Oslo: Utdanningsforbundet. https://www.utdanningsforbundet.no/varpolitikk/kunnskapsgrunnlag/publikasjoner/2019/inntaksordninger-ogstykkprisfinansiering-i-videregaende-opplaring/.
Markussen, Eifred, Berit Lødding, and Solveig Holen. 2012. *De' hær e'kke Nokka for Mæ: om Bortvalg, Gjennomføring og Kompetanseoppnåelse i Videregående Skole i Finnmark Skoleåret 2010-2011 [This Is Not for Me: on Choices, Throughput and Competance Attainment in Upper Secondary in Finnmark in the School Year 2010-2011]*. Report Vol. 10/2012. Oslo: NIFU.
Minde, Henry. 2003. "Assimilation of the Sami – Implementation and Consequences 1." *Acta Borealia* 20 (2):121–146. doi: https://doi.org/10.1080/08003830310002877.
Niemi, Einar. 2017. Fornorskingspolitikken Overfor Samene og Kvenene. [The Assimilation Politics against the Sami and the Kven]. In *Nasjonale minoriteter og urfolk i norsk politikk fra 1900 til 2016*, edited by Nikolai Brandal, Cora Alexa Døving and Ingvill Thorson Plesner, 131–152. Oslo: Cappelen Damm akademisk.
Nordkvelle, Yngve, and Lene Nyhus. 2017. Management by Objectives as an Administrative Strategy in Norwegian Schools: Interpretations and Judgements in Contrived Liberation. In *Administrative Strategies of Our Time*, edited by Noralv Veggeland, 220–260. New York: Nova Science Publishers, Inc.
Onsager, Knut. 2019. Nærings- og Distriktsutvikling -Perspektiver, Politikk/ Virkemidler og Samhandling [Development of Rural Industry, Commerce and Rural Areas -Perspectives, Politics and Interaction]. In *NIBR-rapport [Report] 2019/7*. Oslo: NIBR, Oslomet.
Paulgaard, Gry. 2017. "Geographies of Inequalities in an Area of Opportunities: Ambiguous Experiences among Young Men in the Norwegian High North." *Geographical Research* 55 (1):38–46. doi: https://doi.org/10.1111/1745-5871.12198.
Preston, Jane P. 2012. "Rural and Urban Teaching Experiences: Narrative Expressions." *Alberta Journal of Educational Research* 58 (1):41–57.
Reegård, Kaja, Jon Rogstad, and Kristinn Hegna. 2019. "Stedlige Perspektiver på Skoleliv og Yrkesfag." [Local Perspectives on School Life and Vocational Education]. *Nordic Journal of Comparative and International Education* 3 (3):1–7. doi: https://doi.org/10.7577/njcie.3593.
Regjeringen.no. 2020. Utvalg Skal se på Inntektssystemet for Kommunene [Comitee Will Evaluate the Municipality Funding System]. Press release by Kommunalog moderniseringsdepartementet [Ministry of Local Government and Modernisation]. https://www.regjeringen.no/no/aktuelt/utvalg-skal-ga-gjennominntektssystemet-for-kommunene/id2694169/.
Rød, Daniel A.V., and Unn-Doris K. Bæck. 2020. "Structural Enablements and Constraints in the Creation and Enactment of Local Content in Norwegian Education." *Nordic Journal of Studies in Educational Policy* 6 (3):1–12. doi: https:// doi.org/10.1080/20020317.2020.1802853
Roberts, Philip, and Bill Green. 2013. "Researching Rural Places: On Social Justice and Rural Education." *Qualitative Inquiry* 19 (10):765–774. doi: https://doi.org/10.1177/1077800413503795.
Skinningsrud, Tone. 2013. "Fra Reformasjonen til Mellomkrigstiden. Framveksten av det Norske Utdanningssystemet." [From the Reformation to the Interwar Period. The Emergence of the Norwegian Educational System]. PhD Dissertation, Universitetet i Tromsø.
Skinningsrud, Tone. 2014. "Struktur og Prosess i Norsk Utdanning på 1990- og 2000-tallet; et Makrososiologisk Perspektiv." [Structure and Process in

Norwegian Education in the 1990s and 2000s; a Macrosociological Perspective]. *Norsk Pedagogisk Tidsskrift* 98 (4):222–234.

Skaalvik, Einar M., and Sidsel Skaalvik. 2017. "Still Motivated to Teach? A Study of School Context Variables, Stress and Job Satisfaction among Teachers in Senior High School." *Social Psychology of Education* 20 (1):15–37. doi: 10.1007/s11218-016-9363-9.

Smith, Anne-Marie. 1989. *OECD-Vurdering av Norsk Utdanningspolitikk: Norsk Rapport til OECD: Ekspertvurdering fra OECD [OECD-Evaluation of Norwegian Educational Politics: Norwegian Report to the OECD: Expert Evaluation from the OECD]*. Oslo: Aschehoug.

Solstad, Karl Jan. 2009. *Bygdeskolen i Velstands-Noreg: Om Endringar i Skolestrukturen i Spreittbygde Kommunar i Perioden 1980-2005 [The Rural School in Affluent Norway: on Changes in School Structure in Rural Municipalities 1980-2005]*. Vallset: Oplandske bokforlag.

Solstad, Karl Jan, and Therese Andrews. 2020. "From Rural to Urban to Rural to Global: 300 Years of Compulsory Schooling in Rural Norway." *Journal of Rural Studies* 74:294–303. doi: https://doi.org/10.1016/j.jrurstud.2019.10.034.

Solstad, Karl Jan, and Annika Andræ Thelin. 2006. *Skolen og distrikta: samspel eller konflikt? [The School and Rural Districts: Cooperation or Conflict?]*. Bergen: Fagbokforlaget.

SSB (Statistics Norway). 2019a. Gjennomføring i videregående opplæring [Throughput in Upper Secondary Education]. Online article published by SSB [Statistics Norway]. https://www.ssb.no/utdanning/statistikker/vgogjen.

SSB (Statistics Norway). 2019b. KOSTRA Kommune-Stat-Rapportering [KOSTRA Municipality-State Report]. Online article published by SSB [Statistics Norway]. https://www.ssb.no/offentlig-sektor/kostra/: SSB.

SSB (Statistics Norway). 2019c. Population and Land Area in Urban Settlements. Online article published by SSB [Statistics Norway]. https://www.ssb.no/en/befolkning/statistikker/beftett/aar.

Stein, Jonas. 2019. "The Striking Similarities between Northern Norway and Northern Sweden." *Arctic Review on Law and Politics* 10:79–102. doi: https://doi.org/10.23865/arctic.v10.1247.

Stein, Jonas, and Marcus Buck. 2019. "What Happened in Northern Norway? - A Comparative and Quantitative Analysis of Political and Demographic Development in Northern Norway from 1950 to 2015." PhD Dissertation, UiT Norges arktiske universitet.

Stelmach, Bonnie. 2011. "A Synthesis of International Rural Education Issues and Responses." *Rural Educator* 32 (2):11. doi: https://doi.org/10.35608/ruraled.v32i2.432.

Stronge, James H. 2010. *Effective Teachers – Student Achievement: What the Research Says*. Larchmont, NY: Eye on Education.

Tromsø Kommune. 2015. Sammen for en Framtidsrettet Skole, Kvalitetsutviklingsplan for Tromsøskolen 2015-2020. [Together for a Futureproof School, Quality Development Plan for the Tromsø School 2015-2020]. https://img8.custompublish.com/getfile.php/3065974.1308.effuecqrcd/KUP+til+publisering+på+hjemmesiden.pdf?return=www.tromso.kommune.no.

Ulvestad, Roar. 2018. "Usikker på Om de Nye Læreplanene Vil gi Mindre Stofftrengsel og Mer Metodefrihet." [Uncertainty about the New Curriculum and Decrease in Time Pressure and Methodological Autonomy]. Online article published by Utdanningsnytt [Educational News]. https://www.utdanningsnytt.no/fagfornyelse-laereplaner/usikker-pa-om-de-nye-laereplanene-vil-gi-mindre-stofftrengsel-og-mer-metodefrihet/141922.

Utdanningsdirektoratet. 2019. Fagfornyelsen Utdanningsdirektoratet [The Renewal of Curriculum from the Norwegian Directorate for Education and Training]. https://www.udir.no/laring-og-trivsel/lareplanverket/fagfornyelsen/.

Utdanningsdirektoratet. 2020. Skolebidragsindikatorer for Grunnskolen 2018+19 [School Contribution Indicators for Basic Education 2018+19]. Government statistics edited by Utdanningsdirektoratet [The Norwegian Directorate for Education and Training]. https://www.udir.no/tall-og-forskning/statistikk/statistikk-grunnskole/skolebidragsindikatorer-for-grunnskoler/skolebidragsindikatorer-for-grunnskolen-20182019/.

Vibe, Nils, Mari Wigum Frøseth, Elisabeth Hovdhaugen, and Eifred Markussen. 2012. Strukturer og konjunkturer: Evaluering av Kunnskapsløftet. Sluttrapport fra prosjektet "Tilbudsstruktur, Gjennomføring og Kompetanseoppnåelse i Videregående Opplæring". [Structures and conjunctions: Evaluation of the Knowledge Promotion Reform. Final Report from the Project "Programme Structure, Accomplishment and Attainment of Competence in Upper Secondary Education" within the Evaluation of the "Knowledge Promotion Reform"]. *NIFU rapport [Report] 2012-26*. Oslo: NIFU Nordisk Institutt for Studier av Innovasjon, Forskning og Utdanning. https://www.nifu.no/publications/952162/.

Volckmar, Nina, and Susanne Wiborg. 2014. A Social Democratic Response to Market-led Education Policies: Concession or Rejection? In *The Nordic Education Model, 'A School for All' Encounters Neo-Liberal Policy*, edited by Ulf Blossing, Gunn Imsen and Lejf Moos, 117–131. New York: Springer.

White, Simone, and Michael Corbett. 2014. *Doing Educational Research in Rural Settings: Methodological Issues*. Abingdon, New York: Routledge.

7 Reflexivity and educational decision-making processes among secondary school pupils

Anna-Maria Stenseth and Daniel Andre Voll Rød

Introduction

This chapter is based on data from the research project RUR-ED, funded by the Norwegian Research Council. The project employs a case study design and examines four municipalities in Northern Norway. It uses a mixed methods approach, which includes quantitative analysis, surveys and document and discourse analysis. This chapter is based on qualitative interview data from two of the municipalities included.

This chapter applies the concept of *reflexivity* in analysing how Norwegian lower secondary pupils, in their transition to upper secondary school, deliberate and make educational decisions that influence their futures. In late modern societies, there seem to be endless opportunities for young people to invent and reinvent themselves. The interest in reflexivity has become more widespread in sociological research and debates since the 1990s, following the work of Beck, Giddens and Lash (1994) on social change in modern societies. Scholars often draw upon Giddens and Beck when trying to describe and explain identity formation among young people in fluid modern societies (Beck 1992; Giddens and Schultz Jørgensen 1996). There also seems to be a tension between the subjective experience of freedom to choose and construct identity and the objective opportunities to realize their identity concerns, as the objective opportunities to realize it could be internalized as the product of 'bad choices' or personal fault (Walker 2009, 542). Giddens and Beck's concept of reflexive modernization refers to the embedding of knowledge in the structures of global systems, which, in turn, has an effect on people's everyday lives.

In liquid societies, individuals are not provided with indisputable life models; they need to design these themselves. Hence, vocational development has become a life-designing issue (Guichard et al. 2012). Bauman (2000) argues that liquid modernity is an individualized, privatized version of modernity where the individual has to carry the burden of failure. Liquidity refers to the way established structures and institutions break down or lose their functions. When losing their functions, these institutions fail to provide structures for individual's lives. Following this, the reflexive

DOI: 10.4324/9781003163527-9

process in late modernity prioritizes agency over structure. These points by Giddens, Beck and Bauman are contested; several authors argue that structures still impact peoples' manoeuvring spaces even though people might not perceive them as such (Archer 2003, Furlong 2013). This is probably more evident in youth, as the introduction of a 'youth period' post 1960's with its possibilities for exploring 'ways of life' might have left the impression that structures have less effect (see for instance Furlong 2013). However, as argued by Stenseth and Bæck (2021), structural constraints and enablements have an effect on youths' initial transition and how they perceive local opportunity structures, as some youths are able to stay in their natal community while others have to learn how to stay.

In this chapter, we used Margaret Archer's theory of reflexivity (2003; 2007; 2012). Archer sought to operationalize the concept of reflexivity, incorporating structure, culture and agency through the morphogenetic approach. The aim was to link structure and agency without reducing or conflating agency with structure, which she maintains Giddens and others do (Archer 1995; 2003; 2007; 2012). The concepts of agency and structure have been central in addressing issues relating to people's lives, and the dualism between them has been challenging. Archer contributed to the field by discussing the interrelationships among 'culture', 'social structures' and 'agency'. She argued that rather than giving priority to one side, either structure or agency, one can seek to understand their interplay (Archer 2007).

When conceptualizing the term *agency*, there seems to be a consensus that it refers to a person's ability to act within structural contexts (O'Connor 2014). Researchers seem to agree that both agency and social structures shape people's lives (Archer 1995). They differ, however, with regard to the relative importance of these two explanatory factors. In the literature on youths' *reflexivity*, it is often found that young people's agency operates in different ways, depending on their perceived frames for action and desires (Cairns, Growiec, and Smyth 2012; Christodoulou 2016). Some have argued that young people seem to have little agential power or individual agency, which, in turn, allows few real choices (Cairns, Growiec, and Smyth 2012; Walker 2009; Willis 1977). However, there is a need for young people to be real agents in their own lives because the structures offer less predefined frameworks; vocational choices of the past have become issues of 'life design' (Guichard et al. 2012). Some have voiced concern about the need for young people to become agents to overcome dominant cultural capital and oppression (Curry 2016).

Young people are often confronted with the need to make decisions with far-reaching consequences for their future lives, such as what kind of job and education to aspire to, where to live, etc. Young people's decision-making is often related to how they make context-based decisions that are influenced by family, peers and social networks (Christodoulou 2016; Dyke, Foskett, and Maringe 2008; Walker 2009). Some studies emphasize the difficulties in decision-making processes (O'Connor 2014) and the efforts youth must put into these processes when producing self-narratives and designing their lives (Christodoulou 2016; Guichard et al. 2012). When seeking to explore how young people make decisions, it seems indispensable to focus on how they understand their own circumstances and concerns and how they reflexively deliberate between concerns and opportunities. Some studies explore how working-class adolescents are more reflexive in domains such as personal relationships and sports, but less reflexive in relation to future occupational ambitions (Christodoulou 2016).

Archer states that the fast-changing social world makes it necessary for all of us to become more reflexive. The need to call attention to reflexivity within social theory is found in this premise. 'The subjective powers of reflexivity mediate the role that objective structural or cultural powers play in influencing social action and are thus indispensable to explaining social outcomes' (Archer 2007, 5). In her theory, the internal conversation is presented as the manner in which we reflexively make our way through the world. As reflexive beings, most of us involve ourselves as *active agents*; we develop and determine our ultimate concerns, the things we care about the most.

In addition to reflexivity, this chapter addresses spatial inequalities in education. According to the research literature, place matters; rural youths do worse than their urban counterparts in terms of educational outcomes and encounter a more restricted opportunity structure, which raises the question of spatial equity (Bæck 2016; 2019; Paulgaard 2012; Roberts and Green 2013). 'Opportunity structures are formed primarily by the inter-relationships between family backgrounds, education, labour market processes and employers' recruitment practices' (Roberts 2009, 355). We found that opportunity structures, e.g., access to education and future work, constitute structural constraints on individual educational trajectories for all regardless of the dominant modes of reflexivity. This applies especially to rural youth. Hence, this chapter discusses reflexivity in relation to both spatial inequality and opportunity structures.

This chapter asks the following research questions: (1) can different reflexive modes inform how we understand pupils' reflexive deliberations over their education and life projects? (2) What contextual factors constrain and/or enable these reflexive deliberations?

Theoretical framework

We have chosen to apply part of the three-stage model by Margaret Archer laid out in *Making Our Way Through the World* (2007) as a starting point to examine what is involved when youth reflect and form their own life projects. In critical realism, structure pre-dates the actor, a perspective we find especially true for pupils who have to enter an already existing educational structure. The three-stage model follows below.

Structural and cultural properties *objectively* shape the situations that agents confront involuntarily and inter alia possess generative powers of constraint and enablement in relation to subjects' own constellations of concerns, as *subjectively* defined in relation to the three orders of natural reality: nature, practice and the social. Courses of action are produced through the inner *reflexive deliberations* of subjects who subjectively determine their practical projects in relation to their objective circumstances (Archer 2007, 17).

Archer defines 'reflexivity' as 'the regular exercise of the mental ability, shared by all normal people, to consider themselves in relation to their (social) contexts and vice versa' (2007, 4). Reflexivity is described as the internal conversations individuals engage in when attempting to make sense of and operate in the social world (Archer 2007). All humans are reflexive; however, the particular context and concerns that individuals confront and hold lead to distinct modes of reflexivity. Archer considers that these specific modes of reflexivity have an impact on the ways in which individuals approach and interact with their social context; eventually, this affects social mobility. Thus, different dominant modes of reflexivity tend to produce different patterns of social mobility. Furthermore, human beings have the ability to design and redesign projects they undertake. Archer argued that:

> Our personal powers are exercised through reflexive inner dialogue and that internal conversation is responsible for the delineation of our concerns, the definition of our projects and, ultimately the determination or our practices in society. (2007, 16)

As subjects, people can exercise reflexive powers in different ways; hence, there is no predictable outcome, but, nonetheless, distinctive tendencies in their courses of action. In addition, identities are not exclusively formed by our choosing. People are born in different contexts, with different opportunity structures; hence, every decision they voluntarily make includes a number of involuntary features (Archer 2007; Bæck 2016).

Based on biographical interviews, Archer (2007; 2003) derived a model of four modes of reflexivity, as presented in the table below (Archer 2007, 93).

Table 7.1 Modes of reflexivity (Archer 2007, 93)

Communicative reflexives	Those whose internal conversations require completion and confirmation by others before resulting in course of action.
Autonomous reflexives	Those who sustain self-contained internal conversations, leading directly to action.
Meta-reflexives	Those who are critically reflexive about their own internal conversations and critical about effective action in society.
Fractured reflexives	Those whose internal conversations intensify their distress and disorientation rather than leading to purposeful courses of action.

A two column and four row table explaining the four different modes of reflexivity. The first left column reads communicative reflexives, and the right column describes what it entails. The second reads autonomous reflexives, with an associated description. The third reads meta-reflexives, with an associated description. The last reads fractured reflexives, also with an associated description.

Everyone uses all the modes of reflexivity to a certain degree, and the dominant mode can change with age and circumstances. Archer (2007) argued that the term *communicative reflexives* refer to those who complete their thoughts by engaging in communication with others to work out their problems. Individuals who mainly practice this mode have a strong concern for family and friends and close relationships with people they trust. They may reject opportunities for upward mobility. Their life in society is characterized by 'contextual continuity'. In contrast, *autonomous reflexives* have lone inner dialogues that lead directly to action. When this is the dominant mode of reflexivity, individuals seldom need to seek confirmation or completion from others, because they mainly initiate their own inner dialogue and take responsibility for their own conclusions. These people consider work and employment to be their main concerns. Archer found that autonomous reflexives tend to become upwardly mobile and might experience, but always court, 'contextual discontinuity'. *Meta-reflexives* are more expansive in their self-talk, and they question and answer themselves within internal conversations. Meta-reflexives are often committed to an ideal, be it religious, progressive or otherwise. Whereas the autonomous reflexives are task-oriented, the meta-reflexives are value-oriented (Archer 2007, 132). Meta-reflexives will systematically discount objective costs in their search for an ideal *modus vivendi*, sometimes at the cost of downward social mobility. The last mode is the *fractured reflexives,* who have internal conversations that cause distress and do not enable them to deal adequately with social circumstances.

Study settings

Data for this chapter was collected in two lower secondary schools in two municipalities that are situated above the Arctic Circle in the northernmost county in Norway. The rural school is multi-graded and comprises less than 100 pupils from the first to the tenth grade (ages 6–16). The urban lower secondary school has approximately 400 pupils from the eight to the tenth grade (ages 13–16).

The small, rural municipality, given the fictive name *Coastal Valley,* is a couple of hours' drive from any significantly bigger municipality and has a population of less than 3,000 people. The population is multi-ethnic,[1] comprising Norwegians, Sámi and Kven and people of mixed backgrounds. The municipality is a part of the Sámi administrative area; the Sámi and the Norwegian languages are equal, meaning that everyone has the right to receive answer in the Sámi language when addressing the municipal administration in these areas.

The population is in decline, skewing towards an ageing profile (Leknes et al. 2018), although it has been quite stable over the last couple of years. Most people in this municipality work in public health and social services and in service-related industries. Those who work in the private sector are mainly small-scale farmers, fishermen and small business owners.

Educational decision-making processes 127

The town of Tromsø, with over 70,000 inhabitants, is one of the administrative centres of Northern Norway. Most people work in service-related industries, followed by health and social services, and many also work in education. There is a university and a hospital in the city.

Educational structures in upper secondary education

In Norway, everyone has the right to, but is not obliged to undertake, a free upper secondary education. There are ten years of compulsory schooling before you choose upper secondary education. According to the Education Act § 3-1, pupils have the right to upper secondary education and training until age 24; following this, they have the right to change course once and will then be entitled to more time to complete their studies. Furthermore, § 3-3 states, 'Upper secondary education and training must lead to a university and college admission certificate, vocational qualifications or basic competence' (Opplæringslova 1998).

Pupils can choose either three years on an academic track or a three- to four-year vocational track (VET). Pupils attending VET usually attend school for two years, followed by one to two years of in-house company training to gain their apprenticeship diploma. Municipalities are the school owners of elementary and lower secondary (compulsory) education, and counties are the school owners of upper secondary education. Both school owners have autonomy over their school structure following the municipality reform of 1992 (Solstad 2009; Solstad and Thelin 2006).

Most pupils apply for upper secondary education within their county. However, there are some courses of study that offer nationwide programmes, to which youth can apply regardless of 'Home County'. These courses are state-financed.

Regarding the structure of upper secondary school, today there are five programmes for general studies: (a) general studies itself; (b) sports and physical education; (c) music, dance and drama; (d) art, design and architecture; and (e) media and communication. There are eight vocational education programmes: (1) building and construction; (2) design, arts and crafts; (3) electricity and electronics; (4) healthcare, childhood and youth development; (5) agriculture, fishing and forestry; (6) restaurant and food processing; (7) service and transport and (8) technical and industrial production. In addition, pupils have the right to one year of a supplementary programme for general university admission after they have achieved vocational competence (with or without a trade or journeyman's certificate) (Utdanningsdirektoratet 2020).

Methods

The data is based on semi-structured interviews with 18 pupils, 8 from the rural municipality Coastal Valley and 10 from the urban municipality Tromsø.

The rural/urban continuum or dichotomy is both constructed and contested, as well as difficult to make, at least as a binary (Bæck 2016; Roberts and Green 2013; White and Corbett 2014). The subsection *Study settings* presented the two case municipalities as different. Coastal Valley represents more rural characteristics than the distinctly urban Tromsø, e.g., self-identification of the population as rural, lesser population density, ageing rural demography, distance to urban centres, access to services associated with urban areas such as hospitals and secondary and higher education. As such, there are good reasons for arguing that the two cases are rural and urban, respectively. However, this chapter does not include a working taxonomy of the continuum, but rather uses the two cases to see how place and opportunity structures are relevant to young people's educational choices.

In both schools, we had initial meetings with the head teacher to discuss our project. In the city, the team leader, who is also class teacher for one of the classes, volunteered to participate with her class. The teacher informed the class about the project and pupils who wanted to participate volunteered. Of the pupils who volunteered, ten were selected by the teacher, representing varying socio-economic statuses, grades and gender. In the rural school, pupils in the tenth grade were asked to participate, and all eight volunteered. This made up a total of 18 informants.

The first interviews[2] were carried out when the pupils were in the tenth grade, the final year of compulsory education. Some months after they had transferred to upper secondary school, they participated in a follow-up interview. The topics in the first interview included, amongst other things, expectations of upper secondary school, what track they wanted to choose, and with whom they discussed their decision-making process. The follow-up interviews focused on, amongst other issues, how pupils experienced transition from lower to upper secondary school, if they had entered the track they wanted to attend, and how they experienced upper secondary.

Before participating in the follow-up interviews, the pupils completed 13 fixed response questions on their mode of reflexivity, ICONI, the Internal Conversation Indicator developed by Margaret Archer (Archer 2007). The final indicator accorded individual scores on a scale from one to seven per question. In addition, pupils were asked to list the three most important areas in their life at that moment. The original ICONI was adapted by the researchers to fit the Norwegian context and the participating age group. The adaptation asked the pupils to specify their most important areas of their life, based on predefined categories like relationships to family, friend, school etc., as well as an open-ended alternative. An averaged total score of four and above in any of the four categories of questions assigned a subject to the communicative, autonomous, meta- or fractured category. The highest score over four indicated their dominant mode of reflexivity. Scores over four on fractured reflexivity 'trumped' scores on other modes. Scores on the index were indicative only, as the ICONI was never meant to stand alone. The ICONI results were used to supplement the qualitative interviews (Archer 2007, 330).

Stages in pupils' formation of their educational projects

In this section, we discuss how pupils reflect regarding educational decision-making. Data from the qualitative interviews are analysed to illustrate how youth make their educational choices. First, we present structural conditions that constrain pupils' reflexive deliberations. We then discuss reflexive deliberations, including pupils' educational concerns. In the end, we present the different categories of modes of reflexivity, including the different pupils' concerns, the perceived constraints for these concerns, how pupils deliberately reflect over them and which direction they choose to take as a part of their educational project.

Structural enablement and constraints

The main structural conditions that seem to have shaped the decision-making process of our participants are related to geographical distance from home to the relevant educational institution, perceived future opportunities and relationships to family, friends and teachers/school counsellors. These are presented separately below.

Distance to school

When choosing which upper secondary school to attend, both urban and rural pupils tended to minimize the geographical distance to their home community. The choice of a school at a minimal geographical distance enabled pupils from the urban sample to live at home while attending upper secondary school, while the rural pupils would at least be able to visit their families relatively frequently. Another consideration supporting the decision by rural pupils to choose the nearest school, rather than a city school, was whether the locality of the nearest school was similar to their home community; thus, they would not have to adapt to totally unfamiliar surroundings. A few rural pupils who still opted for a school in the city relied on specific personal preferences or experiences supporting their choice, such as having a consuming interest in a specific sport or drawing on the positive experiences of a family member who had attended an upper secondary school in the city.

Most of the young pupils considered geographical distance to their new school as a constraint. Frida,[3] a pupil from Tromsø who had applied for a programme in an upper secondary school outside the city but had had second thoughts, expressed a general sentiment when saying:

> ...I want to concentrate on my sports, but this means I have to move. If I get my first choice of school here in Tromsø, I do not think I will leave.

Although some urban pupils wanted to enrol in a school outside the city, the majority settled for attending a city school nearby, which enabled them to live at home while attending upper secondary school.

Likewise, for the majority of rural pupils, geographical distance constituted a constraint. Charlotte stated, 'You have to leave family and friends, and if you want to live here, you have to commute, and that is hard'. Recounting the experience of visiting the upper secondary school while still living in her natal rural setting, Charlotte said, 'I got so tired by going back and forth by bus, and you didn't get home until late in the evening. So, one could be away for almost 12 hours, and when one gets home one might not have the energy to do anything'. Few of the rural pupils considered commuting as an option since they would have to spend several hours on a bus every day.

Still, not all the rural pupils considered moving away from home to attend upper secondary school a constraint. To some, it was an enablement, and others were ambivalent. Cody revealed that it would be nice to escape their rural surroundings in Coastal Valley, 'It is exciting to "run away from home", or rather to move and experience something different'. Some admitted that they had mixed feelings.

The rural pupils knew that to attend secondary school at all, they would have to leave their home communities. They seemed to accept this price as unavoidable. *Forsaking education to continue to live in their rural community was never mentioned as an option.*

Perceived future work opportunities

Although it is a difficult question to answer for 15- and 16-year-olds, the pupils were asked what they thought they would be doing ten years from now. Many of them thought they would be studying. Some of those who had chosen vocational tracks thought they would have an occupation. Most of them hoped they would live close to their home community. A few wanted to live in a different place.

Most of the pupils from both areas wanted to live close to their home communities in the future. There was a significant difference between the pupils from the two municipalities regarding perceived future work opportunities. Pupils from the urban area did not pay much attention to this issue. However, in the rural area, most of the pupils thought about future job opportunities, or rather the lack of opportunities, in their locality. They were uncertain about getting a job there when they had completed their education. The main concern for some of them, especially boys, was to pursue an education that would enable them to stay in the rural community. Some of them wanted to 'become something big like doctors, lawyers and engineers', but many changed their minds after a few months in upper secondary school. The pupils explained this change of plans in terms of levels of stress at school and lack of rural job opportunities: 'it would be nice to live here, but there might not be a job for me, therefore I need to move' (Anja). For many of them, the dream was having a job they enjoyed close to their home community; but, for the rural youths, this concern was difficult to achieve as job opportunities were limited.

Educational decision-making processes 131

The introduction presented the concept of local opportunity structures. The two categories presented above, distance to school and perceived future work opportunities, were the two main ingredients in the local opportunity structure for these pupils.

Pupils' interlocutors in the educational decision-making process

The decision-making process the youths underwent regarding the transition from compulsory to upper secondary school received attention in school, at home and amongst peers. Although many of the youth in this study emphasized autonomy in choice of school, they said that this is a topic in school and at home. But many of the pupils emphasized, 'I have thought about this by myself. I know what I want to do'.

Family and friends

Pupils from both communities stated that their family was an important contributor in the decision-making process, or rather in discussing the various options. This has also been found to be the case in other studies (Bæck 2017). Ida, from Tromsø stated, 'No, they [parents] wanted me, in terms of education, to do a vocational track. They knew that if I did an academic one, I would soon get bored'. Anja from the rural community said, 'My dad has told me what to do if I want to become this or that. So, they take a lot of initiative regarding my future and care about what I want to do'. Cody revealed, 'I think my sister has helped me to sort out what is good and not that good [in terms of education]'.

Nonetheless, many of the boys, especially from the rural school, said that they did not talk much about what they intended to do with their parents, teachers or friends. Alan stated, 'We do not really talk that much [me and my parents]', while Ben laughed and stated, 'No, we do not talk about this yet, but they joke about me becoming a doctor'.

Amongst peers, the choice of education did not seem to be a major topic for discussion. This was expressed by Eric as he considered making a project a solitary effort. He said that he did not really feel close to his classmates, although he could talk to them about many things; however, they did not share interests and opinions.

The role of school personnel in pupils' decision-making processes

Many pupils reported that their class teacher or school counsellor had helped them in their decision-making process by suggesting various options regarding tracks, pointing to what subjects they should pursue or explaining the differences between the tracks.

> My teacher helped me choose to become a lawyer. When we spent several days in upper secondary school, I thought about doing natural science, but my teacher advised me to do social sciences, which was good.
>
> *(Anja)*

Pupils who said that they lacked motivation for school and theoretical subjects explained that their teachers had advised them to choose vocational tracks because they liked practical subjects in school (e.g., Arts and Crafts, Home Economics and Physical Education). They claimed, however, that they had decided what to do before talking to their teacher. In 2008, the obligatory subject 'Choice of Education' (*Utdanningsvalg* in Norwegian) was introduced in lower secondary school. The key objectives of the subject 'Choice of Education' were to establish coherence between compulsory and upper secondary school and to enhance pupils' career planning competence on the basis of their ambitions and capabilities (Norwegian Directory for Education and Training 2015). Pupils differed in how they regarded being helped by their teacher on the subject 'choice of education'. We found that some of those who opted for academic tracks in upper secondary school thought that their teachers had offered good advice.

Reflexive deliberation before and after transition to upper secondary school

The last section describes structural constraints and enablements on pupils' forming an educational project. However, a constraint does not exist nor can it be experienced as such if it does not constrain *something*; in this case, this something that is constrained is the pupils' *concern* about what they wanted to achieve in terms of education. Regardless of their mode of reflexivity, many of the pupils revealed that they were uncertain about school choice; only a few were certain. They had all applied for upper secondary school; however, many thought it was a difficult choice to make at their age. As some of them wanted to pursue higher education, their choice of academic track in upper secondary school was based on these requirements. Others applied for the vocational track, but the degree of certainty varied here as well. Their concerns are presented in the sections describing the various modes of reflexivity.

Continuous reflexive deliberations

Many of these pupils regarded making an educational choice as an important stage in life; hence, it seemed crucial to make the right decision. They explained that it was difficult to make an educational decision, and some suggested that it was hard because of their age. Nevertheless, they had to reflexively deliberate what kind of education would be worth pursuing, and for some, what kind of occupation this would lead to, based on their concerns vis-à-vis constraints and enablements. Many of them admitted that they really did not know what to become. Some girls still had an idea of what kind of broader area they would like to study, such as working with people. One girl was the exception as she had made up her mind; she attended vocational track to become a chef.

Anja, who initially had high ambitions, had changed her mind after entering upper secondary school. 'I wanted to become a lawyer, but not anymore. Then I would need such good grades, and that will cause stress'. Those who wanted a more artistic occupation found this ambition hard to sustain. 'I know about someone who was educated to become a photographer, and it's quite an expensive loan and that sort of thing. And I don't want to take out such a high loan' (Jennifer). She found it difficult to pursue this aim due to costs. Another girl said, regarding her occupational ambitions, 'Really nothing [in terms of occupation]. But if one has to commit, then it would be an artist (...). I would rather become a silversmith—I do not know—a sketch artist. If you have to draw and were tired of drawing, you have a deadline, you have to do it' (Greta). She seemed to ponder whether one could have an independent occupation without being restricted; as an artist, one would still need to deal with deadlines, and certain activities, such as drawing, are things one could enjoy as a hobby, not necessarily as an occupation.

In the follow-up interview, conducted almost one year later when they had attended upper secondary school for several months, they had clearer ideas of what to become and how to achieve it; this was especially true of those who had chosen a vocational track and who had been uncertain in the tenth grade. They were able to give an account of the options that were available to them in upper secondary education.

Two of the boys who had thought about pursuing an academic track had changed their minds and followed vocational tracks, both because they wanted less theory and also because they received better information regarding the track. One of them said that he could follow a particular vocational track, which he discovered almost by accident through one of his parents' friends, and still enter university later.

Undoubtedly, some had a well-defined project, especially some of the boys. 'I want to become a professional football player, but if I can't make it, I am going to become a police officer' (Hans), or 'My dream is to design web pages, and I think I can make it' (Isak). One also wanted to walk in the footsteps of a parent and work in a high-status area, while another wanted to do something different from the rest of the family and work in economics. 'All the members of my family work with people, and I want to do something different' (Greg). He wanted this kind of job because he expected to earn a higher salary and have a 'fancy lifestyle', as he put it.

The quotes above show that these pupils had made a start on a life project. What is more interesting is the degree of continuing reflexive deliberation. This means that choice of upper secondary education is not an isolated decision made at one particular point in life but is part of an ongoing internal conversation and for some is a step on the way to formulating their life projects. We will now examine the modes of reflexivity and show how the pupils deliberated between their concerns and various possible projects based on how their concerns activated different structural constraints and enablements.

Categories of reflexivity and their concerns, constraints and educational projects

In following Archer's three-step model and analysing reflexivity amongst pupils, we found it possible to categorize pupils based on their dominant modes of reflexivity. However, it is important to emphasize that each of these pupils showed some signs of every mode of reflexivity and that these modes can operate differently within different contexts. Each person's dominant mode of reflexivity can be subject to change with age and life events. In addition, modes of reflexivity are a sociological concept created to understand the subjective mediation of objective structures. They are not to be understood as a medical typology or diagnostic tool. We must again emphasize that these were young people trying to navigate the education system and about to start their life project; it is important to keep in mind that their reflexivity was developing (see also, Archer 2000, Chs. 8 and 9). For this reason, we have chosen not to discuss the 'fractured' reflexives, as it remains to be seen whether the subjects develop this dominant mode of reflexivity, and it seems difficult to use the 'fractured' category when the reflexivity of the subjects was developing.

Table 7.2 Modes of reflexivity related to decision-making and rural/urban background

Modes of reflexivity	Total	Name[4] Rural pupils in italics	Modes of reflexivity related to decision-making
Communicative	3	Hanna, Jennifer, Odin	None from the rural sample (although some scored high on communicative reflexivity). Some went for 'second best' choice so they could stay home.
Autonomous	11	*Alan, Ben, Birgitte, Charlotte, Cody, David,* Fredrik, Greg, Hans, Ida, Isak	These pupils seemed to have found an educational project, although with varying degrees of confidence.
Meta	4	*Anja, Eric,* Frida, Greta	These pupils struggled to find a suitable educational project, some more than others.

A descriptive table presenting modes of reflexivity related to the analysis. The first column contains the three used modes of reflexivity. The second column contains the total numbers of pupils assigned to each mode. The third contains fictive names of pupils, eight rural and ten urban, sorted by mode of reflexivity and municipality. The last column includes notes about the mode of reflexivity related to decision-making in the specific group of pupils.

Educational decision-making processes 135

The contents of the table will be presented and discussed further in the sections below. There are, however, some general observations and issues that need to be addressed first. We found few gender differences either in our data or in Archer's original study (Archer 2007). These gender differences will not be further addressed in this chapter due to their irrelevance to the main argument.

The various dominant reflexive modes are presented above, including a presentation of these pupils' respective concerns and the structural conditions that constrained and/or enabled them. It also includes their reflexive deliberation when starting to form their educational projects and what they eventually ended up choosing.

Communicative reflexives

Those whose dominant reflexive mode is communicative normally rely on interlocutors they trust. Archer found that this group was in decline due to increases in geographical mobility, higher levels of education and greater cultural diversity (Archer 2012). This is in accordance with our findings, as few of the pupils were categorized as communicative reflexives. At home, all the pupils in this group seemed to have a close relationship with their parents: 'My mum and I do a lot of things together' or 'I like helping mum at home' were common sentiments.

The communicative pupils, all of whom came from the urban school, talked a lot with their parents and family when forming their *concerns* regarding to which educational track to apply. These pupils followed in their parents' footsteps regarding education, work, hobbies or all three, like Odin, who stated, 'I would like to become a captain [on a ship], because it seems like my dad enjoys that, and I have enjoyed it when visiting him'. Another pupil said, 'My dad went to a "folkehøgskole" [folk high school], so I think I will do the same. They have quite a number of tracks I would like to attend' (Hannah).

Although some communicative reflexive girls in the urban sample thought about attending a school away from home, they did not. Instead, they settled for what seemed to be the second best in terms of attending a different school without the preferred track to stay closer to home. In this case, distance to school showed itself as a *powerful constraint* on their concerns, as expressed by Jennifer:

> But I have applied for secondary school in another county. It is an academic track that offers my sport. But I am very uncertain whether to go there, or if I should stay here. If I don't get my first choice here, then I'll move. But if I get a "yes" from both, it will be hard to decide.

In terms of the result of their *reflexive deliberation* together with their peers and families, these communicative reflexives revealed in the follow-up interview that they had chosen to attend the school closer to home and no longer perceived their choice as the second best. Instead, Hannah stated the following: 'I thought that if I'm moving there, I have to be 100% certain that this is what I want to go for, but it wasn't at 100%. Then it's better to stay here so I will not regret it if I quit'. Jennifer stated, 'I would like to go in for my sport (...) but then I have to move and all of that. I have to manage on my own'.

These girls used their interlocutors to a larger degree than the other modes of reflexives. Moreover, some of them said that they would decide which school to attend as late as possible, 'because these schools aren't in the same county, so I get a bit more time to decide'. Furthermore, they had not completely decided on their occupational plans or projects. When asked to talk about their dream occupation, one said, 'Maybe I would be educated as a photographer, but that is expensive, and I would not like to take on that much loan'. These pupils wanted to live close to home after finishing their education. As mentioned above, distance to schools seems to be an important constraint. However, this is also the case with some autonomous reflexives, as shown below. One of the differences between the autonomous and the communicative reflexives is that the latter seemed to talk more to family and friends before making a decision; some said that listening to advice from teachers/school counsellors made the choice easier.

Some pupils, categorized by their ICONI score as communicative, also scored high on autonomous and/or meta-reflexivity, making it difficult to establish what their dominant mode was. They claimed to discuss things with friends and family; however, regarding sport or school achievement, for example, and mulling it over, they seemed to rely on themselves. This could be because they were in a process of 'breaking away' from their parents, feeling they needed some space to make their own decisions and think things over. But they still relied on parents to help them make important decisions. Archer (2012) discussed the *imperative of reflexivity* in societies in constant change, whereby individuals need to be reflexive in contexts that are new to them, and their former skills and habitual actions quickly become outdated. In late modernity, there might be an underlying assumption that people, to take advantage of all options, need both geographical and social mobility. Thus, youth who rely on their parents' advice on educational matters might 'miss out' on some opportunities. This could be the tacit assumption of these girls quoted above. However, they are not the first generation in their families to experience such situational discontinuity. Some of their parents were the first in their family to pursue higher education.

This suggests that communicative reflexives are more vulnerable to and more constrained by the opportunity structure than other modes of reflexives when they are required to live away from home (and their interlocutors) to pursue their primary option in education. Pupils from rural places who invariably have to overcome an even larger structural barrier, in the sense of having to move from their community if they want to obtain an upper secondary education at all, are doubly constrained if they are communicative reflexives. However, those in the rural sample who seemed to be communicative when they were interviewed the first time, in the tenth grade, had become more autonomous when participating in the follow-up interviews and the ICONI survey in the first term in the first grade of upper secondary school. They were worried about not finding a relevant job close to their home communities. 'There aren't many job opportunities here' was a sentiment expressed among pupils from the rural municipality. There are many possible explanations for this change. The obvious is the change of circumstance, as the pupils from the rural sample had to 'become' autonomous in their everyday life as they moved away from home, did their own chores, attended school in a new spatial context and all with less contact with their previous interlocutors. Another contributing cause may be expectation from their families, their old school and the whole rural community that the experience of managing on their own in attending upper secondary was something they had to get used to and endure to obtain an education. This shared knowledge about the costs of getting an education may contribute to fostering an increasing degree of autonomy after the transition has been made. Further inquiry is needed to explore the possible explanations advanced above.

Autonomous reflexives

Autonomous reflexives tend to resolve issues and make decisions based on their own internal conversations and without involving others in their decision making (Archer 2007, 193). When this is the dominant mode of reflexivity, individuals seldom need to seek confirmation or completion from others, because they mainly initiate their own inner dialogue and take responsibility for their own conclusions. These people consider work and employment to be their main concerns (Archer 2003, 213). In this study, most pupils were found to be quite autonomous in the sense that they made autonomous decisions regarding education. This is in line with Archer's findings that the conditions in today's society favour autonomous reflexives. Furthermore, in Archer's study, most of the autonomous reflexives were male, which is also the case in this study.

Some pupils said that they had talked to their parents, or rather informed them, about which track they would like to follow; 'I have talked to my parents and they think it is a pretty good plan'. These boys seemed to have resolved their concerns regarding tracks in upper secondary school. We found elements of autonomous reflexivity in the processes these pupils were undergoing. They knew in which field they would like to work and how to get there. They persistently pursued sport in which they excelled and would like to have a professional sports career. However, they looked upon this as hard to achieve and put quite an effort into doing well at school to get a good education that would lead to well-paid jobs. Some pupils, and especially boys from the urban area, claimed that they knew in which field they wanted to work. 'I want to work with economics. (...) I want to do something different from the rest of my family' (Greg). Another pupil had a specific work aim: 'I'm not the kind of person who can stay in the office for many hours. I could, but as a police officer, I can also be outside doing things' (Hans). These boys seemed to seek upward social mobility. In sum, it seemed that the autonomous pupils had themselves found at least a preliminary educational concern in one way or another. Some uncertainty loomed, but the pupils had deliberately decided on a direction based on what they would like to do. Also, the perceived future work opportunities seemed to work as structural constraints, but not necessarily as deterrents.

Distance to school as a constraint seemed to bother the pupils in this group only to a certain degree. The boys who sought upward social mobility lived in the urban area and did not have to consider leaving the city to get a job that promised social advancement. In the group as a whole, there were also some autonomous girls. One of them, who came from the rural municipality, did not know exactly what to become yet, but she was determined to get higher education and do well in her sport. Birgitte related feeling distant from her home community, having few close friends and wanting to move to get an education and work. 'To live here... It is nice living close to family and all that. But for me, the environment is quite small. Maybe too small, so I am fond of travelling. (...) It is quite nice to travel from time to time'.

The boys in Coastal Valley: An interesting sub-case of autonomy

Some boys in the rural area who were autonomous reflexives had not decided on their plans for future occupations. However, they had all chosen vocational tracks. They had not yet determined which vocational specialization to choose or what to do for a living later. They did not seem to be seeking upward mobility or facing contextual discontinuity, as they had an educational project that they thought would lead to a job in a rural area. School and education did not appear to be their main concern. Their priorities were staying close to family, friends and their home community. They seemed to care about obtaining a job close to home, working in their spare time (while attending school), hanging out with friends and being close to nature. After school hours, many of these boys earned their own money working seasonal unskilled jobs in the primary sector, work which paid a good but irregular income. Some of them said they had quit leisure activities to work. They gave the impression that doing useful work was more important to them than making money. The same boys thought school was too much theory, boring and of little use, even though they acknowledged education as useful in general. Somehow, there seemed to be an ambivalence towards school here. On the one hand, they said, 'Of course, education is important', and on the other, 'I do not think many of the things we learn at school are useful in the future'. They also claimed that they liked practical subjects at school; unfortunately, in the tenth grade, mostly theoretical subjects are offered.

When doing the follow-up interview about what they actually ended up doing, these boys were about to create educational projects for themselves, which they seemed to believe in. This was not the case when interviewed in the tenth grade. These pupils worked after school and/or during weekends; they wanted a practical job and were quite determined to do fairly well in upper secondary school. Here, they enjoyed being able to learn practical work at school, and they even regarded some theoretical subjects as useful, especially those connected to their vocational track – taught in a practical way, using examples from, e.g., car maintenance. Furthermore, they had an idea of what kind of occupation they would like, but there were obstacles to achieving it. They had to deliberate as to whether it was worthwhile moving even further away from home in their second year of upper secondary school to achieve this, or whether they should settle for second best and finish their education closer to home. In the future, the most important thing for them was to earn money and have a job they enjoyed. If they had to, they would consider moving away from their home community to work, but they would prefer to stay. Individuals often have to deal with incommensurable concerns, and it is even worse to get it right without any experience at that age (Archer 2000, 289). However, at this age, a project is relatively corrigible.

Most of these boys had fathers with compulsory school or upper secondary school as their highest education. Most had mothers with higher education, and a few had mothers with upper secondary school as their highest level of schooling These boys did not want to travel, and they regarded spending money on travelling and clothes as 'ridiculous'. They enjoyed motors, being outdoors and working. They wanted to live in the countryside and not in the city, not because the city was expensive but because they did not consider city life as attractive. In upper secondary school, they found themselves an educational project they were motivated to pursue, being able to learn practical skills.

This raises the question: were these boys autonomous? The answer seems to be yes; they did deliberate on their own. Furthermore, they talked about doing things, rather than thinking things over or being interested in theory. They wanted to stay close to their home communities rather than seek upward mobility or face contextual discontinuity. It would be interesting to explore whether there are different ways of being autonomous and whether this is related to context and/or gender. These boys claimed that they did not talk a lot with others about the decisions they had to make. Nor did they use much time to reflect. Instead, they did things. This could mean that they represent an additional type of autonomous reflexivity, which is practical or pragmatic. They were not oriented towards upward social mobility.

In sum, the autonomous reflexives had all decided upon an educational project, mostly by themselves. These pupils were more willing than the communicative reflexives to overcome structural constraints, e.g., they were willing to move away, although not necessarily with pleasure. The pupils in this category seemed to adapt to the educational system better than the other modes of reflexives, whether they were in the academic or vocational tracks. The autonomous reflexives in academic tracks saw school as a step on the way to their occupational aims. The autonomous reflexives in vocational tracks were able to satisfy their concerns through the practical activities that were part of their school life.

Meta-reflexives

Archer defined the meta-reflexive as somewhat similar to the autonomous reflexive, but more oriented towards living up to ideals, and value values (Archer 2007, 230). There were some pupils in our study who seemed to be meta-reflexive as they sought to understand themselves in relation to the rest of the world or to find a deeper meaning in life. They also seemed to be vulnerable in the sense that they had experienced difficulties such as the death or serious illness of a close family member or a parental divorce. It seemed harder for these pupils to find a main *concern* to which they felt they could commit. They appeared to be seeking something they had difficulty finding in the educational system.

These pupils reported being uncertain about what to do. While in the tenth grade, one of them thought about doing the academic track. However, when applying for upper secondary school some months later, the pupil applied for a vocational track. In the follow-up interview, this pupil[5] revealed the following:

> At the start, I thought I should apply for an academic track because I didn't know what I wanted to become. When we were about to apply, I realized I was so tired and bored. I would not have survived the academic track. (...) I find it very satisfying living away from home. I thought it was about time to do things on my own. (...) I could write a book about the things I don't want to become. I don't know what to become (...). Because, working every day, and then go home doing something I like, I don't want that.

This pupil was a ponderer and said it was better to be alone, thinking, than together with people that did not care much about you. The pupil further explained that it was hard to find real, close friends who understood you; one could find many to talk to about things they were interested in, but it was harder to find someone who would understand you.

Some of the pupils in this study could be regarded as meta-reflexives, as they reported thinking about things that were important to them while having difficulty talking to others about many of these issues. At the same time, they seemed to face challenges at school and at home. These pupils felt different from others, and few of them had close friends their own age with whom they could talk. They seemed vulnerable in terms of finding a project within the educational system, as they found it hard to fit in at school, both socially and in terms of finding a project that fit with their concerns. Some of them revealed not having close friends, as their peers did not seem to understand them. Furthermore, they were uncertain of what to make of life. Some wanted to travel and explore the world, not to have a conventional job, etc. However, they did not know whether or how they would make it.

We suggest that these pupils are meta-reflexive, as they were occupied with ideological ideas and values, scored high on meta-reflexivity in the ICONI survey and showed in the interviews that they had not yet found a suitable cause to commit to, and therefore, a fitting educational project. These pupils were mostly concerned with finding a suitable life project, which mostly centred on whether they would succeed in finding an option within the educational system and opportunity structure that would sit well with their own personal concerns. Distance and other interlocutors were not as important to them as actually finding a fitting educational track, and the 'failure' to do so was what worried these pupils the most. None of the meta-reflexive pupils in our sample had found their *major* concerns in life, which might not be surprising due to their age.

Conclusion

We conclude that the current school system seems to be better suited to the autonomous reflexives and those meta-reflexives that find themselves a life project, or at least a project they are happy with. However, as stated above, the meta-reflexives in this study had not found such a project, and we suggest that those meta-reflexives whose developing life projects are incompatible with the educational system's offerings face a harder time in it and perhaps later in the modern labour market. The communicative reflexives are also vulnerable in the transition between lower and upper secondary education, as they will prioritize closeness to their interlocutors and home communities over their own educational concerns and are, therefore, more constrained by local opportunity structures and especially distance to education.

We found that there are a relatively high number of autonomous reflexives in our rural case and wondered what the cause might be. The data suggests that the reasons may be found in their change of environment, as moving away from home forces pupils to live more autonomous lives, living independently, doing their own household chores and being responsible for attending school themselves. It could be that part of the puzzle is found within the family context and in their relations with teachers, as both are cited by the pupils as important influences. It would be interesting to explore how and to what extent the school and/or family prepare and/or enable their young for their future educational project. This requires further investigation, and if parents and teachers are found to play a significant role, it will be informative for future interventions to attain spatial equity in education.

We also found that the opportunity structure, described in this chapter in the categories *distance to school* and *perceived work opportunities*, represented barriers regardless of the dominant mode of reflexivity. This is especially true for pupils from rural areas, who have to move to get an education and possibly also move to get a job, something that their urban counterparts do not have to consider to the same degree. This is hardly surprising, but it is important to note, as educational policy does not seem to give enough attention to such structural inequalities.

Based on our findings, there is a need to consider structures when addressing youth transitions. Even though, in late modernity, young people exercise their reflexivity and make choices based on their concerns, opportunity structures, created by geographical distances and local variations in course options, still have an impact on young people's present and future lives. Place seems to matter; people from rural districts have to move to obtain education and work. The educational system seems to favour autonomous reflexives (those who can and will move).

This raises some important questions that need to be addressed when discussing spatial inequality in education. Does this lead to a scenario where work outside the dwindling primary sector and education that qualifies for higher occupations are harder to obtain if you are not autonomous and/or from an urban place? Are we demanding too much of 15–16-year olds when we ask them to be autonomous, form a life project and move significant distances to obtain education and work? If so, what can be done?

Notes

1. The population comprises members who identify as either Norwegian, Sámi, Kven or of mixed descent. The Sámi are the indigenous people that inhabit the Northern region of Norway bordering on Sweden, Finland and Russia. The Kven is a minority group descended from people who emigrated from Finland to Northern Norway during the 18th and 19th centuries.
2. The year of data collection is not presented in order to keep the identity of the research participants private.
3. Names are identical to those in Table 7.2. We refer to Table 7.2 for an overview of reflexive mode and home community.
4. Names are fictive to ensure privacy and anonymity for the research participants.
5. Neither name nor gender is revealed to protect this participant's anonymity.

References

Archer, Margaret S. 1995. *Realist Social Theory: The Morphogenetic Approach.* Cambridge: Cambridge University Press.
Archer, Margaret S. 2000. *Being Human: The Problem of Agency.* Cambridge: Cambridge University Press.
Archer, Margaret S. 2003. *Structure, Agency and the Internal Conversation.* Cambridge: Cambridge University Press.

Archer, Margaret S. 2007. *Making Our Way through the World: Human Reflexivity and Social Mobility*. Cambridge: Cambridge University Press.
Archer, Margaret S. 2012. *The Reflexive Imperative in Late Modernity*: Cambridge University Press.
Bauman, Zygmunt. 2000. *Liquid modernity*. Cambridge: Polity Press.
Beck, Ulrich. 1992. *Risk Society: Towards a New Modernity, Risikogesellschaft*. London: Sage.
Beck, Ulrich, Anthony Giddens, and Scott Lash. 1994. *Reflexive Modernization: Politics, Tradition and Aesthetics in the Modern Social Order*. Stanford University Press.
Bæck, Unn-Doris K. 2016. "Rural Location and Academic Success—Remarks on Research, Contextualisation and Methodology." *Scandinavian Journal of Educational Research* 60 (4):435–448. doi: https://doi.org/10.1080/00313831.2015.1024163.
Bæck, Unn-Doris K. 2017. "It is the Air that We Breathe. Academic Socialization as a Key Component for Understanding How Parents Influence Children's Schooling." *Nordic Journal of Studies in Educational Policy* 3 (2):123–132. doi: https://doi.org/10.1080/20020317.2017.1372008.
Bæck, Unn-Doris K. 2019. "Spatial Manoeuvring in Education: Educational Experiences and Local Opportunity Structures among Rural Youth in Norway." *Nordic Journal of Comparative and International Education (NJCIE)* 3 (3):61–74. doi: https://doi.org/10.7577/njcie.3274.
Cairns, David, Katarzyna Growiec, and Jim Smyth. 2012. "Spatial Reflexivity and Undergraduate Transitions in the Republic of Ireland after the Celtic Tiger." *Journal of Youth Studies* 15 (7):841–857. doi: https://doi.org/10.1080/13676261.2012.683404.
Christodoulou, Michael. 2016. "Excluded and Dropped in: Habitus and Biographical Identity in Vocational Adolescents' Life Transitions." *Journal of Vocational Education & Training* 68 (3):320–341. doi: https://doi.org/10.1080/13636820.2016.1212248.
Curry, Marnie W. 2016. "Will You Stand for Me? Authentic Cariño and Transformative Rites of Passage in an Urban High School." *American Educational Research Journal* 53 (4):883–918. doi: https://doi-org.mime.uit.no/10.3102/0002831216660380.
Dyke, Martin, Nick Foskett, and Felix Maringe. 2008. "Risk and Trust: The Impact of Information and Experience on the Decision to Participate in Post-16 Education." *Education, Knowledge & Economy: A Journal for Education and Social Enterprise* 2 (2):99–110. doi: https://doi.org/10.1080/17496890802221365.
Furlong, Andy. 2013. *Youth Studies: An Introduction*. New York: Routledge.
Giddens, Anthony, and Søren Schultz Jørgensen. 1996. *Modernitet og Selvidentitet: Selvet og Samfundet under Sen-moderniteten [Modernity and Self-Identity: Self and Society in the Late Modern Society]*. København: Hans Reitzels Forlag.
Guichard, Jean, Jacques Pouyaud, Cecile de Calan, and Bernadette Dumora. 2012. "Identity Construction and Career Development Interventions with Emerging Adults." *Journal of Vocational Behavior* 81 (1):52–58. doi: https://doi.org/10.1016/j.jvb.2012.04.004.
Leknes, S, S. A Løkken, A. Syse, and M. Tønnessen. 2018. Befolkningsframskrivingene 2018. Modeller, Forutsetninger og Resultater [Norway's 2018 Population

Projections. Models, Conditions and Results]. Oslo: Statistisk sentralbyrå [Statistics Norway].

Norwegian Directory for Education and Training. 2015. Læreplan for utdanningsvalg på ungdomstrinnet [The Curriculum for Choice of Education in Lower Secondary School]. https://www.udir.no/lk20/utv01-03.

O'Connor, Christopher D. 2014. "Agency and Reflexivity in Boomtown Transitions: Young People Deciding on a School and Work Direction." *Journal of Education and Work* 27 (4):372–391. doi: https://doi.org/10.1080/13639080.2012.751093.

Opplæringslova. 1998. Lov om Grunnskolen og Den Vidaregåande Opplæringa [The Act relating to Primary and Secondary Education and Training]. https://lovdata.no/dokument/NL/lov/1998-07-17-61.

Paulgaard, Gry. 2012. "Geography of Opportunity: Approaching Adulthood at the Margins of the Northern European Periphery." In *Rural Futures? Finding One's Place within Changing Labour Markets*, edited by Unn Doris K. Bæck and Gry Paulgaard, 189–215. Stamsund, Norway: Orkana Akademisk.

Roberts, Ken. 2009. "Opportunity Structures Then and Now." *Journal of Education and Work* 22 (5):355–368. doi: https://doi.org/10.1080/13639080903453987.

Roberts, Philip, and Bill Green. 2013. "Researching Rural Places: On Social Justice and Rural Education." *Qualitative Inquiry* 19 (10):10.

Solstad, Karl Jan. 2009. *Bygdeskolen i Velstands-Noreg: Om Endringar i Skolestrukturen i Spreittbygde Kommunar i Perioden 1980-2005 [The rural school in a Prospserous Norway: On Changes in the School Structure in Sparsley Populated Municipalities in the Period 1980-2005]*. Hamar: Oplandske bokforl.

Solstad, Karl Jan, and Annika Andræ Thelin. 2006. *Skolen og distrikta: samspel eller konflikt? [The School and Regions: Interaction or Conflict?]*. Bergen: Fagbokforl.

Stenseth, Anna-Maria, and Unn-Doris K. Bæck. 2021. "Being Able to Stay or Learning to Stay: a Study of Rural Boys' Educational Orientations and Transitions." *Journal of Applied Youth Studies* 4 (1):15–30. doi: 10.1007/s43151-021-00038-4.

Utdanningsdirektoratet. 2020. "Videregående opplæring [Upper Secondary Education]." Utdanningsdirektoratet, accessed 23.11.2020. https://www.udir.no/utdanningslopet/videregaende-opplaring/.

Walker, Charlie. 2009. "From "Inheritance" to Individualization: Disembedding Working-Class Youth Transitions in Post-Soviet Russia." *Journal of Youth Studies* 12 (5):531–545. doi: https://doi.org/10.1080/13676260903081681.

White, Simone, and Michael Corbett. 2014. *Doing Educational Research in Rural Settings: Methodological Issues, International Perspectives and Practical Solutions*. Edited by Simone White and Michael Corbett. Oxon and New York: Routledge.

Willis, Paul E. 1977. *Learning to Labour: How Working Class Kids Get Working Class Jobs*. Farnborough: Saxon House.

Part III
External and internal conditioning of educational interaction and practice

8 The impact of PISA on education in Norway
A morphogenetic perspective on structural elaboration in an education system

Terje André Bringeland

Introduction

The Programme for International Student Assessment (PISA) test was introduced in 2000 by the OECD and its first results were published in 2001. The test is 'a triannual international survey which aims to evaluate education systems worldwide by testing the skills and knowledge of 15-year-old students who are nearing the end of their compulsory education' (OECD 2019a). Since the test started in 2000, 90 countries have participated in the assessment. The key school subjects included in the test are reading, mathematics and science. Each year when the test is administered, one PISA subject is emphasized more than the other two subjects. The PISA test aims to assess how well students can apply what they learn in school to real-life situations. Students are also tested in innovative thinking, such as collaborative problem-solving (in 2015) and global competence (in 2018). There is an additional optional test in financial literacy that some countries choose to administer (OECD 2019a). The PISA test takes two hours and includes assignments from each of the above-mentioned subjects. Approximately 5,000 students from each participating country take the test and their results provide the score snapshot. PISA schools are selected for the test, but not entire schools and not entire classes. In addition, there is a student questionnaire that takes about 30 minutes to complete, with questions about family background, attitudes, learning strategies and school learning environment. The schools' managements are also required to answer a separate questionnaire (Sjøberg 2019).

The PISA test has been described as a steering instrument that governs through numbers and comparisons, informing policy recommendations from the OECD to member countries (Sjøberg 2014). The OECD describe their aims as:

> […] to build better policies for better lives. Our goal is to shape policies that foster prosperity, equality, opportunity, and well-being for all. [.]. Together with governments, policy makers and citizens, we work on establishing international norms and finding evidence-based solutions

DOI: 10.4324/9781003163527-11

to a range of social, economic, and environmental challenges. [...]. [W]e provide a unique forum and knowledge hub for data and analysis, exchange of experiences, best-practice sharing, and advice on public policies and global standard-setting.

(OECD 2019b)

PISA effects: International comparisons

The comparative literature has shown that PISA has had different impacts in countries participating in the survey. In the following I will present a sample of studies that demonstrates the wide variety of responses to PISA results. As this is a small sample of studies, my purpose is not to provide a review of the literature on 'PISA effects'. They are chosen to illustrate diversity.

Bieber and Martens (2011) point out in their qualitative study based on policy documents and interview data from experts that the introduction of reforms informed by PISA results depends on whether the OECD policy can solve a locally defined problem in the country. This was the case for Switzerland, where PISA generated internal educational convergence within this federal state (the tendency of policies to grow more alike) and, thus, harmonization between cantons and their schooling. This kind of influence was not the case for the United States (US). The results for the US confirmed what people already believed about their schooling system, namely that it was performing below international standards. However, no new reforms were suggested in the aftermath of the PISA test. This could be due to a lack of interest in PISA, but also to the American system already having many features that corresponded to those recommended by the OECD and PISA.

Grek (2009) draws on interview data and policy documents looking closely at how PISA has affected the education policies of Finland, Germany and the United Kingdom (UK) and why the European Commission considers PISA data as useful. She writes that data from PISA are used to change or support existing educational policies, but the degree of influence varies according to the country's ranking and previous use of surveys. For example, in England, it was a problem to recruit enough schools to participate in the PISA test in 2000 and 2003, primarily because the country already had assessment systems in place. The country had a national organization that processed the data and passed the findings on to the schools. However, due to positive media coverage of the achievement level of students in Scotland, interest in the survey in England increased. Grek (2009) concludes that because of the pre-existing high-stakes tests that had already been established in England before PISA was introduced, '[...] PISA occupies a less central position there' (p. 13). Regarding Germany, Grek (2009), citing Pongratz (2006), describes the impact of PISA on education policy as the strongest since the 1960s, when the country experienced a post-World War II educational crisis, which was associated with the lack of a unified education system. In Germany, following PISA 2000, a proposal was made to intensify the control of students' competence after primary and secondary school. Furthermore, Grek (2009) writes that German teachers encountered increased pressure to deliver results and contribute to the standardization of the education system, in order to enable the comparison of learning outcomes and, thus, assess the quality of the education system. Grek (2009) also mentions that Finland, which scored highly in the first PISA survey, was surprised at the result since the country did not see itself as leading in education, but instead looked toward Germany as a role model for educational reform. PISA, thus, transformed their national self-understanding. Despite their positive results on PISA, the Finnish government still implemented reforms introducing compulsory studies in the comprehensive schools aimed at national uniformity or regional harmonization and placed more focus on the core subjects (Grek 2009, 29).

However, Grey and Morris (2018) have, in their qualitative study of policy documents combined with media analysis, investigated the similarity between the advice provided by the OECD to individual member states (in this case, England) and how the advice has been interpreted/produced/distorted to align with already established education policy. The researchers compared policy advice from the OECD with the public response of politicians and media in connection with the release of the 2012 PISA results. The authors show how central conservative politicians (government members) and right-wing newspapers in England used PISA results to legitimize conservative school policy, and how conservative politicians' interpretations partly went against clear advice from the OECD on how education policy should be changed based on PISA results. The PISA results were used by government representatives to legitimize educational reforms already planned (p. 127) and succeeded in promoting a sense of educational crisis and the need for urgent reforms despite the UK's relatively consistent score on all the PISA tests from 2000 to 2012 (p. 126). The UK scored in the middle range on all subjects in the 2012 PISA test. However, despite this, England reacted directly with a series of reform proposals on the same day the PISA 2012 results were released (3 December 2013). These reforms, which were in line with the already formulated conservative educational policy, were legitimized by the PISA score. But the reforms were not in line with educational advice from the OECD, based on the same PISA results (Grey and Morris 2018, 118–121).

These findings are supported by Baird et al. (2016), who examined reactions to the 2009 and 2012 PISA results in Canada, China (Shanghai), England, France, Norway and Switzerland; these authors write that 'PISA results may play a part in policy-making in England, but it is evident that they do not drive them' (p. 130). Hence, Baird et al. (2016) state that educational policy in England is aligned with PISA, and this shifts the discursive space, with the consequence that the elite's (party) political ideology is 'hidden' and the 'value-free' data from PISA becomes the justification of the reforms.

Breakspear (2012) investigated through an expert survey among members of the PISA Governing Board (PGB), how and to what extent PISA results were being used to evaluate and improve school systems' performance in participating countries. The members of the PGB are individual representatives from the countries participating in PISA, who are formally appointed by their governments, and serve as a link between the PISA project and their Ministries of education.[1] The study concluded that 'PISA seems to have been accepted by policy makers as a valid and reliable instrument for international benchmarking of current system performance as well as changes in performance over time.' (p. 27). Moreover, PISA results have had an impact on reforms in most participating countries. Overall, 64.9% of the respondents said that they see PISA performance as an important indicator of the effectiveness of their school system. The respondents also report that the PISA tests have shaped and legitimized similar national tests (p. 18).

Ringarp and Rothland (2010) studied debates and effects of PISA results in Sweden and Germany, aiming to determine whether real policy borrowing has occurred. In both countries, the PISA results have been a catalyst for policy discussions after the test was introduced (p. 423). The PISA debate in Sweden following its introduction has mainly been linked to the teaching profession and the quality of teacher education, as politicians understood that the PISA results could be related to a lack of teacher autonomy and, in comparison to Finland, the low status of Swedish teachers. Germany, which experienced a 'PISA Shock', i.e., less than expected on the score and ranking list, when the PISA test was introduced – had, since the post-war period, considered Swedish education as a model to be emulated. Although Sweden's post-war educational model had been abandoned in the 1990s, German delegations still went on trips to Sweden to study their system (p. 424). However, Ringarp and Rothland (2010) emphasize that Germany had no real transfer of educational policy from Sweden, but their study trips triggered extensive educational debates, resulting 'in both a more theoretical pedagogical debate and a practical approach in the form of study and informational trips for teachers and other individuals in the field of education' (p. 427).

Sellar and Lingard (2018), in a case study based on document analyses (newspaper articles, reports and White Papers), investigated PISA's impact in Australia and Canada (Alberta). Alberta had an average score of 517 in 2012, reflecting a decline of 32 points from PISA 2003 in mathematics, thus losing its 2003 position as the top-performing Canadian province on PISA. Due to this statistically significant decline in Alberta, a growing anxiety among parents coalesced into the view that Albertan schools faced a mathematics crisis. 'In Alberta, the crisis was produced by a parent-led activist movement for mathematics curriculum reform' (p. 378). The parents feared poor standards and felt compelled to seek out-of-school remedies in response to the declining results. Articles were written and one mother initiated an online petition entitled 'Back to Basics: Mastering the Fundamentals of Mathematics'. The petition was signed by 18,000 individuals (likely mostly parents) and seeded another petition. The Albertan government responded in 2016 with a package of reforms to improve mathematics education. Later, the government confirmed that these reforms were influenced by the reactions to the PISA results. Essentially, the website started by the initiator of the first petition triggered a new governmental policy for mathematics education (p. 374).

In Australia, too, the media and political discourse following PISA 2009 was focused on the declining quality of the Australian school. '[...], the response in Australia focused more strongly on the economic prospects of the nation given its geopolitical location adjacent to Asia' (Sellar and Lingard 2018, 378). The authors write that, despite Australia scoring above the OECD average in 2009 and 2012, the country experienced a decline compared to Asian countries – among them Singapore, Japan and Korea – and this led to anxiety over the prospects of the Australian economy and its human capital. This response was contrasted to responses to the PISA tests in 2000, 2003 and 2006, which received limited but positive media coverage. The PISA scores from 2009, on the other hand, led to two reports: one by a 'consultancy firm, the Nous Group, and the other by a think tank, the Grattan Institute. Both reports received extensive media coverage in 2011 and 2012' (p. 375). The reports addressed the fear of falling behind Asian countries. The former report led to a White Paper being commissioned, and the latter to a roundtable with the Director of the OECD, the Australian Prime Minister, the Federal Education Minister and Asian educational academics. The authors state that the political discourse – which had initially focused on the comparison with Asia and the Australian economy – had extended and become detached from PISA. The new reforms being considered, which were based on conservative initiatives, entailed reduced educational funding, since additional funding apparently had not led to increased PISA scores between 2012 and 2015. Measures that were implemented against declining results were now meant to raise the quality of teacher education and to increase the autonomy of school leaders (principals) (p. 377). The authors argue that the educational crisis in Australia following the PISA results was constructed by political actors playing on anxiety and insecurities regarding Australian education and economic prosperity.

Pons (2017), in his literature review on PISA effects based on 87 references, confirm that PISA has led to a variety of national education reforms worldwide. He points out that PISA is driven by a soft power strategy, which relies on 'numbers and comparisons' to promote policy transfers. This type of influence strongly depends on domestic policy contexts that scholars have tried to capture through different theoretical frameworks. Pons claims that the research on 'PISA effects' suggests few 'overarching theorisations of the political meaning of PISA effects on education governance and policy processes' (p. 131). Hence, he concludes that further research is needed, to better conceptualize these effects. Moreover, 'PISA does not inevitably bring about radical changes in the governance of an education system. PISA is not inevitable *per se* to talk about current educational policy processes' (Pons 2017, 141). Pons calls for a normalization of research on PISA effects, implying that studies thus far have been focused on the novelty of these phenomena. He asks for 'more systematic and cumulative research [...]' (Pons 2017, 131).

Summing up international comparisons of PISA effects

This small sample of studies comparing countries from different parts of the world together with a review article of the PISA literature illustrates the variety of PISA impacts and PISA effects which have been studied since the test was launched at the turn of the millennium. These effects vary from large scale national and federal reforms, to the incorporation of PISA data at various stages of the policy process and adopting it as an international benchmarking tool, an external monitoring of educational quality. Some studies analyse the role of the media and the emotional responses of the public to PISA results, showing that PISA Shocks are not experienced only in low-performing countries. The conception of the policy process following PISA as rational evidence-based decision making where countries are learning from practices in high performing countries, has by many studies been challenged, demonstrating that data may be ignored, misrepresented and used to legitimize policy which is contrary to advice from the OECD. Furthermore, convergence with OECD recommended policy may come about with no reference to PISA results, but as the outcome of an independent policy process in the country concerned.

PISA effects in Norway

After illustrating the great diversity of findings regarding PISA effects on a global scale, the following presentation of PISA studies in Norway will focus more on the explicit and implicit theoretical frameworks of this research.

In a comparative study of PISA effects, briefly mentioned in the previous section, Baird et al. (2016) wanted to find out whether 'policy reactions to PISA results would take similar or the same forms in different countries – especially those countries that have similar results'. Two groups of countries were selected that had different rankings on the PISA test. Canada and China/Shanghai made up the group of high achievers, while Norway, England, France and Switzerland were in the group with average score. Baird et al. claim that their hypothesis on 'policy convergence' is derived from the specialized research literature on this theme that has emerged in connection with the European integration process (Holzinger and

Knill 2005, 780). Baird et al.'s convergence hypothesis was, however, falsified since they found that 'although justifications for policy may, at least partly, be based on PISA results, the form of these policies is not uniform across countries', not even for countries that have the same ranking on the PISA league table (p. 123). Still, they find that in Norway, the PISA Shock 'led to' a series of curriculum and assessment reforms, which were largely justified with reference to PISA (p. 128).

In their case study of Norway, Baird et al. (2016) present the Norwegian educational system as decentralized, 'with many of the decisions made at the central level' (p. 126). Further substantiating this claim, the authors mention the 'wide range of local assessment practices' (p. 127). Addressing possible PISA effects, these authors claim that '[i]n comparative terms, Norway remains a devolved system with only limited direct central intervention' (p. 128).

Commenting on their own explanatory model, Baird et al. notes that 'there are chronological problems with the notion that PISA results [same ranking] responded with different policies, reflecting their different cultural and historical education system trajectory' (p. 121). However, the research team still explains the variety of policy reactions among countries with similar results by 'the different political, historical and cultural practices in those countries' (p. 132). They consider historically rooted domestic conditions as modifying effects on policy reactions to PISA, but apparently find this difficult to reconcile with the notion that PISA has causal effects on policy, because that should entail policy convergence, i.e., becoming more similar (given the same PISA results). However, in accordance with their findings, they maintain that reforms have 'ideological' bases, and therefore, 'the same PISA results could motivate a range of different policy solutions' (p. 121). Their general conclusion being that PISA data is always interpreted and used for political persuasion rather than for evidence-based policy.

Based on her study of how the OECD has influenced Norwegian National Curriculum reforms, Mausethagen (2013) suggests that 'soft governance' should include 'governance by concepts'. Thus, to Mausethagen, soft governance is not just providing comparative statistics, advice and the promotion of certain educational models and policies; it also includes the dissemination of concepts. Studying shifts in the meaning of the concept 'competence' in a succession of Norwegian White Papers from 1995 to 2010, she shows that the meaning of the term has changed from emphasizing collectivism and the transmission of tradition to a more individualistic conception with an emphasis on individual performance; an effect of adopting the OECD DeSeCo[2] competency definitions incorporating them in the Norwegian National Curriculum.

Referring to Elstad and Sivesind (2010), Mausethagen claims that in the first decade of the new millennium, PISA results have been important by legitimizing reforms in basic and teacher education (p. 164), they have 'given impetus to [...] outcome oriented educational reforms' (p. 165), and 'PISA has had a decisive impact on reform efforts' (p. 166). She also mentions that after PISA, some 'form of decentralization' has been introduced that entails allowing teachers to choose their method of instruction (p. 164).

Nortvedt (2018), who studies the policy impact of PISA on Norwegian mathematics education, agrees with Mausethagen and considers the impact of PISA on Norwegian educational reforms as strong, claiming that the PISA Shock 'led to' improvements in quality assessment, testing and a new strategy for mathematics and science teaching. However, referring to research in other countries, which shows that international tests, such as PISA, may be used to 'validate existing policy directions', she claims that this also seems to be the case in Norway (p. 427).

Looking more closely at the changes in the mathematics curriculum, however, Nortvedt notes that they could just be the result of larger international trends because the changes, which are considered to be PISA effects, strongly resemble innovations that were originally developed in Denmark. Thus, alleged PISA effects in Norway may just be a result of ideas that circulate globally and reach individual countries through several channels (p. 436).

Nortvedt also discusses changes in the centralization and decentralization of Norwegian education as possible effects of 'PISA reforms'. She claims that Norwegian educational policy is inconsistent. An amendment to the Education Act and a major curriculum reform in 2006 focused on national achievement goals, but at the same time responsibility was transferred from the national level to the municipalities and the school leaders. Thus, centralization and decentralization at the same time (p. 438).

Sivesind (2019), in her contribution to a volume edited by Waldow and Steiner-Khamsi on 'Understanding PISA's attractiveness', addresses the spread and uses of International Largescale Assessments (ILSAs), including PISA, in the Nordic countries, Norway, Sweden, Finland, Denmark and Iceland. Combining this ILSA survey with a content analysis of 22 Norwegian government policy papers (Green Papers and White Papers) written between 1995 and 2016, she aims to find out how the results of ILSAs are used (in the policy papers). The theoretical framework for her study is from Waldow and Steiner-Khamsi who have suggested the concepts 'reference societies'[3] and 'projections' to capture processes initiated by ILSAs that go beyond merely 'drawing lessons' and 'policy borrowing from countries that top the league' (Waldow 2019, 2).

A reference society is a model to copy, emulate or borrow from. Emphasizing that copying and borrowing do not happen in a straightforward way, the concept 'projection' is suggested. This signifies that policies, systems and practices in 'reference societies' are not generally perceived in an objective fashion, but rather in the way the perceiver wants to see them. In other words, reference societies are perceived and depicted selectively, and sometimes the policy that is 'borrowed' or emulated bears no objective resemblance with the policy in the society from which it is 'borrowed'.

Among a large number of ILSAs used by the Nordic countries, Sivesind found that PISA was the only one that attracted pan-Nordic participation

(Sivesind 2019, 101). It was also the most frequently mentioned ILSA in the Norwegian policy papers, where it was mentioned 100 times (p. 98). Finland was clearly the major reference society, seen by Norwegian policy makers as a country from which to learn (p. 89). Sivesind also finds that when it comes to learning assessment – a core theme in Norwegian policy documents, for which ILSAs are used as the primary source of knowledge – the most-referenced study is PISA.

Sivesind's findings indicate that 'reference societies' like Finland, who top the league, tend to serve not mainly as models to be emulated, but more often as a contrast, that requires further probing about how their conditions for schooling differ from the countries that have them as reference societies. She thinks that in the end, real contextual conditions will decide how information about the reference country is interpreted and translated. Her findings throw doubts on Waldow's 'projection thesis' (p. 102) but elaborates the idea that comparing oneself with 'reference societies' does not necessarily result in 'policy borrowing'.

Summing up studies on PISA effects in Norway

These studies of PISA effects in Norway, all claim that PISA has had effects, even strong effects. Nortvedt describes Norwegian educational policy as 'PISA-driven' (p. 438). The studies on the whole also agree on which Norwegian reforms that were 'PISA effects'. It turns out that they were considered PISA effects because they were justified and legitimized with ideas derived from PISA and PISA results.

These studies emphasize more the adoption of a policy and its justifications, i.e., policy outputs, than the results of a policy, i.e., policy outcomes (Holzinger and Knill 2005). But the Norwegian studies also, to a certain extent, describe and analyse the policy outcomes of reforms that they considered 'PISA effects', i.e., legitimized by PISA. In terms of policy outcomes, Nortvedt and Mausethagen raise the question whether the 'PISA reforms' are a threat to equitable and inclusive education in Norway. And, Baird et al., Nortvedt and, briefly, Mausethagen discuss whether the 'PISA reforms' have contributed to centralized or decentralized education. Baird et al., for example, claim that the Norwegian system is a decentralized one and has remained so after the reforms justified by PISA. Mausethagen (2013, 164) mentions that a major reform in 2006 caused 'some kind of decentralization', giving more freedom for teachers to choose their teaching methods. Nortvedt (2018) claims that the Norwegian system has, in the past decade, been subject to contradictory policies promoting *decentralization* and *recentralization* at the same time. Their criteria for centralization and decentralization seem to coalesce on the conception that decentralization mean devolution of decision making, and centralization entails national uniformity. None of them make the claim that the Norwegian educational system is centralized.

The quest for a theoretical framework – Applying Archer's morphogenetic approach

Given this tentative assessment of the state of the art of PISA effect research, Margaret Archer offers a fresh restart with her theory of state educational systems, their inherent mechanisms and her model of morphogenetic cycles – as well as her conceptualizations of centralized and decentralized systems. These are tools that may be applied in the study of PISA effects or the lack of them (Archer [1979] 2013; 1984; 1995). Instead of primarily studying PISA effects as policy outputs (the adoption of reforms/policies that are justified by PISA), policy outcomes (the results of policy) can be theoretically analysed by applying Archer's concepts. Policy outcomes may be conceptualized as structural processes that exist in all state educational systems, which in Archer's theory are identified as unification, systematization, specialization and differentiation; the relative prevalence of these processes determines whether the system is centralized or decentralized.

Applying Archer's model of morphogenetic cycles, entails seeing the Norwegian PISA debate, which will be presented later in this text, as the middle phase (sociocultural interaction) in a morphogenetic cycle, where previously existing structures and structural processes are elaborated resulting from sociocultural interaction. In the interaction phase of the cycle, agents confront each other's conflicting ideas and vested interests. The morphogenetic cycle can simply be depicted as:

> structural conditioning (T1) → sociocultural interaction (T2-T3) → structural elaboration/morphogenesis (T4).
> *(Archer [1979] 2013, 1984, 1995)*[4]

Archer's definition of state educational systems is presented in Skinningsrud's article in this volume and will, therefore, not be repeated here. But below I will present the mechanisms of the system shortly. These concepts will be used in the analysis of structures and processes in the Norwegian education system before and after the PISA debate.

Unification has two aspects: *intensive unification* refers to structures and processes that facilitate political efficacy in the sense of a streamlined implementation of state policy, *extensive unification* produces uniformity by state policy being effectively implemented in all localities. S*ystematization* entails that the different parts of the system are connected, bottle necks are removed and new elements, which have previously been external, are incorporated into the system. *Specialization* refers to the diversity of provisions, including recruitment bases, internal processes, and output competences. *Differentiation* refers to the autonomy of the system, which has to do with the self determination of incumbents of the system in deciding upon their system activities and operations. And finally, *centralized* and *decentralized* systems differ in the relative predominance of the various systemic structures and processes. In centralized systems, the processes of *unification* and *systematization* predominate, while in decentralized systems, *specialization* and *differentiation* play a more important role (Archer [1979] 2013; 1984).

Clearly, Archer's definitions of centralized and decentralized educational systems rest on her identification of macro structures and ongoing processes in educational systems, and thereby differ from the definitions in the literature that has been examined so far.

Research questions

My aim is to find out whether the Norwegian educational system was impacted by the first PISA results, the Norwegian PISA Shock and the PISA reforms and interventions, i.e., measures that were justified by the PISA results, in such a way that the system was fundamentally changed. For this purpose, I will employ Archer's model of morphogenetic cycles and her conceptualizations of structures and processes in state educational systems. I therefore ask:

> After the introduction of PISA, the following public debate and the implementation of reforms justified by PISA, was there a change in which kinds of structures and processes that predominated in the system?

To answer the overall research question, I ask the following subsidiary questions:

1 What kinds of structures and processes predominated in the Norwegian educational system in the decade before the introduction of PISA?
2 Who were the protagonists in the public debate after the release of the first PISA results, and what were their concerns and projects?
3 Which systemic structures and processes were strengthened and which were weakened by the reforms legitimized by PISA results?

In my discussion towards the end of the chapter, I will discuss how empiricist and critical realist thinking differ in their conceptions of causality, introducing the notion of counterfactual reasoning. I will also discuss what consequences the critical realist notion of 'open systems' has for thinking about PISA effects.

Method

This research is a case study based on document analysis and the research literature on PISA effects. Danermark (2003, 123ff) argues from a critical realist stance that case studies in research on open systems can reveal mechanisms that may be found in other cases. Case studies are suitable for comparative research and for identifying mechanisms rather than for making empirical generalizations. This research uses abduction as a way of reasoning, using theoretical concepts to recontextualize and analyse empirical data. Thus, Archer's concepts of structures and processes in educational systems are used to recontextualize and analyse the implications/policy effects of educational reforms and other changes in the Norwegian educational system that were introduced before and after the release of the first PISA results in 2001 and the following PISA debate.

The scope of this research covers a period of two decades, 1990–2010, which will be analysed as one limited morphogenetic cycle to determine whether there has been a transformation or reproduction of systemic structures following the introduction of PISA.

Systemic structures and processes before PISA (1990–2000)

In the following, I will, in chronological order, describe the major educational reforms and interventions that were made during the decade 1990–2000 and analyse the kinds of processes they were part of, drawing on Archer's concepts of unification, systematization, specialization and differentiation.

Skinningsrud (2014) argues that, in the 1990s, processes of systematization and unification characterized the Norwegian education system, thus supporting the claim that it was a centralized system. In their 1989 assessment, however, the OECD claimed that the system had become too decentralized. The OECD pointed to changes made in the funding mechanism for education in 1986, when funding of education was changed from direct earmarked state funding to block-grant funding of the municipalities. In addition, in 1987, changes were made to the National Curriculum guidelines, requiring schools to work out local adaptations of the National Curriculum. Both changes entailed a transfer of decision-making from the national to the local level. The OECD advised central Norwegian authorities to reclaim their control of education and make the system more uniform. The OECD's report from 1989 expresses surprise at the lack of national data and systems of quality control of outputs relevant for the assessment of reform policies (OECD 1989, 168).

St. Meld [White Paper] No. 37 (1990–1991), 'On the Organization and Management of the Education Sector', which was issued as a follow-up to the OECD's (1989) report, introduced the concepts of management by objectives (MbO) in the education sector in Norway. This White Paper also introduced other measures that contributed to increased central control of education. The move was spearheaded by the Labour Party's Minister of Education Gudmund Hernes, who, during the 1990s, played a leading role in initiating reforms effecting a more unified and systematized system (Skinningsrud 2014).

In 1991, general teacher education (*allmennlærerutdanningen*) was expanded from three to four years, and the following year new framework plans[5] (*rammeplaner*) were introduced. New framework plans introduced the university's weighting scheme (*vekttallsordning*) and provided opportunities to incorporate study units from other higher educational institutions in the four-year teacher education program (Skjelmo 2007, 228). The new plans entailed a harmonization of the curriculum of teacher education with the curriculum of higher education in general. This expansion of teacher education was part of a new joint legislation for higher education that included both universities and colleges. Thus, teacher education was incorporated in the 'sub-system' of higher education, which meant increased systematization of the education sector, i.e., the closer integration of an element by establishing new links to other parts of the system.

The Municipal Act (*Kommuneloven*) from 1992 gave the municipalities the freedom to choose their own organizational solutions based on local assessments. 'Desectorization' was encouraged, which meant that school matters could now be redistributed between several municipal committees or assigned to multi-purpose committees which handled several different policy areas. Professional educational qualifications were no longer required to deal with educational matters at the municipal level. This practice was in line with NPM principles, which claim that leadership is a distinct skill independent of knowledge of the specific field in which it is executed (Skinningsrud 2014). This side-lining of educational expertise at the municipal level reduced professional input in municipal decision-making and fragmented the local professional community (Helgøy 2003), reflecting reduced professional autonomy and a weaker differentiation of the education system.

The Leadership Development in School (LUIS) programme in 1992 was a follow-up of White Paper No. 37 (1990–1991) 'About the Organization and Management of the Education Sector'. This programme of leadership education for leaders in the school system worked in parallel with the reorganization of the central education administration. The two previous leadership programmes, Leadership in School (LIS) and Leadership in Upper Secondary School (LEVIS) had targeted leaders at different levels in the system, but LUIS was a joint program for leaders in compulsory schools and in upper secondary education (Møller 2016, 12–13). The LUIS program was initiated by the Ministry and its curriculum framework was also defined by the Ministry (Møller 2016, 13). The establishment of a joint program for school leader training in primary and secondary school was meant to facilitate the implementation of the overarching National Curriculum framework, thus ensuring that state policy was enacted effectively. Drawing on Archer's concepts, this programme-reduction in leadership development and the merging of the programmes meant increased unification (extensive and intensive) by making leadership education uniform across levels and ensuring state control of its content.

The Upper Secondary Education Reform of 1994 (Reform 94) meant major changes to the course offerings in basic vocational education. The transformation and elimination of more than 100 locally designed and industry-specific introductory vocational courses, which were replaced by 13 nationally uniform course offerings, similar across the country, helped to make vocational training more uniform and general and reduced early specialization (Skinningsrud 2014). Thus, the reform promoted increased extensive unification and reduced specialization.

In the 1990s, the higher education sector was systematized. As previously mentioned, universities, university colleges and colleges had been governed by separate legislation. However, in 1989, a new act on universities and university colleges was passed (NOU [Green Paper] 2020:3, 50). In 1991, the Parliament decided on a merger of colleges of higher education in accordance with the principle of geographical proximity. Colleges of nursing and colleges of teacher education became separate departments in newly merged higher education colleges. Through this decision, the number of colleges in the nation was reduced from 98 to 26 (NOU [Green Paper] 2020:3, 51). A new act on universities and university colleges, passed in 1995, included all state-funded higher education institutions (NOU [Green Paper] 2020:3). In most places, teacher education was now organized as 'departments' under a joint College Board. This new act meant that the direct management channel to the Ministry was severed. Teacher education, like other professions, now had to deal with a common regional college management. The reduction in and merger of regional colleges meant that the system increased its extensive unification by reducing the uniqueness of specialized professional programmes, among them teacher education.

The Basic Education Reform Act of 1997 (Reform 97), initiated by Hernes and the Brundtland III (third) government, extended compulsory education from 9 to 10 years by lowering the school entry age from 7 to 6 years. The Act also introduced a new National Curriculum for basic education. In the 1990s, two education acts contributed to extending the length of education for Norwegian citizens. Reform 94 had entitled all 16- to 19-year-olds to 3 years of upper secondary education, and Reform 97 extended compulsory education from 9 to 10 years (Bergesen 2006, 33). The curriculum (L97) that followed the reform was extremely detailed and gave little freedom to the teachers (Hovdenak 2004). The research leader and evaluator of the reform stated:

> Many of the projects conclude that much is as it has been in the work in the school. In several areas where L97 has changed in line with previous plans, the researchers do not find that the school has changed its practice to any great extent. [.]. The school mostly focuses on teacher-led classroom teaching, with instruction and question – answer sequences. The students are very passive recipients, they get to give short answers to questions from the teacher and they work individually with assignments. Orientation around the textbooks is strong. Overall, the conclusion is that activity [child centred] pedagogy is more strongly rooted ideologically and rhetorically than in practice.
>
> *[author's translation] (Haug 2004, 254–255)*

The expanded length of school attendance with a detailed National Curriculum at all levels ensured a system with strong uniformity.

In 1998, the Teacher Education Council (*Lærerutdanningsrådet*), formerly known as the Teacher School Council (*Lærerskolerådet*), which was mandated to suggest framework plans for the National Curriculum governing teacher education, was made part of the Norwegian Network Council (for higher education) (*Norgesnettrådet*). The inclusion of the Teacher Education Council in the Norwegian Network Council for higher education meant increased uniformity (extensive unification) since the latter dealt with a range of professions in addition to the teacher profession, for example, engineering, health and social services. The Norwegian Network Council, however, was discontinued in 2001 and replaced by other government bodies. The process of reorganizing and establishing new bodies for advisory and government control functions in Norwegian higher education as a unified sector continued after the 2001 PISA results and debate.

In 1998, a new teacher education reform (*allmennlærerutdanning*) arrived, with a revised framework plan (*rammeplan*). The mandate of the committee preparing the reform proposal was to adapt teacher education to the previously introduced reforms of basic education (Telhaug 1997, 234). This signalled an intent at systematization, in terms of a closer fit between basic education and the education of teachers. The committee proposed a stronger national standardization of content and structure in teacher education across the country, noting that local curriculum plans at the time showed little uniformity and besides did not reflect the national framework plans to a sufficient degree. Furthermore, the diversity of local models hindered standardized reporting and statistics to be collected by national authorities (Telhaug 1997, 241–242). The 1998 revised framework plan reduced the number of choice options for students in teacher education and made the first three years nationally uniform in terms of content. The curricula for each subject were detailed, specifying the content as well as teaching and assessment methods (NOKUT 2006, 16). This revision of the framework plan for teacher education increased national uniformity and facilitated the implementation of national policy (the National Curriculum), thus strengthening both extensive and intensive unification, beside its contribution to systematization.

In 1998, European universities sought to develop an integrated market for higher education through the European Higher Education Area (EHEA), an initiative led by the Council of Europe (CoE), which several educational ministers agreed and committed to in the Bologna Process. In addition, ambitious reforms later emerged to create an integrated European research area before 2010 – this was advocated by the EU after the Lisbon meeting in 2000, as a parallel to the Bologna Process that would bring more comparable, compatible and coherent structures to higher education (Helsvig 2017, 229). Here, the main objective was to approach the flexibility and differentiation of the North American higher education and research system to equip Europe for ever tougher and knowledge-driven competition with the growing economies of the South and East. The Bologna Process was used to legitimize and drive changes that had previously been difficult to achieve within a nation state framework (Helsvig 2017); it sought to increase mobility for students and teachers between the different countries and universities and to ensure commensurability between levels and grades. In Norway, it was the Green Paper NOU [Green Paper] 2000:14 and the St. Meld [White Paper] No. 16 (2001–2002) that introduced the Norwegian Quality Reform for higher education (*Kvalitetsreformen*) and the requirements related to the policy on EHEA. The Quality Reform's introduction of a new degree structure also had consequences for teacher education which were outlined in St. Meld [White Paper] No. 16 (2001–2002), recommending that the same degree structure should be adopted in teacher education. These changes in teacher education which meant full integration into higher education was a clear expression of extensive unification – all higher education should have the same structure. The process started before and continued during and after the discussion following the release of the first PISA results.

The 1998 Education Act, by including basic education (primary and lower secondary education) and upper secondary education in one single education act (Opplæringslova [Education Act] 1998), entailed increased systematization. Previously, basic education and upper secondary education had been regulated by separate acts. In the revised Education Act, of 1999 (§ 9–9), the schools were told to carry out school-based assessment: to regularly assess the extent to which the school organization and teaching and learning activities contributed to the goals set in the curriculum. The municipalities were responsible for ensuring that the assessments were carried out, and thus to enable control of goal achievements in terms of government policy – intensive unification (Helgøy 2003, 73).

Summing up the educational structures before the introduction of PISA

During the 1990s, changes, through legal reform acts and other initiatives, were taking place in all domains of the system. Reform acts were implemented in basic education (1997), in upper secondary education (1994) and in higher education at several points during this decade. The changes in higher education affected teacher education, which had formerly been outside the higher education sector. But this sector was now systematized, and universities, university colleges and regional colleges were, by the end of the 1990s, more closely integrated into the same structure and systematized under the same legislation. This process created more uniformity (extensive unification) in the higher education sector in which teacher education was gradually included. The integration of the advisory Teacher Education Council into the Network Council for Higher Education was part of the integration of teacher education into the structure of higher education, further increasing systematization. This integration of advisory councils also meant increased uniformity, i.e., increased extensive unification of education for various professions, which were now overseen by the same national council. The process of integrating teacher education in the higher education sector, which started before the PISA Shock and the PISA debate, continued with new legislation following the PISA debate.

Another government initiative, which did not involve legislation, was the education for school leaders. LIS, LEVIS and LUIS were courses in school leadership, which gradually became more unified and uniform (extensive unification), through the merger of courses targeting compulsory and upper secondary education, and they were more intensively unified by the Ministry defining their content.

In the 1990s, the processes of differentiation and specialization were weakened by the Municipal Act in 1992, which reduced the opportunity for professional input in municipal decision-making, and by the reform act on upper secondary education in 1994, which replaced a large number of highly specialized introductory courses in vocational education with a much smaller number of nationally uniform courses.

The predominance of processes of unification and systematization going on in the system and the tendencies towards weaker differentiation (autonomy) and specialization indicate that the system, by Archer's definition, was a centralized system during the 1990s.

The 'PISA Shock' and the PISA debate

In 2000, Norway participated in the first PISA survey. The Minister of Education at the time, Kristin Clemet, was from the Conservative Party under the Bondevik II government (a centre-right coalition government). Clemet later stated on her blog that 'the first time we were asked, [the Labour Party's] Gudmund Hernes was the Minister of Education, and it was therefore he who first said yes to Norway's participation. Since then, all education ministers have said the same thing—whether they came from the SV [Socialist Left], the Labour Party or the right' [author's translation] (Clemet 2014). In the 1990s, Hernes, from the Labour Party, was known for introducing MbO into the education system, advocating a strong state and planned political governance (Thuen 2010, 282). Hernes wanted more focus on structure, training, discipline, standardization and knowledge in the schools and higher ambitions among students and parents (Bergesen 2006, 32).

As Clemet claims in her blog, the PISA test had already been mentioned in government circles in 1996. A Norwegian Green Paper (A Norwegian Official Report – NOU) from the same year, ordered by the Labour government, refers to an upcoming international test (PISA), and that Norway will be joining it: 'Investigations under the direction of the OECD. The OECD is working on the question of regularly collecting data on the level of achievement in reading, mathematics, and science. As the committee understands, Norway is among the countries that will participate' [author's translation] (NOU [Green Paper] 1996:22, 134). Historically, the education policy of the Labour Party has been criticized for paying too little attention to knowledge transmission and too much attention to collectivist attitudes and social change (amelioration). This collectivism was attributed to the Social Democrats' project of ensuring the right to education for all individuals, regardless of their social background. The Social Democrats' project also entailed a tension between focusing on educational aims for the individual and collective aims for society as a whole (Bergesen 2006, 23, 27–31). The Socialist Left Party (SV) was criticized by the Conservative Party for their resistance to exams and grades; in turn, SV claimed that the Conservative Minister Kristin Clemet, in the government's (2004) White Paper 'Culture for Learning', was bringing the school back to the 1960s, focusing too heavily on memorization of instrumental (fact-based) knowledge (Bergesen 2006, 82). During her election campaign in the summer of 2005, Kristin Halvorsen, the leader of SV and Member of Parliament, proclaimed that her party was more focused on Bildung [formation] in a broader sense than just knowledge-transmission and had a broader view of education, given her party's ideology (Bergesen 2006, 81–82).

Helge Ole Bergesen (the Secretary of State in the Ministry of Education and Research from 2001 to 2005 under the Minister of Education Kristin Clemet) stated in his autobiographical book about the introduction of PISA in Norway that 'the stage was set for the big Norwegian settlement on knowledge in the school. For those of us who had just taken over the political leadership of the Ministry of Education and Research, the PISA results were a "flying start"' [author's translation] (Bergesen 2006, 41f). Bergesen claims that, previously, there had been no tradition of requesting results or quality indicators; politics had generally been based on politicians' ideologies and assumptions about the system (p. 42). This was to be changed, as failing competencies and average results were no longer loose accusations put forward in the conservative election platform. Bergesen describes how the message to the public, connected with the 'flying start' mentioned above, was moderated to prepare the ground for reforms that had not yet been presented to Parliament:

> From a political point of view, however, this became a little too much of the good [for us]. [...], gradually, the negative impression became so dominant that it threatened to paralyze those who could in practice improve the school—namely, the 100,000 teachers [...]. How would they manage to keep their chins up and be motivated for a new reform process when the media was constantly full of bad news about the school? It was imperative to balance the message [...]. [...]. It also became important to choose the right words when commenting on knowledge failure. We decided to use the term 'medium good' results, not 'mediocre'.

[…]. When this survey [PISA] was conducted, our reforms had not been presented to the Parliament, and they were not yet ready for practical implementation in the school. [author's translation].

(Bergesen 2006, 46–47)

In a press release dated 6 December 2004, Clemet, the Minister of Education and Research, stated that the 2003 PISA results had indicated that Norwegian schools did not perform as expected. 'The PISA study confirmed that the Norwegian school faces major challenges, especially in relation to students' learning. The new reform of basic education, which will be implemented from 2006, appears even more necessary' [author's translation] (Utdannings-og forskningsdepartementet [Education and Resarch Department] 2004).

The average results caused a PISA Shock in Norway. In the Norwegian social-liberal newspaper *Dagbladet*, the results were contrasted with Norway's top performance in the Winter Olympics. It was further claimed that schools received too many resources (i.e., input), without this being matched by the results (i.e., output). Bergesen points out that the PISA results elicited few reactions from other politicians, although later mentioning that he met a number of teachers who were not fans of the test (Bergesen 2006, 41–43). Only the teacher organizations responded to the test results from PISA. 'We are good enough', said Helga Hjetland, the leader of the educational association *Utdanningsforbundet*. She declared that the school must have self-confidence and stay with its mission. The leader of the teachers' union *Lærerforbundet*, Anders Folkestad, commented that 'this is too stupid, it's groundless and unscientific to say that the Norwegian school gets too much and gives too little. Well-being is important for long-term learning' (Bergesen 2006, 41). In addition, Professor Stefan Hopmann, at the pedagogical institute at the Norwegian University of Science and Technology (NTNU), claimed that the PISA test said nothing about the quality of Norway's schools, and indicated that he was dissatisfied with the test (Telhaug and Mediås 2003, 327).

Clemet, the Minister of Education and Research, in a Parliamentary debate on 17 January 2002, underlined the seriousness of the test results and described the situation as disturbing.

> Finally, a few words about the OECD survey that Representative Reikvam also included in his main address. How relevant is it to Norwegian conditions? My impression is that the Norwegian researchers who have been involved in this work—and I emphasize that this is very solid research—emphasize that this is actually quite relevant for Norwegian curricula. It may not be equally relevant for all countries, but for Norway this is actually quite relevant. The second thing—I just have to mention it—is that I have seen a lot of newspaper articles indicating that these somewhat poor results, that we are average, is

because we have integrated virtually all children and young people into Norwegian schools, and that this makes it a little difficult to stay on top. But this factor is considered in the final assessment of the results, so you can say that from a purely research standpoint, it has been corrected for the fact that you have slightly different school systems and different school policies. In my opinion you can always discuss how bad it is or how disappointed you are about achieving average results. [author's translation].

(Stortinget [The Parliament] 2002, 1315)

The Education Minister, Clemet, wanted to replace detailed management from the centre with decentralized responsibility. The Conservative Party had previously been criticizing the Labour Party for strong centralization and bureaucracy in the education system (Bergesen 2006, 25, 31–32). In a document published by the Ministry of Education and Research in 2002, 'The School Knows Best', (*Skolen vet best*), the message was: 'We must decentralize responsibility, increase quality control and allow more influence from the users. The school must be governed from below, not from above, [but] within nationally decided aims' (Telhaug 2005, 67). The Minister followed this up in 2003 by proposing amendments to the Education Act (Ot. Prp. Nr. 67 (2002–2003), which allowed the organization of students into smaller groups, and decided that each student should have a contact teacher (Telhaug 2005, 67). The stated aims of this initiative were to grant more autonomy to schools and teachers to be innovative in their teaching practices to raise the quality of schooling. When the White Paper '[A School] Culture for Learning' (*Kultur for læring*) (St. Meld. Nr. 30 (2003–2004) was presented in April 2004, the new policy of decentralization was launched as a 'systemic change':

> In order for the schools to succeed, a systemic change is needed in the way the schools are governed. National authorities must allow greater diversity in the solutions and working methods that are chosen, so that these are adapted to the situation for the individual student, teacher, and school. The state shall set goals and contribute with good framework conditions, support, and guidance. At the same time, trust must be shown in the school and the teachers as professionals. We will mobilize for greater creativity and commitment by giving [them] more freedom to take responsibility [author's translation].

(Telhaug 2005, 68)

Summary of the PISA debate in the aftermath of the first PISA results

The participation in the PISA test was announced by the Labour Party (the Brundtland III government) in 1996 (NOU [Green Paper] 1996:22, 134).

However, in 2001, when the first PISA results were published, a coalition centre-right government was in power, with a Conservative Minister of Education, Kristin Clemet; she claimed that the first PISA results supported conservative educational policy. The debate following this PISA Shock became a heated confrontation between the educational politics of the right and the left parties. The conservatives blamed the former Labour government for the weak PISA results (Bergesen 2006). The Conservative Party claimed that basic schooling had been under the influence of the Labour Party's softer educational policy. Although the Labour Party had already made a shift in their education policy in the 1990s, under the leadership of Education Minister Hernes, the party was criticized for not emphasizing school leadership, knowledge transmission and quality indicators. The leaders of the educational association and the teachers' union (*Utdanningsforbundet* and *Lærerforbundet*, respectively) and a professor from NTNU's pedagogical institute participated in the debate, trying to tone down the importance of PISA results as a quality indicator for Norwegian education. The interaction and debate in the period before and after the introduction of PISA was still ideologically charged with ideas and opinions that could be identified with party politics.

Structural elaboration after PISA

On 5 October 2001, the Labour government's Prime Minister Jens Stoltenberg appointed a committee for the preparation of a Green Paper suggesting procedures for quality improvement in basic education. The PISA results were the justification for commissioning the Green Paper and its mandate. Due to a change of governments soon afterward, from Labour to a centre-right coalition with the Conservative Minister of Education (Kristin Clemet), the committee's mission statement was slightly altered and some of its members replaced. Furthermore, on 6 March 2002, the commission was requested by Minister Clemet to deliver, within three months, a partial instalment of its recommendations. The Minister was explicitly asking for an outline of a National Quality Assessment System (NQAS) and other educational improvements related to 'international projects and initiatives in this area (among others from the OECD) and systems developed in other countries' (NOU [Green Paper] 2002:10, chapter 1.9). The original mandate had not mentioned that the OECD's initiatives should be considered, only that Norwegian basic education should be viewed in a broader international context.

As mentioned earlier, during the Norwegian PISA debate, the Ministry in 2002 issued a policy paper 'The school knows best' (Skolen vet best! 2002), with a foreword, signed by Minister Clemet, announcing that the Ministry had initiated a comprehensive modernization of Norwegian basic education (compulsory and upper secondary). Pointing to the current mismatch between the input of resources, 'which in Norway is among the highest in the world', and the average results on international tests, her solution is decentralization, quality control and user influence; in her own words: 'governance from below', though within the framework of 'nationally determined goals'.

The NQAS, requested by Minister Clemet as part of her modernization project, included the introduction of National Tests which did not exist in Norway at that time. In the Green Paper (NOU [Green Paper] 2002:10, chapter 1.9), containing national recommendation for strategies – among them a NQAS – to improve the quality of Norwegian schools, the term 'quality' (*kvalitet*) is mentioned 623 times. 'PISA' is mentioned seven times and 'OECD' eight times.

The Norwegian NQAS was established in 2003. The purpose was to contribute to 'quality development, transparency, and dialogue' in the education system by providing 'knowledge to support central and local decision-making and local quality assessment and development'. The components in the NQAS included national and international tests, diagnostic tests, exam results, user questionnaires, and national inspection'. In addition, a website for publishing these educational data was established (Udir [DfE] 2009).

A later research-based evaluation study of the Norwegian NQAS pointed out that the quality assessment system serves both a control function, by providing data for decision makers, and a learning function, in providing useful knowledge for quality improvement at the local level. The study concludes that the current NQAS has its focus on control, while learning for quality improvement receives less attention. The main emphasis is on national and international tests, among them PISA (Udir [DfE] 2009). The evaluation also showed that the NQAS tends to be more positively valued by people in central positions, while teachers find them less useful (Udir [DfE] 2009).

Drawing on Archer's conceptualizations, the Norwegian NQAS, which was justified by Norway's result on PISA and other international tests, promotes unification of the system. It provides information on educational outcomes to policy makers, enabling management by national objectives and central monitoring, while holding local school owners accountable for the results.

The Norwegian Directorate of Education and Training (*Utdanningsdirektoratet, Udir*) was established in 2004. It represented a new level in the stratification of the system. Its main task is to drive the implementation of national policy and supervise the system on behalf of the state. This entails that the directorate undertakes supervision and enforces regulations, develops curricula, exams and tests and works to address school development in general. It aligns with and designates several education-related responsibilities to local municipalities. It also launches the National Tests in basic reading, English and mathematics skills in Norwegian compulsory schooling. In addition, it suggests entry requirements for teacher education and administers the approval of private schools (Udir [DfE] 2020). Thus, it contributes to intensive and extensive unification in the education system by ensuring that national policy is implemented in all regions of the country.

St. Meld [White Paper] No. 30 (2003–2004) 'Culture for Learning' announced the plan for the reform that would 'modernize' compulsory and upper secondary education, the Knowledge Promotion Reform (K06). The White Paper stated the need for a 'systemic change' of Norwegian education in view of Norway's poor performance on international tests and the challenge of the 'knowledge society'. The White Paper put forward three principles for systemic change: clearly stated national goals, clearly assigned responsibility for outcomes, and increased local freedom (p. 25). The White Paper sees the NQAS as a valuable instrument for the new system of governance. But the effectiveness of the new system would depend on competent teachers and school leaders with a positive attitude to change (p. 9). PISA is referred to 17 times in this White Paper (Møller and Skedsmo 2013, 343).

The main principles of the K06 reform were approved in Parliament in 2004, and information was disseminated to the education sector by a circular from the Ministry (Rundskriv F-13/04) outlining the visions of the coming reform. These were to create a 'culture for learning', develop new National Curricula for all school subjects describing national goals in terms of competences and incorporate 'basic skills' in every school subject at each level of the system. The government would also initiate competence development among teachers, school leaders and instructors by organizing courses targeting these groups.

A pamphlet informing the public about the K06 reform issued by the Ministry in 2005, the Knowledge Promotion Reform – in compulsory and upper secondary education ('Kunnskapsløftet – reformen i grunnskolen og videregående opplæring') repeats the White Paper's justifications for initiating the reform referring to 'international studies' having shown that the performance of Norwegian students in basic skills, reading, writing and mathematics is lower than in countries 'we would like to compare ourselves with'. Beside introducing the notion of competences and the emphasis on 'basic skills', the pamphlet mentions that the reform will allow more local freedom, enabling teachers to choose methods of instruction (Utdannings-og forskningsdepartementet [Education and Research Department] 2005).

Regarding upper secondary education, a central concern in the St. Meld [White Paper] No. 30 (2003–2004) 'Culture for learning' was the need for a 'simplification' of the vocational course options, meaning that a reduction in the number of courses from many specialized ones to fewer general courses would entail simplification. The White Paper proposed to reduce the number of vocational programs, reflected in the number of first year options, from twelve to eight. A reduction of the current 102 second year options to 35–50 courses was also suggested (p. 68–72). In the end, K06 entailed nine vocational programs as first year options and 52 as second year options. The chosen solution entailed reduced specialization in initial vocational education. The decision to reduce the number of options and thereby reduce early specialization is the expected outcome in a centralized system, where uniformity and reduced specialization tendentially predominate.

The evaluation studies of the K06 reform pointed out that the expressed intention of the reform, that it would create decentralized education, had not materialized. In their assessment, the education system remained centralized (Karseth, Møller, and Aasen 2013).

As previously mentioned in the section on pre-PISA structural processes, in 2001, teacher education was subjected to a new revision. St. Meld [White Paper] No. 16 (2001–2002) suggested that teacher education should adopt the common European degree structure proposed by the EHEA policy and the Bologna Process to harmonize the structure of higher education in European countries. This meant that teacher education would adopt the same degree structure as the higher education sector in Norway and the rest of Europe. 'PISA' is mentioned three times in this White Paper as a reference for legitimizing the new teacher education *(Allmennlærerutdanningen)*. The EU standard for the calculation of credits, ECTS, was also introduced. The new proposal regarding teacher education was part of the new Quality Reform in Norwegian higher education. The 2001 teacher education legislation was the first since 1890, which was decided without the preparatory step of commissioning a Green Paper, implicating that the teaching profession was excluded from exerting influence on the formulation of the act (Karlsen 2005, 410). This teacher education reform signalled the weakening autonomy of the teacher profession. At the same time, it represented an increased systematization, continuing the process from the 1990s by incorporating teacher education in the degree structure of higher education.

Education in school leadership was also subject to structural change in the aftermath of the PISA Shock. In 2002, the Ministry of Education and Research announced funds to stimulate the university and college communities to develop education at the master's level for school leaders.[6] The work was organized through the Central Agency for Flexible Distance Learning *(Sentralorganet for fleksibel fjernundervisning – SOFF)* in 2004 (Møller 2016, 15).

St. Meld [White Paper] No. 30 (2003–2004) 'Culture for Learning' had emphasized the changing role of school leaders and their crucial importance for students' learning outcomes: 'For the school to meet the challenges from a more knowledge-driven society, a systemic change is needed, where management is to a greater extent based on clear national goals, clear responsibilities and increased local freedom of action' (p. 8–9), 'A learning organization requires powerful leadership that conveys explicit expectations related to the school's goals' (p. 26–27); […]. 'Experience shows that good school management is crucial to the work on quality development in the school' (p. 99).

St. Meld [White Paper] No. 31 (2007–2008), 'Quality in School' followed up the intention behind the Knowledge Promotion Reform (K06) which was outlined in 'Culture for Learning' by emphasizing quality improvement and at the same time responding to the OECD's recommendations on education for school leaders. The OECD study of school leadership in 22 countries, entitled 'Improving School Leadership' (2006–2008), had proposed that school leaders should be offered leadership courses on a regular basis (Møller 2016, 15–16). In the White Paper 'Quality in School', the Ministry delegated the responsibility for the course to the Directorate of Education, which would define the framework plan and select higher education institutions to deliver the course (St. Meld [White Paper] No. 31 (2007–2008, 66). The study programme for educational leadership was weighted at 30 credits and would be delivered as a part-time distance learning course that extended over a period of one and a half to two years. The 30 credits could be incorporated in a master's degree programme for those who wanted a full degree in educational leadership. Initially, the education was to be offered to newly appointed school leaders who had no formal leadership education. The Directorate of Education gave four higher education institutions the mandate to start a school leader master's programme in autumn 2009, and in autumn 2010, two new academic institutions received similar mandates (Hybertsen et al. 2014, 15–16; Møller 2016, 16).

This school leader education meant increased systematization since a national master's-level programme for school leaders had not been offered before but was now fully incorporated as a part of the system. Today, master's-level education in leadership is often required to obtain a position as school leader in a Norwegian school.

Summing up structural elaborations after the introduction of PISA

In the document '*Skolen vet best*' [The School Knows Best, 2002] the Ministry declared its intention to effect 'a systemic change' and establish a decentralized education system. A major justification for this new policy was Norway's PISA results. However, reforms that were implemented after the introduction of PISA maintained and reinforced the processes of unification and systematization which had already prevailed in the system before the introduction of PISA. Arguably, processes of systematization that integrated teacher education into higher education – by establishing relationships with other higher education institutions, programmes and courses, and the initiation of programmes and degrees for educational leadership – were continuous processes that had started before PISA and continued after PISA. Increased intensive unification (the effective implementation of state policy) was ensured in the already centralized system by the establishment of the Education Directorate in 2004. Also the reduction of specialization in vocational education effected by K06 (after PISA) continued the same tendency as in Reform 94 (before PISA), and the lack of professional participation in the preparation of the 2001 teacher reform act continued the trend of reduced professional autonomy and system differentiation initiated by the Municipal Act of 1992 (before PISA).

Discussion

Studies of 'PISA effects' often claim that PISA has 'led to this and that'. However, it is always agency (groups or individuals) that mediates such influence. Postulating that 'PISA League Table' ranking is a cause is entirely empiricist and in opposition to theorizing based on generative mechanisms. Seeing PISA results as a cause exemplifies *associational* thinking, which is based on correlations, i.e., an assumption that because events occur simultaneously or one after the other in time, there is a cause–effect relationship between them. This is an empiricist conception of causality derived from a Humean constant conjunction of events model linked to a flat ontology. In opposition to using associational thinking to make inferences about causation, critical realism uses *counterfactual* thinking because causality is not conceived as a correlation, but as a necessary connection, i.e., the result of mechanisms that belong to a deeper stratum in reality than the actual and the empirical (Bhaskar [1975] 2008, 12; Sayer 2000, 85).

Also, it is important to acknowledge that PISA alone, as a single cause of change in an open system, is impossible. This is also what my analysis of pre- and post-PISA processes of systemic change has indicated. Nevertheless, PISA may influence the course of events (policy and reforms) when (individual or group) agency can make use of the results to underpin their educational ideas and/or interests – as my limited analysis of the Norwegian PISA debate illustrates.

A counterfactual question that aims to find the causal effect of PISA, for example, whether the introduction of the Norwegian NQAS was a 'PISA effect', would be to ask whether the NQAS would have occurred without PISA. An associational question, by contrast, would ask whether the NQAS came after PISA. The answer to the counterfactual question will probably be that NQAS could have come about without PISA, and there was no necessary connection between PISA and the NQAS. PISA was one of many possible justifications. NQAS could have been introduced for many other reasons, such as to enable the effective implementation of national policy, ensuring the uniformity and quality of provisions, etc. Hence, the NQAS could have come into being without PISA.

A more comprehensive question about causal effects, which could be answered by posing counterfactual questions, is whether the Conservative Minister of Education caused the introduction of PISA and thereby the subsequent alleged PISA effects in Norway. The interaction (debate) that produces reforms has a power aspect – propositions involving references to PISA carry more weight when they are presented by members of the government, who are thereby setting the tone of the public debate. This also entails defining a problem, or *the* problem. This was the case in Norway, when the first PISA results from 2000 were published. The Conservative Minister of Education exploited these results to legitimize her party's policy. However, imagining that the Minister of Education had not been a member of the

Conservative Party when the first PISA results were published, the PISA results might not have been portrayed as a shock or have even contributed to the subsequent reforms. This does not mean that these centralizing reforms would not have been implemented, especially since the system was already centralized before PISA was introduced and was already characterized by processes of systematization and unification. Beside this counterfactual argument about the likelihood of PISA and the centralizing reforms being implemented by any other Minister of Education, the factual evidence is that Ministers from other political parties have continued Norway's participation in the PISA survey every third year since 2000.

As previous research has shown, there has been no uniform PISA effect throughout Europe, or even Scandinavia. This is especially important to underline as there is a strong tendency in Europe and the US to treat Scandinavia as one homogeneous area (as with the case of the 'welfare state'). The previous literature on PISA effects indicates that various agents have mediated PISA results in ways that benefit their educational interests.

In Norway, processes that were already ongoing in the 1990s, such as systematization and unification, continued after the introduction of PISA. Hence, PISA did not affect the dominant structures of the education system in Norway. The education system remained a centralized system – despite Clemet's expressed intention to create a decentralized system, announced in 'Skolen vet best' [The School Knows Best]. Given my analysis and arguments, educational development in Norway did not take a new turn with the implementation of reforms legitimized by PISA results. Alleged PISA effects (for example NQAS, K06, etc.) have not changed the Norwegian education system significantly, as the education system was already centralized prior to the PISA test. After PISA, structures that entailed stronger centralization emerged through new elaborations of systemic macro structures that characterize a centralized system and a weakening of the macro structures and inherent mechanisms that enable stronger professional autonomy in schools.

Another counterfactual question which may be posed about details in the process of introducing PISA is whether the Education Minister at the time caused Norway's participation in PISA by enrolling Norway in the PISA 2000 test. Imagining that the Educational Minister had decided not to enrol Norway in the first PISA test, this might have had the consequences of reducing the credibility of (inter-) national testing and thereby the policy recommendations and processes already ongoing in the system; there were already processes in motion at the beginning of the 1990s that focused on change in the governance of education. The OECD recommended more centralization with stronger unification, especially more evidence-based policy and systemic evaluative structures (OECD 1989). Participation in the PISA test had already been suggested in 1996 under a Labour Party government. Thus, another Education Minister from another political party would most probably have enrolled Norway in the test.

Another scenario is if Norway had decided to opt out of the PISA test at some point. That would have been a missed opportunity to evaluate and compare Norwegian results with other countries' results, which, according to the OECD, could have consequences for socioeconomic development, since they are a measure of the country's human capital. Opting out would have been an unlikely choice for any Norwegian government.

Based on the arguments above, the answer to the counterfactual question whether another minister in another government, led by other parties, would have introduced PISA, and whether they would have rejected the possibility of opting out, the answer is yes. PISA would have been introduced by other parties, who would also have continued to participate, as the opposite choice – not introducing PISA and receiving the following series of PISA results – would have been too risky for the vested interests in education. It follows from the counterfactual reasoning above that there was no necessary connection between the Conservative Minister and her government, on the one side, and the initial and continued PISA participation, on the other. Consequently, the Conservative Minister and her government could not have been the cause of Norway's initial and continued participation in PISA.

Other ways of reasoning about PISA effects deal specifically with the role of ideas in mediating PISA results. PISA as a set of ideas can be argued to have affected the macro, meso and micro levels of the education system through its influence on agency, given that some agents find this set of ideas beneficial for their educational projects. The influence may be partly positive or negative 'washback effects', generating various assertions through which agents legitimize their interests with ideas that are compatible with them. Structural positions and mandates may generate frictions and interactions between individuals or groups that adhere to different ideologies defending and legitimizing conflicting interests. PISA has at the macro level, understood as the transnational and national decision-making levels, contributed with ideas that impact the policy and rhetoric of politicians and also the selective use of PISA results that often becomes detached from the original narrative (Grey and Morris 2018; Sellar and Lingard 2018).

A reason for this free and sometimes distorted use of PISA results in the policy debate at the macro level is that the soft governance from the OECD, directed at the national (macro) level of policymaking, consists of providing information and advice on policy. Soft governance does not entail the use of sanctions because the OECD cannot impose national legislation. It can only provide comparative statistics to national authorities and make recommendations for policy. For OECD ideas to be adopted as a national policy, they must be accepted and implemented by national authorities. However, at lower regional and municipal (meso) levels, national policy is implemented by means of legislation and resource allocation as well as information. Both legislation and resource allocation entail the use of sanctions for breaching rules. To the extent that OECD policy is adopted and implemented at the national level, sanctions may be activated at lower levels, if new legislation and new systems of resource allocation are transgressed. This also entails that various forms of sanctions at the micro level (the schools) may be activated if support of national policy (acceptance of PISA) is withheld by single individuals or groups.

When teachers conduct the PISA test in their class, that itself is an obvious PISA effect on agency, as the test is being mediated, creating certain events. This argument justifies the claim that PISA effects operate but in different ways at different levels of the education system. However, PISA effects exercised through agency will not be the only generative mechanism creating particular events in everyday schooling, as other more substantial systemic powers contribute to the actualization of most school event, such as conducting a PISA test.

Conclusion

During the period I have investigated, the Norwegian system remained centralized, in the sense that processes of unification and systematization continued to predominate. Hence, the introduction of PISA could not have effected change in these characteristics of the system. PISA became influential in Norway because the Educational Minister at the time seized the opportunity created by the 'PISA Shock' to promote the educational policy of the Conservative Party, advocating educational reform. It must be noted that a previous Labour government, in 1996, had decided that Norway should participate in the PISA test. Before that, in 1989, the OECD had recommended a stronger role for the state and improvement in the educational statistics providing feedback to policymakers. The question is: would another government have resisted the OECD's advice and/or withdrawn Norway's PISA participation? Probably not, since OECD advice is generally heeded by the Norwegian political elite, across political parties. Norway's participation in PISA had been initiated by a Labour government, but the 2001 PISA results turned out to be useful in legitimizing the educational policy of the Conservative Party. Arguably, in Norway, the systemic processes that predominate in a centralized system seem to have been maintained by various left and right coalition governments, before and after the introduction of PISA.

Notes

1. The PGB overseeing PISA 2012 had 65 members and 37 of them responded to an e-mail questionnaire about PISA effects in their own country. The Norwegian representative on the PGB is from the Directorate of Education and Training, and other countries' representatives are from similar government affiliated agencies (Breakspear 2012, 9).
2. DeSeCo is an abbreviation of 'Definition and Selection of Key Competencies', the outcome of an OECD project running from 1997 to 2003, 'Definition and

Selection of Competencies: Theoretical and Conceptual Foundations' (Mausethagen 2013, 170).
3. The concept 'reference societies' is adapted from 'reference groups', originally used in the discipline of social psychology, where it designates groups which are a reference for comparison. It was later modified by the sociologist Reinhard Bendix and applied to whole societies, i.e., 'reference societies' (Waldow 2019).
4. The notation T1–T4 indicate successive points in chronological time.
5. A framework plan (*rammeplan*) is a centrally decided general outline of the National Curriculum at different levels of schooling, allowing supplementary details to be included at a later date.
6. The term 'school leader' is used here as an equivalent to the term 'principal', designating the head or leader of a unit. One reason for this choice of terminology is that, in the Norwegian context, the term 'principal' is considered outdated as a consequence of recent structural changes in the Norwegian education system, which entail more external control mechanisms and expectations of 'transformative leadership'.

References

Archer, Margaret S. 1984. *The University Edition of Social Origins of Educational Systems*. London: Sage Publications.

Archer, Margaret S. 1995. *Realist Social Theory: The Morphogenetic Approach*. Cambridge: Cambridge University Press.

Archer, Margaret S. [1979] 2013. *Social Origins of Educational Systems*. London: Sage.

Baird, Jo-Anne, Sandra Johnson, Therese N. Hopfenbeck, Talia Isaacs, Terra Sprague, Gordon Stobart, and Guoxing Yu. 2016. "On the Supranational Spell of PISA in Policy." *Educational Research* 58 (2):121–138. doi: 10.1080/00131881.2016.1165410.

Bergesen, Helge Ole. 2006. *Kampen om Kunnskapsskolen [The Battle for the Knowledge-School]*. Oslo: Universitetsforlaget.

Bhaskar, Roy. [1975] 2008. *A Realist Theory of Science, Classical Texts in Critical Realism*. London: Routledge.

Bieber, Tonia, and Kerstin Martens. 2011. "The OECD PISA Study as a Soft Power in Education? Lessons from Switzerland and the US." *European Journal of Education* 46 (1):101–116.

Breakspear, Simon. 2012. The Policy Impact of PISA: An Exploration of the Normative Effects of International Benchmarking in School System Performance. OECD Education Working Papers (71).

Clemet, Kristin. 2014. "Pisa i Morgenbladet [Pisa in Morgenbladet]." Civita, Last Modified 07.09.2014, accessed 29.09.20. https://www.civita.no/2014/09/07/pisa-i-morgenbladet.

Danermark, Berth. 2003. *Att Förklara Samhället [Explaining Society]*. 2nd ed. Lund: Studentlitteratur.

Elstad, Eyvind, and Kirsten Sivesind, eds. 2010. *PISA: Sannheten om Skolen? [PISA: The Truth About School?]*. Oslo: Universitetsforlaget.

Grek, Sotiria. 2009. "Governing by Numbers: The PISA 'Effect' in Europe." *Journal of Education Policy* 24 (1):23–37.

Grey, Sue, and Paul Morris. 2018. "PISA: Multiple 'Truths' and Mediatised Global Governance." *Comparative Education* 54 (2):109–131. doi: 10.1080/03050068.2018.1425243.

Haug, Peder. 2004. "Sentrale Resultat frå Evalueringa av Reform 97 [Key Results from the Evaluation of Reform 97]." *Norsk Pedagogisk Tidsskrift* 88 (4):248–263.

Helgøy, Ingrid. 2003. "Fra Skole til Tjenesteleverandør? Endringsprosesser i Norsk Grunnskole [From School to Service Provider? Change Processes in Norwegian Primary and Lower Secondary school]." *Norsk Statsvitenskapelig Tidsskrift* 19 (1):55–79.

Helsvig, Kim G. 2017. *Reform og Rutine: Kunnskapsdepartementets Historie 1945–2017 [Reform and Routine: The History of the Ministry of Education 1945–2017]*. Oslo: Pax.

Holzinger, Katharina, and Christoph Knill. 2005. "Causes and Conditions of Cross-National Policy Convergence." *Journal of European Public Policy* 12 (5):775–796. doi: 10.1080/13501760500161357.

Hovdenak, Sylvi Stenersen. 2004. "Et Kritisk Blikk på Reform 97 og Dens Grunnlagstenkning [A Critical Look at Reform 97 and Its Basic Thinking]." *Norsk Pedagogisk Tidsskrift* 88 (4):316–330.

Hybertsen, Ingunn Dahler, Bjørn Stensaker, Roger Andre Federici, Marit Schei Olsen, Anniken Solem, and Per O. Aamodt. 2014. *Ledet til endring: Nasjonal rektorutdanning i grunn- og videregående skole: Endringer på skolene, måloppnåelse og anbefalinger. Sluttrapport fra Evalueringen av den nasjonale rektorutdanningen [Led to Change: National Principal Education in Primary and Secondary School: Changes in Schools, Goal Achievement and Recommendations. Final Report from the Evaluation of the National Principal Education]*. Oslo: Nordic Institute for Studies in Innovation, Research and Education.

Karlsen, Gustav E. 2005. "Styring av Norsk Lærerutdanning—et Historisk Perspektiv [Management of Norwegian Teacher Education—A Historical Perspective]." *Norsk pedagogisk tidsskrift* 89 (6):402–416.

Karseth, Berit, Jorunn Møller, and Petter Aasen. 2013. *Reformtakter: Om Fornyelse og Stabilitet i Grunnopplæringen [Reform Measures: On Renewal and Stability in Basic Education]*. Oslo: Universitetsforlaget.

Mausethagen, Sølvi. 2013. "Governance Through Concepts: The OECD and the Construction of "Competence" in Norwegian Education Policy." *Berkeley Review of Education* 4 (1):161–181.

Møller, Jorunn. 2016. "Kvalifisering som Skoleleder i Norsk Kontekst: Et Historisk Tilbakeblikk og Perspektiver på Utdanning av Skoleledere [Qualification as a School Leader in a Norwegian Context: A Historical Review and Perspectives on the Education of School Leaders]." *Acta Didactica Norge* 10 (4):7–26. doi: 10.5617/adno.3871.

Møller, Jorunn, and G Skedsmo. 2013. "Modernising Education: New Public Management Reform in the Norwegian Education System." *Journal of Educational Administration and History* 45 (4):336–353.

NOKUT. 2006. *Evaluering av Allmennlærerutdanningen i Norge 2006: Del 1: Hovedrapport*. Oslo: NOKUT.

Nortvedt, Guri A. 2018. "Policy Impact of PISA on Mathematics Education: The Case of Norway." *European Journal of Psychology of Education* 33 (3):427–444. doi: 10.1007/s10212-018-0378-9.

NOU [Green Paper] 1996:22. "Lærerutdannning. Mellom krav og ideal [Teacher Education. Between Demand and Ideal]." https://www.regjeringen.no/contentassets/f755d28da8164d8cb0e8a504c1c550c6/no/pdfa/nou199619960022000dddpdfa.pdf.

NOU [Green Paper] 2000:14. "Frihet med ansvar — Om høgre utdanning og forskning i Norge [Freedom with Responsibility — About Higher Education and Research in Norway]." https://www.regjeringen.no/no/dokumenter/nou-2000-14/id142780/.

NOU [Green Paper] 2002:10. "Førsteklasses fra første klasse—Forslag til rammeverk for et nasjonalt kvalitetsvurderingssystem av norsk grunnopplæring [First Class from the First Class—Proposal for A Framework for A National Quality Assessment System of Norwegian Basic Education]." https://www.regjeringen.no/no/dokumenter/nou-2002-10/id145378/sec1.

NOU [Green Paper] 2020:3. "Ny lov om universiteter og høyskoler [New Law for Universities and Colleges]." https://www.regjeringen.no/contentassets/65a475004027495a8009b359e253b19e/no/pdfs/nou202020200003000dddpdfs.pdf.

OECD. 1989. *OECD-vurdering av norsk utdanningspolitikk: Norsk rapport til OECD: Ekspertvurdering fra OECD [OECD Assessment of Norwegian Education Policy: Norwegian Report to the OECD: Expert Assessment from the OECD]*. Translated by A.-M. Smith. Oslo: Aschehoug.

OECD. 2019a. "About the OECD." Accessed 06.02.19. http://www.oecd.org/about/.

OECD. 2019b. "Who we are." Accessed 26.09.19. http://www.oecd.org/about/.

Opplæringslova [Education Act]. 1998. "Lov om Grunnskolen og den Vidaregåande Opplæringa [Act on Primary and Secondary Education]." http://lovdata.no/dokument/NL/lov/1998-07-17-61/KAPITTEL_1#KAPITTEL_1.

Pons, Xavier. 2017. "Fifteen Years of Research on PISA Effects on Education Governance: A Critical Review." *European Journal of Education* 52 (2):131–144. doi: 10.1111/ejed.12213.

Ringarp, J, and M Rothland. 2010. "Is the Grass Always Greener? The Effect of the PISA Results on Education Debates in Sweden and Germany." *European Educational Research Journal* 9 (3):422–430.

Sayer, Andrew. 2000. *Realism and Social Science*. London: Sage.

Sellar, Sam, and Bob Lingard. 2018. "International Large-scale Assessments, Affective Worlds and Policy Impacts in Education." *International Journal of Qualitative Studies in Education* 31 (5):367–381. doi: 10.1080/09518398.2018.1449982.

Sivesind, Kirsten. 2019. "Nordic Reference Societies in School Reforms in Norway: An Examination of Finland and the Use of International Large-Scale Assessments." In *Understanding PISA's Attractiveness: Critical Analyses in Comparative Policy Studies*, edited by Florian Waldow and Gita Steiner-Khamsi. London: Bloomsbury Publishing Plc. https://ebookcentral.proquest.com/lib/tromsoub-ebooks/reader.action?docID=5720861.

Sjøberg, Svein. 2014. "PISA-syndromet—Hvordan Norsk Skolepolitikk blir Styrt av OECD [The PISA Syndrome—How Norwegian School Policy is Directed by the OECD]." *Nytt Norsk Tidsskrift* 31 (01):30–43.

Sjøberg, Svein. 2019. "PISA—internasjonal skoletest [PISA—International School Test]." Store Norske Leksikon, Last Modified 19.12.2019, Accessed 29.09.2020. http://snl.no/PISA.

Skinningsrud, Tone. 2014. "Struktur og Prosess i Norsk Utdanning på 1990- og 2000-tallet—Et makrososiologisk Perspektiv [Structure and Process in Norwegian Education in the 1990s and 2000s—A Macrosociological Perspective]." *Norsk Pedagogisk Tidsskrift* 98 (04):222–234.

Skjelmo, Randi Hege. 2007. "Endringer i Norsk Allmennlærerutdanning—Mot en Sterkere Enhetlighet: Desentralisert Allmennlærerutdanning i Nord-Norge

1979-2006 [Changes in Norwegian General Teacher Education—Towards A Stronger Uniformity: Decentralized General Teacher Education in Northern Norway 1979-2006]." PhD dissertation, University of Tromsø, Tromsø, Norway. http://munin.uit.no/bitstream/handle/10037/1391/thesis.pdf?sequence=1.

St. Meld [White Paper] No. 16. 2001-2002. "St. Meld. 16. Kvalitetsreformen Om ny Lærerutdanning: Mangfoldig—Krevende—Relevant [Quality Reform About New Teacher Education: Diverse—Demanding—Relevant]." https://www.regjeringen.no/contentassets/ae31935c94ff4c169cc1c378e4a1be1d/no/pdfa/stm-200120020016000dddpdfa.pdf.

St. Meld [White Paper] No. 30. 2003-2004. "St. Meld. 30. KULTUR for Læring [Culture for Learning]." https://www.regjeringen.no/contentassets/988cd-b018ac24eb0a0cf95943e6cdb61/no/pdfs/stm200320040030000dddpdfs.pdf.

St. Meld [White Paper] No. 31. 2007-2008. "St. Meld. 31. Kvalitet i Skolen [Quality in School]." https://www.regjeringen.no/contentassets/806ed8f81bef4e03bccd-67d16af76979/no/pdfs/stm200720080031000dddpdfs.pdf.

St. Meld [White Paper] No. 37. 1990-1991. "St. Meld. 37. Om Organisering og Styring av Utdanningssektoren [About the Organization and Management of The Education Sector]." https://www.stortinget.no/no/Saker-og-publikasjoner/Stortingsforhandlinger/Lesevisning/?p=1990-91&paid=3&wid=c&psid=DIVL402&s=True.

Stortinget [The Parliament]. 2002. "Stortinget—Møte torsdag den 17. januar 2002 kl. 10. Forhandlinger i Stortinget nr. 88. 17. Jan.—Interp. fra repr. Reikvam om å legge til rette for forsøk i skolen der all evaluering skal ha læringsstøtte som mål. Interpellasjonsdebatt i Stortinget 17. Januar 2002. Stortingsforhandlinger. Nr. 13, 15–17. Januar. Sesjonen 2001–2002 [The Parliament—Meeting on Thursday 17 January 2002 at 10. Debates in the Storting no. 88. 17 Jan.— Interp. from Rep. Reikvam to Facilitate Experiments in Schools Where All Evaluation Should Have Learning Support As A Goal. Interpellation Debate in the Parliament 17 January 2002. Parliament Negotiations. Nr. 13, 15–17. January. Session 2001–2002]." https://www.stortinget.no/globalassets/pdf/referater/stortinget/2001-2002/s020117.pdf.

Telhaug, Alfred Oftedal. 1997. *Utdanningsreformene: Oversikt og Analyse [The Education Reforms: Overview and Analysis]*. Oslo: Didakta Norsk Forlag.

Telhaug, Alfred Oftedal. 2005. *Kunnskapsløftet—ny Eller Gammel Skole?: Beskrivelse og Analyse av Kristin Clemets Reformer i Grunnopplæringen [The Knowledge Promise—New or Old School?: Description and Analysis of Kristin Clemet's Reforms in Basic Education]*. Oslo: Cappelen Akademisk Forlag.

Telhaug, Alfred Oftedal, and Odd Asbjørn Mediås. 2003. *Grunnskolen som Nasjonsbygger: Fra Statspietisme til Nyliberalisme [Primary School As A Nation-Builder: From State Pietism to Neoliberalism]*. Oslo: Abstrakt Forlag.

Thuen, Harald. 2010. "Skolen—Et liberalistisk prosjekt? 1860–2010 [The school—A liberal project? 1860–2010]." *Norsk Pedagogisk Tidsskrift* 94 (4):273–287.

Udir [DfE]. 2009. "Nasjonalt kvalitetssystem [National Quality System]." Last Modified 20.01.2010, Accessed 29.09.2020. https://www.udir.no/tall-og-forskning/finn-forskning/rapporter/Evaluering-av-Nasjonalt-kvalitetsutviklingssystem/.

Udir [DfE]. 2020. "Våre oppgaver [Our Tasks]." Last Modified 04.03.2020, Accessed 29.09.2020. https://www.udir.no/om-udir/vare-oppgaver/.

Utdannings-og Forsknings Departementet [Education and Resarch Department]. 2004. "Norsk Skole Trenger et Kunnskapsløft [Norwegian Schools Need a Boost in Knowledge]." Regjeringen.no, Last Modified 06.12.04, Accessed 29.09.2020. https://www.regjeringen.no/no/aktuelt/norsk_skole_trenger_et_kunnskapsloft/id252942/

Utdannings-og Forsknings Departementet [Education and Research Department]. 2005. "Kunnskapsløftet – Reformen i Grunnskolen og Videregående Opplæring [KnowledgePromotionReforms–inCompulsoryandUpperSecondaryEducation]." https://www.regjeringen.no/globalassets/upload/kilde/ufd/prm/2005/0081/ddd/pdfv/256458-kunnskap_bokmaal_low.pdf.

Waldow, Florian. 2019. "Understanding PISA's Attractiveness: Critical Analyses in Comparative Policy Studies." In *Understanding PISA's Attractiveness: Critical Analyses in Comparative Policy Studies*, edited by Florian Waldow and Gita Steiner-Khamsi, 1–22. London: Bloomsbury Publishing Plc.

9 School leaders' reflexive mode in their internal conversations on PISA

Terje André Bringeland

Introduction: Educational testing for accountability and learning

Despite the sizeable number of studies on the effects of PISA (Program for International Student Assessment), prior studies have primarily investigated PISA impacts at the macro-level of national policy making. The present study starts to fill the knowledge gap on PISA effects at the micro level of the school. This study is of school leaders and how they mediate PISA influence through their reflexivity; 'reflexivity' in the sense defined by Margaret Archer as the mental ability, shared by all normal people to consider themselves in relation to their (social) context and vice versa (Archer 2007, 4). My intention is not to explore how the notion 'reflexivity' may be incorporated into general theories of school leadership. That would be a task which is beyond the scope of this chapter. The purpose of the chapter is to demonstrate in greater detail how Norwegian school leaders, in a country that has participated in PISA since its beginning, deliberate in internal conversations about its possible usefulness to their school.

The importance of school leaders for improving students' learning is emphasized in international research reviews. After the teacher, the effect of leadership practices is considered the next most important factor in improving students' learning (Leithwood, Sun, and Pollock 2017) – although Leithwood, Sun, and Pollock (2017, 353) do acknowledge that 'leadership is not always effective and, even when it is, its influence on students is largely indirect (or mediated)'. The study presented in this chapter is about how school leaders in Norwegian lower secondary schools deal with the challenge of using standardized tests for the improvement of learning in their school. Focus for this investigation is PISA, the international achievement test, which has been developed by the OECD (Organization for Economic Co-operation and Development). Research conducted in the United States primarily suggests that school leaders should take an evidence-based approach to improving their own competencies and educational practices (Sun, Przybylski, and Johnson 2016); which means that they among other data should base their work on test results.

DOI: 10.4324/9781003163527-12

In recent decades, educational quality indicators, such as scores on achievement tests have increasingly been developed and adopted on a national and international scale, and results have been recorded over time. With this has come an increased emphasis on educational comparison and competition, both domestically in each country (between schools and regions) and internationally (between countries). In Norway, the municipalities – who own the compulsory schools (basic and lower secondary) – are reported to be explicitly expressing rising expectations concerning local students' results on national and municipal tests, holding teachers and school leaders accountable (Skedsmo and Møller 2016). In lower secondary schools, school leaders, in particular, are held accountable for what is done and achieved at their school (Møller and Ottesen 2011).

After the introduction of the Norwegian Quality Assessment System, in 2004, students' achievements measured by standardized tests were increasingly seen as an indicator of quality in the compulsory school (Skedsmo and Mausethagen 2017). Skedsmo and Mausethagen argue that the introduction in the 1990s, of management by objectives (MbO) as a principle in public administration (including the education sector), justified increasing reliance on testing and measurements of learning outcomes. The use of standardized tests in schools has come to serve a double function, both as instruments for increased accountability and for learning. The accountability function entails that agents at different levels of the education system are subject to control and held accountable for students' learning, measured by outputs. The learning function entails the use of test results for feedback to improve learning at all levels of the system. Accountability involves control and benchmarking of quality between schools, municipalities, regions, as well as between nations, while learning for improvement may in principle take place at all levels of the education system, i.e., from the political-administrative level to classroom practices. Though, the major focus for learning is the individual student in the classroom. A central feature of the Norwegian Quality Assessment regime is that schools and teachers are trusted to use test results for the improvement of learning without introducing incentives or sanctions. This high level of trust, however, contains a paradox in the sense that at the same time as the improvement of individual learning from assessments is emphasized, the national control regime is tightened through uniform national guidelines for school and student assessments (Skedsmo and Mausethagen 2017, 176).

The pressure on teachers, school leaders and others involved in education to improve measurable results in terms of learning outcomes is produced by cultural and structural conditions, the idea of performativity as the supreme indicator of educational quality and the demand from superiors in the system to raise students' performance levels. This has effects on what is focused on in schools, how things are done and potentially why school leaders and others do what they do.

Since the implementation in 2006 of a competence-based National Curriculum (The Knowledge Promotion Reform, K06), the government has initiated clarifications and improvements of assessment rules and regulations. The changes have entailed an increased emphasis on formative assessment, or assessment *for* learning, in comparison with summative assessments, which is assessment *of* learning[2] (Tveit 2014). Despite the acknowledged distinction between summative and formative assessments, Norwegian guidelines are not entirely consistent in upholding it. National Tests are, for example, expected to serve both summative and formative assessment purposes. They are expected to provide summative assessments for the purpose of monitoring quality in the education system as a whole, but they are also expected to help teachers and schools to identify individual students' strengths and weaknesses. However, while school owners and school leaders have found summative scores on national tests useful for decision-making, many teachers report that these tests are not helpful for giving feedback to individual students. As Tveit (2014, 233) points out, summative and formative assessments have different purposes and the two are hard to combine in one single instrument.

The Norwegian government's prioritization of formative assessment is expressed in several initiatives. The requirement to provide formative assessments is specified in the Norwegian Education Act as a responsibility for the municipalities, as school owners. The act mentions four principles for formative assessment, which entail that in the practice of teaching, the student must be made aware of: (1) what s/he is expected to learn, i.e., be clear about the learning goals, (2) must be given informative feedback about the quality of his/her work, (3) be given advice on how to improve/reach the learning goals and (4) become involved in the learning process and in self-assessment (Hopfenbeck et al. 2013, 28). Hopfenbeck et al. (2013) conducted a case study of Norway as part of the OECD-project 'Governing Complex Education Systems' and followed the implementation of the Norwegian government programme 'Assessment for Learning' (Vurdering for læring, 2010–2014). The programme itself involved nearly 900 schools across 184 municipalities representing every county in the nation. Hopfenbeck et al.'s study of the programme implementation included a sample of nine schools from four different municipalities (Hopfenbeck et al. 2013, 12–13). These researchers found that Norway has adopted a particular approach to formative assessment (assessment for learning), which differs from many other countries', i.e., by emphasising feed-back and self-assessment rather than, for example, the need to reconcile formative and summative assessment or improving the quality of questioning (Hopfenbeck et al. 2013, 25).

Tveit (2014, 225), referencing both the OECD and other Norwegian researchers, claims that '[c]ompared to many other countries, Norwegian teachers tend not to articulate learning goals to their students or to follow up students systematically'. Several OECD reviews of Norwegian education (OECD 2008; 2011) stressed the need for improvement of formative assessment practices, especially providing feedback to students. In the literature, external observers like Hopfenbeck et al. (2012, 421–422) claimed that '[t]here is a profound absence of systematic assessment practices in Norwegian classrooms' and 'a lack of focus on explicit assessments'. Tveit (2014, 230) traces the historical roots of this state of affairs, i.e., the indifference to formal assessments in Norwegian schools. He refers to the disputes in the 1970s, when formal grades were abolished in Norwegian primary education by Parliamentarian decision. The same was suggested for upper secondary schools but was not accepted by Parliament. The assessment policy of avoiding formal grading was enabled by curriculum plans that did not specify competency goals but emphasized a broader notion 'holistic competence' which also included collaborative skills and work effort. This broad notion of competence continued to be used until 2006, when the Knowledge Promotion Reform introduced a competency-based curriculum which defined learning objectives more precisely, enabling formative assessments related to learning goals. The Norwegian tradition of avoiding formal assessments as to where students stand in relation to achievement goals clearly required a recalibration to fit in with the more recent emphasis on precise measurements of the level of achievement.

The mentioned study by Hopfenbeck et al. (2013) found that the implementation of the 2010–2014 initiative 'Assessment for learning', which promoted formative assessment, encountered many problems. One of them was that Norwegian teachers resisted being held accountable for their teaching methods and considered it a lack of trust from the state. Trust goes both ways, and an investigation by Skedsmo and Mausethagen (2017) indicated that Norwegian teachers have a high level of trust in the state, and they do not object to increasing external controls in education as long as these controls are seen to be in line with their own professional work and support professional values.

However, the extensive use of testing has been subject to criticism from teachers as well as school leaders. Gunnulfsen and Møller (2017) in a recent study found that school leaders consider the current national tests to be mere 'symbolic action', since the test results only confirmed what they already knew about their students. In addition, school leaders stressed that they are above all accountable for ensuring that each student receives a good education; their mandate is not merely to raise the average score on academic achievement. This view is supported by the Norwegian compulsory school's official mandate, which is two-pronged: instrumental and formative (Slagstad 1998), the former referring to knowledge transmission and the latter to personal formation.

In Norway, the use of National tests for learning purposes has in many respects not been as successful as planned. Aas and Brandmo (2018), in their study of Norwegian school leaders, found that while the leaders do initiate discussions about test results, many of these discussions do not lead to new practices in the classroom, mainly because school leaders encounter what they perceive as resistance from the teachers. However, another suggested explanation for why test results often do not generate new practices is that school leaders in Norway find it difficult to prioritize and carry out short- and long-term planning of their work and also to define what is a 'good' result (Skedsmo 2009). In the international context, the lack of learning benefits from testing has been attributed to teachers' and school leaders' lack of knowledge on how to use test results to improve their teaching practice (Sun, Przybylski, and Johnson 2016). Thus, the school leader's potential indirect influence on student learning is not necessarily actualized. Lack of knowledge among school leaders on how to use test results for formative assessments, in particular, is underlined in a review of studies made in the United States and Canada (Hornskov, Bjerg, and Høvsgaard 2015). These findings about lack of knowledge on how to use test results to improve learning outcomes has resulted in a discussion about 'data literacy', which many school leaders and teachers seem to lack, and which appear to be crucial at a time when evidence-based practice has become an imperative. It has been argued that upgrading school leaders' data literacy could increase their ability to learn from test results and thereby improve their students' learning.

However, Sun, Przybylski, and Johnson (2016, 29) conclude their literature review of 'data-informed instruction', largely based on reported practices in the United States, fully embracing data-informed teaching practices, by arguing that teachers themselves should decide what kinds of data they need. They should be provided with user-friendly data analyses that are useful for instructional decision making. The data should be generated on request from teachers and schools but produced by dedicated specialized school personnel or external expertise.

PISA, PIRLS[3] and TIMSS[4] are all international tests included in the Norwegian Quality Assessment System. The purpose of including international tests for quality assessment is to enable comparison of Norwegian students with students in other countries. The following presentation focuses on PISA. PIRLS and TIMSS are only mentioned in passing.

PISA

In 2000, the PISA test was introduced in the Norwegian educational system. The results from this first test were publicly announced in December 2001. PISA is a triannual international survey which 'assesses students' knowledge and skills in reading, mathematics and science; each assessment focuses on one of these subjects and provides a summary assessment of the other two' (Schleicher 2019). Moreover, PISA professes to measure how well students at the end of their compulsory schooling can apply what they have learned. In the words of Andreas Schleicher, the officer in charge of PISA in OECD, 'the world no longer rewards people for what they know […] but for what they can do with what they know' (Schleicher 2016, 2). Unlike the other two international tests that are included in the Norwegian Quality Assessment System, TIMSS and PIRLS, which are based on the curricula in participating countries, thus applying a 'curriculum approach', PISA has adopted a 'literacy approach'. This means that test items in PISA are independent of school curricula and instead claim to measure 'literacy' in the domains of reading, mathematics and science, i.e., knowledge and skills that are needed among members of contemporary society for the future. A conceptual framework for the construction of the test, defining what literacy means in the various domains, what kinds of competences and skills it includes, is worked out by OECD appointed experts from several countries. Attempting to test students' ability to apply knowledge by solving problems in 'authentic real-life situations', PISA items in the mathematical domain may ask students to solve a problem from everyday life by using mathematical reasoning. The real-life contexts that were mentioned in the conceptual framework for the 2018 mathematical literacy test were personal, occupational and scientific.[5] Since its start in 2000, with 32 participating OECD-countries, the number of PISA-participants has steadily increased to 72 countries in 2007 and 90 participants in 2018, including non-OECD countries (Aursand 2018).

PISA consists of a two-hour test with assignments from each of the domains mentioned; it also comes with a student questionnaire that takes about 30 minutes to complete, with questions about family background, attitudes, learning strategies and the learning environment at school. (The schools' management staff are also required to answer a questionnaire each time the PISA test is administered [Sjøberg 2014a].) The PISA test is meant to be a snapshot and, thus, does not follow students over time. Each country randomly selects a representative sample of approximately 5,000 students; individual schools and individual students in these schools are selected to participate, but not entire schools or classes. Apart from testing 'key foundational skills' in reading, science and mathematics, PISA is also assessing broader cognitive and social skills. In 2015, this included 'collaborative problem solving', and in 2018, 'global competence'. PISA has offered optional tests in financial literacy since 2012 (OECD 2019).

Despite its widespread use, PISA's attained position as the 'global standard' of international testing, and its acceptance as a reliable instrument for benchmarking student performance worldwide (Breakspear 2012), severe criticism has been waged against the test. Sjøberg and Jenkins (2020) discuss some weak points in the test and its applications. Concerning the validity of the test they point out that the presentations of 'authentic situations' make extensive use of verbal text, regardless of which domain is being tested: reading, mathematics or science. The use of verbal descriptors puts a premium on competence in reading. This may entail that PISA measures reading skills as much as skills in science and mathematics. The high correlation of individual scores on reading, mathematics and science across all countries, which varies between 0.77 and 0.89 (OECD 2005, quoted in Sjøberg and Jenkins [2020]), may indicate that much the same competence is being measured by all the tests. Sjøberg and Jenkins also discuss the problems associated with translations of the test from one language to another, providing examples of how some translations of questions together with their multiple-choice answers might have favoured students in some countries. The scores and consequent ranking of countries may also be influenced by the different degree of involvement and motivation among students in achieving good results on the test. These problems indicate that PISA is not a neutral instrument, which is impartial to the variety of cultures and languages represented by participants taking the test.

The serious doubts raised over PISA's claim to neutrality and impartial assessment of students all over the world, signalled by its 'literacy approach' as against the 'curriculum approach', may undermine the assertion made by OECD reports that a country's PISA score indicates its economic growth potential. An OECD report from 2010 by Hanushek and Woessman titled 'The High Cost of low educational performance. The long run economic impact of improving PISA outcomes', estimates how much individual countries would gain by improving their PISA-score. The authors assert, for example, that an increase of 25 PISA points over time would increase Germany's GDP by 8,088 million USD (OECD 2010, p. 25, quoted in Sjøberg and Jenkins [2020, 8]). Thus, PISA is effectively staging a high stakes competition between countries, which concerns their future prosperity.

The assumption that quality of schooling measured by PISA results may crucially affect the nation's future generates an increased interest in improving educational quality and students' learning outcomes. Consequently, OECD also engages in country reviews of national educational systems and provides policy advice, focusing on how to improve student achievements. Norway, in 2011, together with other OECD countries, enlisted in a review of its educational evaluation and assessment system and practices. Among several challenges confronting Norwegian education, summed up by the OECD evaluation team, they mentioned: 'Many schools and school owners struggled to use data effectively for school improvement', 'School leadership could play a stronger role in driving quality improvement in schools' and 'Formative assessment needs to be more firmly embedded in regular teaching practice' (Nusche et al. 2011).

Research on PISA has mainly been concerned with its influence on national educational policy (Bieber and Martens 2011; Breakspear 2012; Grek 2009; Meyer and Benavot 2013; Ringarp and Rothland 2010; Sjøberg 2014b). There is little empirical research in Norway on how the PISA test affects school personnel. Sjøberg (2014a) has called for more research on PISA's effect in schools. Eggen (2010), in her qualitative study among Norwegian school leaders and teachers, found no indications that PISA results were being used in schools for summative or formative assessment. Instead, the use of PISA consisted exclusively of general reflections and discussions among school personnel, which did not result in action. Some school leaders complained that that they felt exploited by the PISA survey, since they do not receive direct knowledge of the results from their own school.

In 2008, the Norwegian Education Association conducted a survey among members employed in the compulsory schools, concerning teachers' and school leaders' knowledge and opinions about the PISA test (Utdanningsforbundet 2008). Nearly 50% of the school leaders (principals, inspectors, heads of department etc.) answered that they are familiar with the PISA items, and that school leaders have more general knowledge about PISA than teachers. About 75% of the school leaders say they are familiar with the PISA survey and what it measures, while approximately 50% answer that they have read some of the PISA reports. About 70% of the respondents among school leaders 'completely or partially agree' with the statement: 'the PISA results and the PISA debate are discussed at my workplace' – what the discussions are about and for what purpose is uncertain, due to the design of the survey. Furthermore, 60% of teachers and school leaders 'completely or partially disagree' that the PISA results can give extra inspiration to schools, teachers and students. Nearly 80% disagree 'completely or partially' with the statement that 'the PISA results provide a correct overall picture of the quality in the Norwegian school'. In addition, about 50% of the school leaders 'completely or partially disagree' with the statement that 'PISA items are measuring central aspects of the Norwegian school'. A minority, about 30%, of the school leaders 'completely or partially agree' that 'the PISA study succeeds in measuring the skills required for future society', against the 60% who 'completely or partially disagree' with this statement. The remaining 10% do not know. Approximately 80% of the school leaders are 'completely or partially in agreement' with the statement 'the PISA survey tells little about what to do to improve the quality of the Norwegian school'. Finally, nearly 90% of the school leaders 'completely or partially agree' that 'the most positive thing about the PISA survey is that it puts the school on the political agenda'.

Summing up, previous research on PISA effects in Norway indicates that the PISA test is not used in assessment for learning (*formative assessment*) in lower secondary schools. It is a test that the school is instructed to administer as part of the National Quality Assessment System – a decision made at higher levels of decision-making (i.e., at the level of national policymaking). Among the effects that are mentioned is that the test creates space for reflections and discussions among staff members on educational matters. It seems that the utility of PISA is assessed differently by agents holding different positions within the educational system. High level experts close to the government tend to view the test as very influential on educational change (see, e.g., Breakspear 2012). In contrast, 80% of Norwegian school leaders, responding to a survey conducted by the Norwegian Education Association, replied that PISA says little about how to improve the quality of Norwegian schools. Some school leaders have even stated that they feel exploited by the test. Researchers have pointed out the lack of knowledge regarding the effects of PISA in Norwegian schools. Thus, as the test is administered every third year, and it is part of the National Quality Assessment System, it is pertinent to ask how school personnel are affected by the test and what kinds of practices it may trigger.

Reflexivity

When Archer introduced the concept of reflexivity in her theoretical toolbox, she emphasized that reflexivity has for decades been an unacknowledged condition of social life. It has not, however, been understood correctly. In the past, reflexivity has been conceptualized as either subjectivism or consciousness (Archer 2007, 1). Archer (2007, 4) defines reflexivity as 'the regular exercise of the mental ability, shared by all normal people, to consider themselves in relation to their (social) contexts and vice versa'.

In Archer's conception, reflexivity mediates between structure and agency, as well as culture and agency, and it operates in our internal conversations. The internal dialogues in which 'people talk to themselves within their own heads, usually silently and usually from an early age' vary between persons (Archer 2007, 2). We deliberate about our circumstances in relation to ourselves and decide on our own personal courses of action in society in fundamentally different ways.

A central premise in critical realism and Archer's morphogenetic approach is that structure and culture precede agency and their causal powers constrain and enable agents (Bhaskar [1979] 1998, 31ff; Archer [1979] 2013; [1988] 1996; 1995; 2000; 2003; 2007; 2012). How to realize future projects in the face of these enabling and constraining forces is one of the things that the internal conversation is about (Archer 2003; 2007; 2012). Archer (2007, 17) sums this up in three propositions:

1 Structural and cultural properties *objectively* shape the situations that agents confront involuntarily, and *inter alia* possess generative powers of constraint and enablement in relation to (the sentence continues in the next numbering).
2 Subjects' own constellations of concerns, as *subjectively* defined in relation to the three orders of natural reality: nature, practice and social.
3 Courses of action are produced through the *reflexive deliberations* of subjects who *subjectively* determine their practical projects in relation to their *objective* circumstances.

Archer (2007, 5) further states that 'subjective powers of reflexivity mediate the role that objective structural or cultural powers play in influencing social action and are thus indispensable to explaining social outcomes'. Arguing that the subjective powers of reflexivity are indispensable to explanations of social outcomes, she mentions other theories, apart from social realism, that require a reflexive first-person (Archer 2003, 42). Economic models based in conceptions of individuals as maximisers of self-interest need reflexivity to explain the pursuit of preferences and the maximization of utility. Likewise, functionalism is another example of such requirement, when expectations are overturned by contingencies and when unscripted performance is required, reference to reflexivity cannot be evaded. Reflexivity is genuinely an interior phenomenon that underwrites the private life of the social subject. Its subjectivity has a first-person ontology that precludes any attempt to render it in the third person. Furthermore, it possesses causal efficacy. Archer states that 'only if the "internal conversation" can be upheld as an irreducible *personal* property, which is real and causally influential, can the exercise of its powers be considered as the missing mediatory mechanism that is needed to complete an adequate account of social conditioning'. Reflexivity is a personal property (PEP) that, through the 'projects' that subjects pursue, activates the causal powers of social structures (SEP), as well as contradictions and complementarities inherent in their cultural surroundings (CEP). This means that enablements and constraints in pursuing a chosen course of action, as well as the adoption, rejection and modification of ideas, depend on how persons deliberate in their internal conversations about their circumstances (Archer 2007, 64).

Reflexive modes

We do not all exercise our reflexivity in the same way, and our internal conversations are, therefore, not identical. The different modes of reflexivity practised in internal conversations go beyond personal idiosyncrasies and are consistently different ways of deliberating what to do, and how to achieve our goals and projects in given social circumstances. Throughout life, people are conditioned by different structures and cultures that trigger a variety of internal conversations. Archer (2003) has identified three modes of reflexivity: communicative, autonomous and meta-reflexivity. The inability to hold such an internal conversation without inciting distress and disorientation is referred to as fractured reflexivity. Archer acknowledges that there may be other forms of reflexivity that may not be actualized at a given time due to the lack of relevant social conditions. The reflexive modes are all elaborated in this anthology by other authors that are utilizing them in their analysis. They will, therefore, not be described in further detail here. Their main characteristics are summarized in Figure 9.1.

Research questions

The interview data analysed below are focused on the theme of PISA, i.e., what the school leaders know about PISA, what role it plays in their school and how it affects their practice as school leaders. I will aim to identify all the various modes of reflexivity that might be practised by one and the same person. I base my analysis on the assumption that the three modes of reflexivity are personal and that all of them may potentially, and to various extents, be activated in each person – depending upon their knowledgeability and

Autonomous mode	Communicative mode	Meta-reflexive mode	Fractured reflexivity
Individualistic individuals with their own concerns, strategies and choices to reach the results and outcome they seek. They are characterized by Archer (2003) as being strategic agents.	Individuals who are traditionalists, and support the established customs or beliefs of a group. These individuals consult and interact with others before deciding. They are characterized by Archer (2003) as being conformist agents.	Critical and ethical individuals. Meta-reflexives are idealists that can never be pleased by the private or public sector. They are characterized by Archer (2003) as being subversive agents.	Agents to whom things merely happen, with an inability to sustain 'projects'. They are characterized by Archer (2003) as being passive agents.
Oriented to tasks.	Oriented to trust.	Oriented to values.	Disoriented.

Figure 9.1 The three reflexive modes and fractured reflexivity.

situation, moreover, that they may be selectively triggered by specific circumstances related to PISA.[6]

Prior to my analysis of the data material, I anticipated that school leaders would turn out to be either predominantly autonomous reflexives or meta-reflexives. As mentioned above, one reason for expecting them to be autonomous reflexives is the nature of society in late modernity, how rapidly it changes and the increasing expectations of agents' performance and output; after all, recent reforms in Norwegian education have stressed performativity. Another reason why school leaders might be autonomous reflexives in their work context is their position and role in schools, as these come with the corresponding expectation that they will be 'in charge'. However, the school leaders might also be communicative reflexives, at least to some extent, since they depend on a good working relationship with their staff of teachers, thus valuing a collaborative environment and emphasizing consensus as the basis for decision-making; however, the leaders do not need confirmation from their teachers for every task they perform. The school leaders could also be predominantly meta-reflexive, since there are always aspects that can be criticized at different levels of the educational system, including the micro, meso and macro level. Finally, a reason for expecting the school leaders to be predominantly meta-reflexive regarding PISA is the nature of the PISA test and the widespread criticism it has received. Given their position, I did not expect the school leaders to be predominantly fractured reflexives.

Since it may be assumed, as Archer does in her theory, supported by her empirical findings, that all normal people engage in reflexivity, reflecting upon their environment and deliberating between their personal projects and the structural constraints and enablements they may encounter, it may also be assumed that school leaders engage in reflexivity. But the question is whether a certain mode of reflexivity predominates among them.

My research questions in analysing the interviews were the following:

1 Which reflexive modes are activated in the three school leaders when they engage in internal conversations about PISA?
2 Which is the dominant reflexive mode of each school leader (regarding PISA)?

In the 'discussion' I will present some arguments about how the structural position as school leader may influence the predominant reflexive mode elicited among school leaders.

Study design and research method

This research had a multiple case-study design and consists of three cases (Yin 1994). Yin (1994) recommends case studies as particularly suitable for testing and developing theories; moreover, Danermark et al. (2002) argue that case studies are well-suited to critical realist research, since critical realist investigations aim to uncover mechanisms rather than make empirical generalizations, which requires representative samples.

The research method used was secondary analysis of qualitative data (Heaton 2008, 35). The interview data were originally collected as part of my master's thesis, which was about the informants' knowledge about PISA and its purpose, and whether PISA had had an effect on their school and on their practical work in teaching mathematics, including formative evaluation. I made use of these qualitative data for a secondary analysis by applying other theoretical concepts to and raising other research questions regarding the same data.[7]

The interviews were conducted during March and April 2015 with three school leaders in three different lower secondary schools in one Norwegian municipality.[8] Each of the schools had between 400 and 600 students. I used (1) semi-structured interviews, which were recorded, and (2) the participants were e-mailed for information about their age and educational background after the interview. The theme of the research and the interview guide were made available to the school leaders beforehand, and they had the opportunity to consult with their staff (mathematics teachers). All three interviews were conducted in Norwegian and then transcribed; the transcriptions were later translated into English. The identification of reflexive modes was not the purpose of my original investigation.

In my presentation of the school leaders and the schools, I use the term 'school leader' as a common designation for several administrative positions in the school, including head of department, assistant school leader and school leader. The school leaders' age and years of work experience have been rounded up or down, as a strategy to preserve their anonymity.

School leaders' reflexive mode 193

Autonomous mode	Communicative mode	Meta-reflexive mode
School leaders' focus on results, accountability and outcome with and without PISA as a trigger.	School leaders' interaction with others, specifically their colleagues/staff, when deciding the role and use of PISA for their schools.	School leaders' ethical and critical perspective on PISA (in view of the schools' mandate and connected to their professional values)

Figure 9.2 School leaders' reflexive modes manifested in their internal conversations on PISA.

In both my primary and secondary analysis of the data, I employed abduction, which means that the theoretical concepts I used contextualized the data. In my secondary analysis, I used different theoretical concepts from the ones I used in my primary analysis. The reasoning of abduction, opens up to, as Danermark (2003, 179ff) has stated, applying different theoretical interpretations that can lead to new insights, such as types of mechanisms operating *in situ*.

In my analysis, where I identified the different modes of reflexivity in school leaders' internal conversations on issues related to their work, and specifically on their opinions and use of PISA results, I used the indicators described in Figure 9.2.

Case 1: Roman

A brief description of case 1

Roman was in his 50s and had worked for nearly 20 years as a school leader in various schools. Before becoming a school leader, he worked for about 10 years as a teacher. He had a degree in management and pedagogy. Roman describes PISA as an international survey that is sufficiently general in content to cover many countries. He believed that the school's role is to translate the general validity of PISA surveys into his own school context. Roman claimed he used PISA wisely to develop his school, but he did not give concrete examples of what was done locally as a result of the PISA reports.

Analysis: Modes of reflexivity

Compared to the other respondents, Roman was very quick in his replies to questions asked by the interviewer, and he did not ponder over his answers.

He always knew how to answer and where to be heading with the topic in the interview.

Roman was concerned with improving learning outcomes in his school, which coincides with what he perceives as a general change that had taken place in Norwegian education:

> Yes, there has been a change in the view that learning is our mandate, and in learning lies professional competence and social competence, and we are probably more concerned with academic results now than we were 10 years ago. [...].
>
> *(Transcript A, pp. 1, 2)*

In his role as school leader, Roman had a clear plan for the use of PISA as well as other tests. He believed they should be used to improve teaching and thereby students' learning:

> We use [PISA] wisely to develop ourselves. [...] I am for PISA, national tests, and diagnostic tests, and I am in favour of that—also publicly. But they must be used wisely so that we take advantage of the results that are there. [...]. It's very easy to see whether this school has gone up or down [on national tests results]: fine when we go up, a little worse when we go down. Whether we go up or down, we must sit down and ask what is good and why, and what can be better and how. If we fail to use the educational results that help us develop pedagogically, if we stop trying to do better, then we stop being good.
>
> *(Transcript A, p. 2)*

Roman acknowledged that a major impact of PISA is placing schools and education on the public agenda. He admitted that his staff is challenged when trying to use PISA results for formative evaluation, since the test is international. However, he felt it is the job of the teachers to make it relevant in the Norwegian context:

> PISA has had an impact in the sense of publicity. At the same time, issues, questions, and challenges have been discussed internally at the school, and we are more concerned with results than we once were. [...] our challenge is to get teachers to use the test results in a sensible way, in seeing their own students and promoting positive development.
>
> *(Transcript A, p. 1)*

> [...]. PISA asks more or tries more in some areas than in others: PISA is also a test of reading and understanding. PISA is international and is suitable for many countries with different school cultures, different school traditions, different curricula, different teaching, knowledge premises, yes, the whole package, and it becomes more general than the

[national test] made only for Norway. We must take that into account and look at what they are learning in England, Australia etc. […]; it is our role to translate the universal validity to our school.

(Transcript A, pp. 1, 2)

Roman discussed PISA and its use with the teachers in his school. He acknowledged their problems in implementing PISA results but does not succumb to the problems raised by the teachers. He did not seem to be concerned about reaching agreement with his staff, i.e., his 'friends and family', on how to deal with PISA. Instead, he tried to convince them to agree with him. He wanted PISA results to be implemented by the teaching staff despite acknowledging their difficulties in doing so. However, he did talk about himself and the staff as 'we', and as having a common aim. This might indicate a tendency to engage in *communicative reflexivity*, i.e., seeing the staff as 'similars' ('we'). But since he insisted on using PISA results despite some resistance from his staff, his communicative mode seemed largely subdued. He remained 'the boss' who made decisions on his own. Regarding *meta-reflexivity*, Roman was aware of the criticism that had been voiced against PISA, but he made the point that he had publicly endorsed PISA and the use of standardized tests. Roman did acknowledge problems in applying the PISA results, albeit this did not demonstrate *meta-reflexivity*, since he did not reconsider his position on the use of PISA in view of the criticism raised against the test. In fact, he did not voice an explicit critique of PISA and the expectations about its use in his school. An autonomous reflexive thinks he/she can work out a solution him/herself. Roman had a plan for dealing with PISA, i.e., to get teachers to use it more, in order to improve students' learning. However, although Roman conveyed decisiveness in planning to make the teaching staff implement improvements based on PISA-results, he was not specific about how this could be done. When his professed, but still quite empty strategy is interpreted in the light of interviews with the other school leaders, one may wonder whether he, like the other two, was at a loss about how to use PISA to improve learning in his school, i.e., for formative assessment. PISA is part of the Norwegian Quality Assessment System, and schools are obliged to learn from it for quality improvement. Being a strategic leader and wanting to give a good impression to the interviewer, Roman may have chosen to display his decisiveness in making the staff use PISA results, while he himself, in fact, was quite unsure about how to go about it. There is no way of confirming whether this interpretation is correct regarding Roman's subjective experience. However, researchers have pointed out the difficulty of using summative assessments, such as PISA and National Tests for formative purposes. Likewise, Norwegian teachers have expressed dissatisfaction with the National Tests for not providing adequate information for formative assessment (Tveit 2014).

Summing up case 1, the analysis indicates that Roman activates mainly the autonomous mode. His stated intent to use PISA for formative assessment without specifying how this could be done, apart from delegating the job to the teachers, could indicate that his reflexivity was inadequate to the task. Roman's dominant mode was clearly the *autonomous mode* in being performance and outcome oriented.

Case 2: Gillian

A brief description of case 2

Gillian was in her 50s and had worked for around 20 years as a school leader at different schools. Before becoming a school leader, she worked for over 25 years as a teacher. She had a broad educational background in management and pedagogy. Gillian believed that the PISA test indicates how students are doing in school, both nationally and internationally. She also felt that PISA is valuable for comparison with other countries, though she expressed an awareness of cultural differences regarding views on education, highlighting variations in how students are regarded and how and what they should learn. She was against the use of PISA results in her school. She said that the school lacks ownership in the survey and pointed out that it is an external study that has had greater impact on national education policy than on teaching practice in individual schools.

Analysis: Modes of reflexivity

Gillian was oriented towards outcomes in her work as a school leader. Her talk changed through the interview, from being rather general at first, touching upon philosophical questions and later addressed her project as a school leader. Gillian started the conversation by asking open questions while trying to respond to mine. She was thinking and talking as the interview progressed.

Although strategically oriented to achieving results, Gillian seemingly did not have a clear strategy regarding PISA, other than declining to use PISA results in her school. Her reason for this was partly that PISA results were 'external data', since they had not been collected in her school, and partly their 'remoteness' to Norwegian competence goals for mathematics education:

> [...] we have not even participated in PISA: participants are picked randomly, so then they will be someone else's data. So, there's something about that—just how much time can we spend in the school on external results? Not just time, but how can we justify using it? That's a bit of it.
> *(Transcript B, p. 4)*

Despite her rejection of PISA on the grounds that its data is 'remote' from her school and its content is based on other competencies than those in the Norwegian curriculum, she was still interested in obtaining information about how to use PISA. She talked about attending information meetings in the future:

> [...] now there are offers for guidance, erm, this spring, yes, this semester they have organized information meetings in many places, where you can sign up to receive guidance. We would have liked to attend it this year, but it conflicted with other things, and we could not attend. But we are now very aware of it and want to attend them, but unfortunately not this spring. So, I assume that those meetings provide guidance for how [...] the results could be used in schools. [...].
>
> *(Transcript B, p. 1)*

According to Gillian, PISA had not directly influenced her and the mathematics teachers' role, but her role as a school leader had been influenced by a generally increased emphasis on learning outcomes, tests, requirements and expectations that the school must use test results.

In response to the question as to whether PISA had affected her role, she replied:

> Not PISA directly, but it has probably affected my role as a school leader that in recent years there has been an increased focus on learning outcomes and different ways of testing students, and requirements and expectations that the school must use those results.
>
> *(Transcript B, p. 3)*

Gillian's project was to improve students' learning and to make school management and teachers assume a greater responsibility for learning outcomes. She emphasized that the school personnel should do what society demands and take responsibility for students' results.

> [...] both the school management and the teacher must acknowledge that it is they who are responsible for the students' results. And then what is learning? What is the teacher's role? How to not only guide, but work with school learning so that students achieve the competence that society demands in the competency goals?
>
> *(Transcript B, p. 2)*

Gillian was oriented towards ethical questions but did not criticize PISA. Instead, she talked about the questionable legitimacy of using external results that were not generated by her school, and she pondered about what learning is, what the teacher's role should be and how to promote learning. She talked about the 'remoteness' of PISA and how to legitimize its use:

> 'Does this apply to us?' is a question that always comes up when you read about results- 'Are these good enough goals?' 'Are they relevant?' 'How can we use it?', really.
>
> *(Transcript B, p. 4)*

Later in the interview, Gillian seemed rather ambivalent when she said that she wanted to attend PISA information meetings. Her main concern, which could be seen to promote professional values (*meta-reflexive*), was expressed when she asserted that 'only one plan is valid', meaning the National Curriculum:

> [...] if you are a teacher then there is one [curriculum] that applies, and [the job of the teacher is to find out] how you can get the students to learn this.
>
> *(Transcript B, p. 2)*

Gillian did not criticize PISA or the educational system in a disloyal way, as one might expect from *meta-reflexives*, nor did she engage in *communicative reflexivity*, as she expressed that there was just one plan to be followed – no discussion needed. On this issue, she did not seek consent from her closest 'friends or family' (i.e., her colleagues at her school).

In making her staff take responsibility for the students' acquiring competencies defined by the National Curriculum and emphasizing that there was only one valid curriculum, Gillian practiced the *autonomous reflexive mode*. Her opinions on these issues were non-negotiable. She did not seem willing to adapt her views to protests or other opinions that may have prevailed among her staff and did not, in this sense, practise *communicative reflexivity*. Regarding the use of PISA, her firm opinion was that it could not, for several reasons, be applied in her school. Regarding the application of PISA results, however, her standpoint was ambivalent and open to revision. She seemed to acknowledge that she might need more information about the test, so, she planned to attend PISA information meetings in the future. She admitted – when asked – that she could not specify which domains within mathematics education were covered by the PISA test. She also found it challenging to explain in what sense PISA might be relevant for the teaching of mathematics in her school: 'It is kind of hard to answer that, really' (Transcription B, p. 1).

Regarding the use of PISA, on the one hand, she was opposed to the use of PISA results in her schools, for several reasons, and she could not describe how it might be relevant or how its content was related to the official curriculum. On the other hand, she considered attending PISA information meetings in the future, which might give her knowledge and reasons for some usage of PISA results. Wanting to know more is typical of *meta-reflexives*, who reflect upon their own reflections – i.e., always critical to some extent, or if one prefers, recognizing their fallibility. However, seeking more knowledge and information could also express the instrumental interest of an autonomous reflexive in improving students' achievements.

Summing up case 2, the analysis shows that Gillian activated two different reflexive modes when reflecting on PISA: autonomous and meta-reflexive. She was autonomous in assessing the relevance of PISA for her school, rejecting its use without consulting the staff. By not involving the staff in her decision, she did not activate communicative reflexivity. Her seeking more information about PISA by attending the information courses could indicate a meta-reflexive mode, being ready to change her mind based on new information. However, her meta-reflexivity did not result in a subversive stance to her social context (including PISA). Her lack of knowledge on how the items of the PISA test relate to the content and competencies in the National Curriculum made her uncertain of how to use the test in her school, but she would seek more knowledge to find out. Thus, one could argue that she demonstrated meta-reflexivity, to a certain extent. Gillian's dominant mode of reflexivity was the autonomous mode. She made decisions on her own, based on what she assumed would promote good results in her school.

Case 3: Louise

A brief description of case 3

Louise was in her 40s and had worked as a school leader for about 10 years at the same school. Before becoming a leader, she worked as a teacher for nearly 10 years. She was educated as a teacher. Louise stated that PISA is an international project that measures whether the school is emphasizing the right things. She thought that PISA results have had an indirect impact on schools in centrally decided curriculum change and changes made in the form of examinations: PISA has, thus, become a national assessment system that is used at a higher level than the individual school. According to Louise, her school is unable to absorb and study the magnitude of the data and research material available for use, and the PISA study is too large to be used directly in her school. She felt that the national and local surveys and tests are more helpful to her own school than PISA; nevertheless, Louise believed that PISA is sensible and has value in itself.

Analysis: Modes of reflexivity

Louise emphasized that PISA is external and distant from her school since data are not specific to the students in her school.

> [...] going straight into PISA and then straight into our school, is too much of a distance because it is not our students who have responded. We must constantly relate to the students we have here and now.
> *(Transcript D, p. 2)*

Still, she considered PISA to have general merits by providing input to educational policy at the national level. By virtue of impacting upon national policy, it also has an impact on her school. Louise explained that what is being signalled by PISA has influenced her school, how they conduct their teaching and what their students achieve; however, the major impact is at the higher political and managerial levels of the educational system:

> PISA is sensible and has value in itself [...]. Clearly, we are part of the Norwegian school system, so, it is clear that what is signalled in PISA also has an impact on our school, and how we conduct our teaching, and what our students achieve—it has. [...] But it is more on the management level, in comparing what Norwegian students are not sufficiently good at, and what we can improve on, and what we are good at. So, it becomes more about overall management.
>
> *(Transcript D, p. 2)*

Louise explained that the teachers are results-oriented and that she herself had attended a PISA course. Like Gillian, she was somewhat sceptical towards using PISA for information about her own students and to improve her own practice. For this purpose, national and local tests are more useful:

> I was on a PISA course just before Easter, and it was very interesting. But again, it is so big. [...] if I am going to use [the PISA results] directly in school, it will in the first place be amongst my own students [if the PISA results will tell about this particular school], to see where we are as a school, what our students are getting and not getting, and what we have to change here. And the national and other local tests are more suitable to do that, than the PISA results.
>
> *(Transcript D, p. 2)*

Like Gillian, Louise had no answer to the question about which areas of mathematical knowledge PISA covers, claiming that 'it is terribly difficult to say' (Transcript D, p. 1). When asked whether PISA covers the competence goals in the Norwegian mathematics curriculum, she responded by saying, 'Well...', in the uncertain and thoughtful tone one might use when saying 'Hmm' (Transcript D, p. 1).

One element that distinguished Louise from the other cases was her emphasis on broader learning. Louise expressed disagreement with the current selective focus on specific subjects and teaching practice in these subjects. She regretted that the school seems to forget that, in compulsory education, broad knowledge and basic skills are important.

> [...] one forgets in a way that we are a compulsory school, and it should transmit the basic skills students should have when graduating. There is too much focus on some subjects [...]. [...]. It is the breadth [i.e., all subjects] we should work on and get the students prepared for moving ahead [in life and further education]. They will learn more later in their educational pathway; they will not become good realists or philologists

in compulsory school. That is not the goal. There is a bit of a danger with testing, that there is simply too much focus on the individual subject.

(Transcription D, p. 3)

Louise may be characterized as a predominantly *autonomous reflexive* (strategical) who was oriented to outcome, since she clearly expressed being oriented to various tests and the use of them in her own school. She also clearly expressed her own non-negotiable concerns – which she wanted to implement regardless of what her staff may think. She was sceptical towards the utility of PISA in her own school and had a clear conception of how she, herself, might try it out in her own class or school if the results were to become more relevant for her school. She did not seem to engage in *communicative reflexivity* in the sense of trying to reach an agreement or submitting to staff opinion on pedagogical issues. Her criticism of the current emphasis on specific school subjects, advocating the importance of a broader education and basic skills, could indicate that she engaged in *meta-reflexivity*. However, she did not oppose PISA, despite not wanting to use it in her own school. She thought the test has merit and is valuable in and of itself. While Louise criticized the selective focus on specific school subjects, paradoxically, she did not criticize PISA or other tests, even though PISA is one of the tests that focuses on specific subjects. Like Gillian, Louise could not describe the areas of knowledge and the competence goals of PISA in relation to the Norwegian curriculum. Both Gillian and Louise seemed at a loss about how to implement PISA-results in their school, which they both felt obliged to do. Both leaders seemed to overcome their sense of not knowing what to do by seeking more knowledge in a PISA course.

Summing up case 3, Louise activated two different modalities in reflecting on PISA, autonomous and meta-reflexivity. Like Gillian, Louise made autonomous decisions without consulting the staff and did not engage in communicative reflexivity with them. She was critical to current educational policy, which favours certain school subjects, and doubted the utility of PISA for her school. Still, she had attended a PISA course, which indicated her meta-reflexivity; wanting to re-examine her own standpoint. But having attended a PISA course, she was still doubtful about its utility for her school. Autonomous reflexivity was her predominant mode.

Discussion

Regarding the research question (1) on which modes of reflexivity that were activated among school leaders by PISA issues, two modes, the autonomous and the meta-reflexive, were detected. Regarding research question (2), the predominant mode among all three leaders was autonomous reflexivity, in the sense that they emphasized leadership efficacy and were preoccupied with tasks to be completed. They were actively trying to deal with their environment.

However, determining which reflexive mode was the predominant one in each case entailed some challenges. In the beginning, it was difficult to determine whether a school leader was predominantly autonomous reflexive or predominantly meta-reflexive. Initially, I categorized Gillian and Louise as predominantly meta-reflexives. My recollection of the tone and atmosphere in the two interviews predisposed me towards this categorization. However, when I studied the content of the interviews more closely, I arrived at a different conclusion and classified them as predominantly autonomous reflexives. My final classification was based on the assessment that not using or declining to use PISA as a tool in formative evaluation is not necessarily based on meta-reflexivity. Gillian and Louise, who claimed they would have used PISA in their formative work if only they knew how to do so, could not be classified as predominantly meta-reflexives because they were not fundamentally against the use of PISA. Another example that precludes categorizing Louise as predominantly meta-reflexive was her conviction that there is too much focus on certain school subjects, which is something meta-reflexives might say, but without her mentioning alternatives, possible solutions, or ways of counteracting the emphasis on certain subjects. Neither did her concerns stop her from attending a PISA information meeting organized by the Norwegian Directorate of Education and Training (*Utdanningsdirektoratet*). In essence, she did not reject the PISA test, nor its emphasis on specific school subjects.

The primary indicator for classifying all three school leaders as predominantly autonomous reflexives is that they explicitly expressed a desire to use PISA in their professional work as school leaders, and they made other statements about PISA, which excluded them from being considered as meta-reflexives. Their PISA critique was moderated and toned down. Meta-reflexives, also characterized as subversive agents, would most likely not have considered attending PISA information meetings organized by the Norwegian Directorate for Education and Training. Such participation might be seen by meta-reflexives as problematic or irrelevant; moreover, meta-reflexive agents would likely also find it difficult to emphasize positive aspects of the test. A subversive agent might have become upset or annoyed when the issue of the test was raised and would likely have voiced protest against and dissatisfaction with the test. However, none of the school leaders expressed negative emotions when discussing PISA. Hence, none of the cases could be classified as predominantly meta-reflexives, even though Gillian and Louise were rather sceptical about the usefulness of PISA for improving mathematics education in their school.

Based on the content of the interviews, autonomous reflexivity was the predominant mode for each of the school leaders. However, the possibility of a social desirability bias (Callegaro 2008) in the interview data must be mentioned. Since 2007 and onwards, the emphasis in Norwegian educational policy has been on assessment *for* learning (formative assessment) as one of the most effective ways to improve students' achievement. Evidence from Norwegian researchers on a 'weak culture' for formative assessment in Norwegian schools (Tveit 2014, 226) and rising expectations from municipal leaders regarding the improvement of school results (Skedsmo and Møller 2016) may have prompted self-presentations among the school leaders, which over-emphasized their valuing of the PISA test and their optimism about being able to use it. The three school leaders all expressed a positive attitude to PISA as at least having 'a value in itself', if not immediately useful in their own school. But they may have exaggerated their valuing of the PISA test. Their optimism about eventually being able to use it could have been mobilized to create a positive image of themselves and their school. All this may have prompted self-presentations among the school leaders, which led to an under-estimation of their meta-reflexivity and an over-estimation of their autonomous reflexivity.

The analysis shows that certain aspects of the PISA phenomenon (using PISA for formative assessment and how PISA items are related to the Norwegian National Curriculum) seemed to trigger uncertainties in two of the respondents. Two of the leaders, Gillian and Louise, did not encourage the use of PISA for formative evaluation in their schools and found it hard to understand how it could be used to improve mathematics education. They were at a loss for answers when questioned about how the content of the PISA test related to the competences specified in the Norwegian mathematics curriculum and whether PISA could be of any help to improve teaching practice. But they did not completely discard that PISA might be of use. Both indicated that they might need guidance in using PISA for their teaching. They believed that PISA could possibly serve as a tool for formative assessment but expressed uncertainty about how this should be done. Louise had been on a PISA course to become better informed – and Gillian wanted to attend such a course in the future. Arguably, Roman might also be seen to harbour this uncertainty about how PISA results might be applied in his school. Although he insisted on his eagerness to do this, his plans seemed rather vague and unspecific. One might suspect that he was covering up his own uncertainties regarding the use of PISA, when his plan consisted in assigning the job to his staff, without further specifications. Gillian's and Louise's uncertainties combined with their willingness to learn and re-assess their beliefs could indicate meta-reflexivity (reassessing their beliefs about PISA), but might equally well express the concerns of an autonomous reflexive seeking information wanting to improve students' performance.

Why was autonomous reflexivity the dominant mode among the school leaders? And why did they adopt an instrumental stance to the use of the PISA-test in their school, assigning the job of 'learning from the test results' to their staff without further guidance, or attending or planning to attend courses in the Directorate, while meanwhile prohibiting any use of the test in their own school. Previous studies have explained the limited use of tests by school leaders as a result of their lack of knowledge on how to use test results (Eggen 2010), or as caused by resistance from teachers (Aas and Brandmo 2018). Another possible explanation that might be hypothesized is that the school leaders are actually meta-reflexives: as meta-reflexives, they would acknowledge the inherent limitations of the test and not see the point of trying to use it to improve their teaching practice (formative assessment). However, this explanation is not supported by the present investigation, which indicates that all three school leaders were not predominantly meta-reflexives regarding PISA. In one way or another, each endorsed the PISA test.

A different explanation, suggested by Archer's theory and the present data, is that the school leaders are driven by their concern for 'performative achievement', that is, 'task performance at a level which satisfies external standards of assessment', which is the deeper personal concern that fuels autonomous reflexivity. Autonomous reflexives tend to adopt a strategic stance towards their structural and cultural context and to be accommodative, since 'to them, context is a means towards the realization of their concern, which is task performance' (Archer 2003, 265–266). But the school leaders presented here were not only being accommodative because they were able to realise their basic concern, 'to perform well', in addition, they were compliant to avoid negative sanctions. By virtue of their leadership position, school leaders must be loyal to the decisions on educational policy made by national authorities in Norway, even while their gut feeling as former teachers might tell them that 'something is not right'. For school leaders, taking a stand against PISA would not have been a strategic way to deal with their environment, since this could result in sanctions from their superiors. Strategic action would instead entail using PISA to the extent that is expected and in the way it is prescribed by superiors in the system. For the three school leaders, the prospect of negative sanctions for non-compliance adds to the effect of their inner concerns for performance and results.

It is significant that the three school leaders were each previously teachers – two of whom taught for a considerable length of time. A counterfactual question would be: If they had still been teachers, would their predominant mode of reflexivity regarding PISA have been different? Furthermore, would they, as teachers, have been meta-reflexives? Would they have adopted a more principled stance on the futility of using PISA results? My impression from two of the interviews was that these leaders, at least to some extent, engaged in meta-reflexivity regarding PISA. This indicates that as teachers, and not constrained by their present leadership position, they might have been meta-reflexives. Their position as school leaders seems to be a necessary condition for their expressing a desire to learn how to use PISA as a tool for formative evaluation, instead of flatly acknowledging the inherent limitations of the test.

Efforts made by Norwegian educational authorities to organize PISA information meetings seem to build on the assumption that the limited and strategic use of PISA in schools is due to a lack of knowledge on how to use PISA. This explanation is underscored by Eggen (2010), who points out that schools need the right frameworks and knowledge to use PISA for formative assessment. Tveit (2014), however, in a study of National Tests, argues with reference to Skedsmo (2011) that summative evaluation based on group results, and formative assessment, providing diagnostic information about individual students, are hard to combine in one single type of test. Summative evaluations are useful for holding municipalities and school accountable for students' results, while formative, diagnostic assessments are more useful for teaching practice. The current messages of Norwegian educational authorities, who claim that the two functions may be served by the same tests may, according to Tveit (2014) and Skedsmo (2011), prompt unrealistic expectations as to what purposes the National Tests can serve.

The same concerns could be raised regarding PISA. The three school leaders in the present study find other tests than PISA more interesting and valuable for formative work. Gunnulfsen and Møller (2017), however, found a more consistent rejection of all external tests, showing that school leaders, like the teachers, considered national tests to be 'symbolic action', since the results merely confirmed what they already knew about their students. The widespread attention given to test results despite their 'irrelevance' seems to indicate that the educational policy emanating from the centre – which requires the dissemination of PISA results and the use of national tests – is out of touch with the school personnel's own assessments regarding how to improve the quality of teaching in Norwegian schools.

Conclusion

PISA is one of an increasing number of tests (i.e., diagnostic, local, national and international) used in schools, and it has been administered in Norwegian schools every third year since 2000. Researchers have pointed out that standardized tests serve two major functions. The first is to increase control and hold agents at different levels of the system accountable for students' achievements. The second is to improve the quality of schooling and, more specifically, to facilitate formative assessment for better learning. Test results also enable competitions, which are staged between individual schools and regions as well as between countries based on the assumption that competition will lead to quality improvement.

This research confirmed that all three reflexive modes were exercised in the school leaders' internal deliberation on PISA issues, though all modes were not activated by each one of the leaders. The predominant mode engaged in by all three leaders was autonomous reflexivity. Two of the school leaders claimed, when asked whether and how the PISA test relates to Norway's National Curriculum and its competency goals, that they could not tell. These two school leaders had decided that PISA could not be used for formative evaluation and they did not encourage the use of PISA results for teachers in their school. On the one hand, they discouraged the use of PISA in their school on the grounds of it being external to their school and unrelated to the National Curriculum. On the other hand, both had attended or planned to attend PISA courses organized by the Norwegian Directorate of Education and Training, hoping to acquire know-how regarding future use of PISA for teaching practice.

In Archer's theory, reflexive modes are personal properties that mediate the influence of structures on individual action, so that identical objective situations may produce different kinds of action from different persons. Archer (2003; 2007; 2012) has suggested that certain social structures may encourage some reflexive modes more than others, and therefore, different reflexive modes have predominated in various historical periods, due to changes in structural and cultural configurations. Interestingly, Archer (2007, 320–321) has suggested that the practice of autonomous reflexivity is expected 'to rise considerably as globalisation intensifies' since globalization 'remains capitalist in nature' and the autonomous reflexive mode seems 'supremely compatible with early capitalist entrepreneurship in its practical concerns, self-reliance, instrumental rationality, and exchange relations'. Autonomous reflexivity fits well with managerial jobs, which currently proliferate in the caring professions and in education. The autonomous reflexives 'are vested in the institutional order that provides the contextual outlet for their performative skills, their main effect is to augment goal-achievement in different part of the social system' (Archer 2003, 357). However, in her most recent publication on reflexivity, Archer (2012, i) asserts 'that modernity is slowly ceding' towards the predominance of meta-reflexivity, 'at least amongst educated young people'.

In the discussion of my findings, I have argued that the position of school leader entails constraints on PISA critique, since the test is endorsed by the highest level of educational policymaking in Norway. I have also argued, on counterfactual grounds, that the position of school leader may be a necessary condition for the predominance of autonomous reflexivity rather than meta-reflexivity on PISA-related issues among the school leaders. I posited that, had the school leaders still been teachers (as they had been for many years), they might well have been meta-reflexives and rejected PISA. All of them were familiar with PISA critiques and two had taken a stand against using PISA in their school. Their currently subdued meta-reflexive mode and the predominance of autonomous reflexivity may be a new stage in their personal (and professional) development.

Since it can be difficult to identify a person's dominant reflexive mode, further research on modes of reflexivity might benefit from validation by supplementary data sources. I suggest that Archer's (2007) Internal Conversation Indicator (ICONI) may serve this purpose. An additional data source, combined with the ICONI, might be to present the results for verification by the respondents themselves. This could strengthen the validity of the findings and/or provide additional data that may ground a more accurate identification of modes of reflexivity.

Notes

1. The term 'school leader' is used 'as an equivalent to the term "principal", designating the head or leader of a unit. One reason for this choice of terminology is that, in the Norwegian context, the term "principal" is considered outdated as a consequence of recent structural changes in the Norwegian education system, which entail more external control mechanisms and expectations of "transformative leadership"' (Bringeland, cited from the paper in this anthology with the title 'The impact of PISA on education in Norway: a morphogenetic perspective on structural elaboration in an education system').
2. Formative assessment, or evaluation, typically involves providing students with qualitative feedback rather than just scores on their assignments. It is conducted 'in process' by teachers to modify learning and teaching activities to improve students' achievements. The terms 'formative assessment' and 'summative assessment' were coined by Scriven (1967) and later developed by Bloom, Madaus, and Hastings (1971), and also integrated in Blooms concept of 'mastery learning' (Bloom 1971).
3. Progress in International Reading Literacy Study
4. Trends in International Mathematics and Science Study
5. *Personal contexts* might involve, e.g., food preparation, shopping, transport etc. *Occupational contexts* might involve measuring or quality control. *Societal contexts* (including local, national or global), might involve voting systems, public transport, demographics and advertising. *Scientific contexts* could involve mathematics applied to the natural world, in science and technology, or weather, climate, ecology or medicine. The scientific context might also include intra-mathematical problems (OECD 2019, 88).
6. For an example provided by Archer, which shows how one phenomenon, toothache, may activate all types of reflexive responses in the same person within a short time span, see Archer (2012, 12).
7. The informants whose interviews I am using all gave written consent to future use of these data. Unfortunately, when I began the secondary analysis, three recorded interviews with school leaders—one of which had been transcribed—were accidentally deleted. Since much of these data had been preserved in my master's thesis, I used these in my secondary analysis.
8. Initially, there were four respondents, but one school leader withdrew his consent to making the data material available for future research.

References

Aas, Marit, and Christian Brandmo. 2018. "Assessment Results for Transforming Practice: School Leaders' Role." *Nordic Studies in Education* 38 (2):174–194. doi: 10.18261/issn.1891-5949-2018-02-06.

Archer, Margaret S. 1995. *Realist social theory: The morphogenetic approach.* Cambridge: Cambridge University Press.

Archer, Margaret S. 2000. *Being human: The problem of agency.* Cambridge: Cambridge University Press.

Archer, Margaret S. 2003. *Structure, agency and the internal conversation.* Cambridge: Cambridge University Press.

Archer, Margaret S. 2007. *Making our way through the world: Human reflexivity and social mobility.* Cambridge: Cambridge University Press.

Archer, Margaret S. 2012. *The reflexive imperative in late modernity.* Cambridge: Cambridge University Press.

Archer, Margaret S. [1979] 2013. *Social origins of educational systems*. London: Sage.
Archer, Margaret S. [1988] 1996. *Culture and agency: The place of culture in social theory*. Cambridge: Cambridge University Press.
Aursand, Leah Rose. 2018. "What [Some] Students Know and Can Do: A Case Study of Norway, PISA, and Exclusion." Master's Thesis, Department of Education, University of Oslo.
Bhaskar, Roy. [1979] 1998. *The possibility of naturalism: A philosophical critique of the contemporary human sciences*. 3rd ed., Critical realism. London: Routledge.
Bieber, Tonia, and Kerstin Martens. 2011. "The OECD PISA study as a soft power in education? Lessons from Switzerland and the US." *European Journal of Education* 46 (1):101–116.
Bloom, Benjamin S. 1971. "Mastery learning." In *Mastery learning: Theory and practice*, edited by James H Block, 47–63. New York: Holt, Rinehart & Winston.
Bloom, Benjamin S, George F Madaus, and John Thomas Hastings. 1971. *Handbook on formative and summative evaluation of student learning*. New York: McGraw-Hill.
Breakspear, Simon. 2012. The policy impact of PISA: An exploration of the normative effects of international benchmarking in school system performance. OECD Education Working Papers (71), 31 pages.
Callegaro, Mario 2008. "Social desirability." In *Encyclopedia of survey research methods*, edited by P. J Lavrakas, 826–827. Thousand Oaks, CA: SAGE Publications.
Danermark, Berth. 2003. *Att förklara samhället [Explaining society]*. 2nd ed. Lund: Studentlitteratur.
Danermark, Berth, Mats Ekström, Liselotte Jakobsen, and Jan Ch. Karlson. 2002. *Explaining society: Critical realism in the social sciences, Att förklara samhället*. London: Routledge.
Eggen, Astrid Birgitte. 2010. "PISAs gyldighet blant skoleledere og lærere [PISA's Validity among School Leaders and Teachers]." In *PISA: Sannheten om skolen? [PISA: The Truth About the School?]*, edited by Kirsten Sivesind and Eyvind Elstad, 281–297. Oslo: Universitetsforlaget.
Grek, Sotiria. 2009. "Governing by numbers: The PISA 'effect' in Europe." *Journal of Education Policy* 24 (1):23–37.
Gunnulfsen, Ann Elisabeth, and Jorunn Møller. 2017. "National testing: Gains or strains? School leaders' responses to policy demands." *Leadership and Policy in Schools* 16 (3):455–474.
Heaton, Janet. 2008. "Secondary analysis of qualitative data: An overview." *Historical Social Research* 33 (3):33–45.
Hopfenbeck, Therese N., Inger Throndsen, Svein Lie, and Erling Lars Dale. 2012. "Assessment with distinctly defined criteria: A research study of a national project." *Policy Futures in Education* 10 (4):421–433. doi: 10.2304/pfie.2012.10.4.421.
Hopfenbeck, Therese, Astrid Tolo, María Flórez Petour, and Yasmine El Masri. 2013. *Balancing trust and accountability? The assessment for learning programme in Norway, governing complex education systems case study*. Paris: OECD.
Hornskov, Søren, Helle Bjerg, and Laura Høvsgaard. 2015. *Review: Brug af data i skoleledelse [Review: Use of data in school management]*. København: UCC.
Leithwood, Kenneth, Jingping Sun, and Katina Pollock. 2017. *How school leaders contribute to student success: The four paths framework*. Vol. 23, Studies in Educational Leadership. Cham: Springer International Publishing.

Meyer, H.D, and A Benavot, eds. 2013. *PISA, power and policy - The emergence of the global educational governance*. Oxford: Symposium Books.
Møller, Jorunn, and Eli Ottesen. 2011. "Styring, ledelse og kunnskapsutvikling i skolen [Management, Leadership and Knowledge Development in the School]." In *Rektor som leder og sjef: om styring, ledelse og kunnskapsutvikling i skolen [Principal As Leader and Manager: On Management, Leadership and Knowledge Development in the School]*, edited by Jorunn Møller and Eli Ottesen, 15–26. Oslo: Universitetsforlaget.
Nusche, Deborah, Lorna Earl, William Maxwell, and Claire Shewbridge. 2011. *OECD reviews of evaluation and assessment in education: Norway 2011, OECD reviews of evaluation and assessment in education*. Paris: OECD Publishing.
OECD. 2008. *Teaching and Learning International Survey (TALIS). Resultater fra OECDs internasjonale studie av undervisning og læring [Results from OECD's international study of teaching and learning]*. Paris: OECD.
OECD. 2011. *OECD reviews on evaluation and assessment in education – Norway*. Paris: OECD.
OECD. 2019. *PISA 2018 assessment and analytical framework*. Paris: OECD Publishing.
Ringarp, J, and M Rothland. 2010. "Is the grass always greener? The effect of the PISA results on education debates in Sweden and Germany." *European Educational Research Journal* 9 (3):422–430.
Schleicher, Andreas. 2016. "Challenges for PISA." *RELIEVE e-Journal of Educational Research, Assessment and Evaluation* 22 (1):1–7.
Schleicher, Andreas. 2019. *PISA 2018: Insights and interpretations*. Paris: OECD Publishing.
Scriven, Michael. 1967. "The methodology of evaluation." In *Perspectives of curriculum evaluation*, edited by Ralph W Tyler, Robert M Gagné and Michael Scriven, 39–83. Chicago: McNally.
Sjøberg, Svein. 2014a. "Hva PISA-testen måler [What the PISA Test Measures]." *Bedre Skole* (04):70–75.
Sjøberg, Svein. 2014b. "PISA-syndromet—Hvordan norsk skolepolitikk blir styrt av OECD [The PISA syndrome—How norwegian school policy is directed by the OECD]." *Nytt Norsk Tidsskrift* 31 (01):30–43.
Sjøberg, Svein, and Edgar Jenkins. 2020. "PISA: A political project and a research agenda." In *Studies in Science Education*, 1–14. London: Routledge. doi: 10.1080/03057267.2020.1824473.
Skedsmo, Guri. 2009. "School Governing in Transition? Perspectives, Purposes and Perceptions of Evaluation Policy." PhD dissertation, University of Oslo, Faculty of Education, Oslo: Unipub.
Skedsmo, Guri. 2011. "Vurdering som styring av utvikling og overvåkning av resultater [Assessment as management of development and monitoring of results]." In *Rektor som leder og sjef: Om styring, ledelse og kunnskapsutvikling i skolen [Principal as leader and manager: On management, leadership and knowledge development in the school]*, edited by Eli Ottesen and Jorunn Møller, 74–94. Oslo: Universitetsforlaget.
Skedsmo, Guri, and Sølvi Mausethagen. 2017. "Nye styringsformer i utdanningssektoren—spenninger mellom resultatstyring og faglig-profesjonelt ansvar [New forms of management in the education sector—tensions between performance

management and professional responsibility]." *Norsk pedagogisk tidsskrift* 101 (2):169–179.

Skedsmo, Guri, and Jorunn Møller. 2016. "Governing by new performance expectations in Norwegian schools." In *New public management and the reform of education: European lessons for policy and practice*, edited by Helen M Gunter, Emiliano Grimaldi, David Hall and Roberto Serpieri, 53–65. London: Routledge.

Slagstad, Rune. 1998. *De nasjonale strateger [The national strategists]*. Oslo: Pax Forlag.

Sun, Jingping, Robert Przybylski, and Bob J Johnson. 2016. "A review of research on teachers' use of student data: From the perspective of school leadership." *Educational Assessment, Evaluation and Accountability* 28 (1):5–33.

Tveit, Sverre. 2014. "Educational assessment in Norway." *Assessment in Education: Principles, Policy & Practice* 21 (2):221–237. doi: 10.1080/0969594X.2013.830079.

Utdanningsforbundet. 2008. "Spørreundersøkelsen om PISA blant Utdanningsforbundets medlemmer [The Survey on PISA among the Members of the Education Association]." Accessed 14.01.2021. http://www.utdanningsforbundet.no/upload/Diverse/Pdf-filer/Publikasjoner/Unders%C3%B8kelser/Rapport%20 PISA_111108_web.pdf.

Yin, Robert K. 1994. "Case study research: Design and methods." In *Applied social research methods series*, 2nd ed., Vol. 5. Thousand Oaks: SAGE Publications.

10 The worldwide language issue in education

Birgit Brock-Utne

Introduction

It may seem out of place to begin a chapter about the Norwegian educational system, serving a population of 5 million, by comparing it with similar policies, practices and outcomes on the continent of Africa. However, since my central focus is upon the relationship between indigenous languages and those used in teaching and learning, the similarities between the two are greater in this respect than is commonly recognized. So, too, are some of the international agencies that now exert powerful external influences, both political and financial, upon the form and content of educational development, which were non-existent when the Norwegian system was first taking shape.

In terms of the language of instruction, such influences were and are both structural and cultural. They can be roughly grouped as the following six points, although their impacts are interdependent with one another. The list could be longer or shorter but cumulatively it points to the fact that the continuing erosion of the importance of the Norwegian language in education threatens to make similarities with developing nations even more marked.

- Increased privatization of educational institutions, often at all levels.
- The privileging of English as the language of instruction, regardless of what mother tongue is dominant in a region and spoken in the home.
- In school, pupils now confront the double task of simultaneously learning new subjects and skills in a new language.
- In higher education students meet the full brunt of the internationalization of studies to prepare them for the global labour market in the new millennium.
- Higher rewards go to academic publications in English, Norway having developed a points-based system that ranks Publishers and Journals, which has been contested but unsuccessfully.
- Together the local variants on the above protect and protract the linguistic heritage of the original colonial power in Africa and promote the interests of neo-liberalism within Norway.

DOI: 10.4324/9781003163527-13

Language was never culturally neutral and, in the past, reflected the lower status of North Sami compared with those speaking Norwegian. In the new millennium, the two crucial social divisions that are hardened by the educational incursion of the English language into teaching, examining and publishing are between the rich and poor and urban versus the rural dwellers.

In my presentation, I shall focus on languages of instruction in many countries, on languages that are threatened as academic languages or not used in education at all, even though these are the languages people speak. The theme cannot be understood unless one looks at the capitalist policy ruling the world today, increasing differences between people, making the rich richer and the poor poorer. When it comes to Africa, it is also necessary to look at the colonial history of the continent. The role of the elites adhering to private schooling for their own children has to be understood. A focus will be on Norwegian policy, both towards developing countries and within our own country.

Privatization of education in Africa through Norwegian 'development' aid

In an article on the 'Worldbankification' of Norwegian development assistance to education, I note that even in a period with a Minister of Development from the Social Democratic Party, money given to the World Bank to assist secondary education in Tanzania was granted on the condition that the money should be used for private schooling only (Brock-Utne, 2007a). This was against the official policy of Tanzania at the time as well as against the policy of the Social Democratic Party of Norway. When in 1989 the Minister of Development, Kirsti Kolle Grøndahl, who had earlier been the Minister for Education, proposed that support to the education sector in Tanzania be expanded, she probably had not foreseen that the $US 8 million that was granted, based on her initiative, would be given to the World Bank to create a new non-governmental organization which would be disliked by many officials in the Tanzanian Ministry of Education. Nor would she have predicted that this organization would further the privatization of the secondary school sector whose outcome created larger disparities between regions and groups of people in Tanzania. The World Bank established an NGO called the National Education Trust Fund (NETF) totally financed by Norway, but run according to the neo-liberal policies of the World Bank. A frank consultancy report prepared for NORAD (Norwegian Agency for Development Cooperation) on the Fund stated: 'There is lack of local support for the Fund. The Fund is designed for dependency on donor support. Without donor support the Fund would be non-existent' (Galabawa and Alphonse, 1993, 3). Most of the programme officers I interviewed in the Ministry of Education in the spring of 1992 disliked the NETF because the support was only supposed to go to private secondary schools, thus weakening the government sector (Brock-Utne, 2000). The officers I talked with in the CCM headquarters were especially annoyed at the NETF, claiming that it would lead to greater disparities in the country, disparities between regions, between religions and between the rich and the poor. In a clear protest against NETF, the CCM office started another fund they named the Nyerere Educational Trust Fund – using the same acronym – NETF. This NETF was to support able students coming from very poor homes to get to secondary school.

After Nyerere's term in office, the way was clear to adopt the 'Education and Training Policy' (MOEC, 1995), which opened private primary schools. Lene Buchert (1997) reported that many of the government officials as well as bilateral aid agencies and people from the academic environment saw 'a determined World Bank hand behind it'. One of her interviewees said about the Education and Training policy of 1995: 'It has been stuffed down the throat of the Government by the IMF and the World Bank' (Buchert, 1997, 52).

These private primary schools use English as the language of instruction. The richest parents in Tanzania send their children to very costly private primary schools, where there is plenty of instructional material, DVDs, videos and teachers who have English as their first language. For these children too it would have been better had the language of instruction been the one with which they are most familiar, but in competition with children in less expensive schools they have an advantage. Also middle-class and even some lower-class parents send their children to private, English medium primary schools, but schools where they pay less, there is not enough instructional material and the teachers are not fluent speakers of English, some hardly master the language at all, neither the oral nor the written form. These pupils run into insurmountable problems. Their parents have not understood the difference between learning a foreign language as a subject and having the foreign language as the language of instruction. For these children it would have been a much better alternative to have had all their lessons in Kiswahili, a language they master well, and learnt English as a subject from teachers who are trained in teaching English as a foreign language.

Norway's lack of support to mother tongue instruction for development

There seems to be general agreement that children learn better when they understand what the teacher is saying! In Africa, this is not the case. Instruction is given in a foreign language, a language that children do not normally hear around them. Difficult subjects are taught in this foreign language, often by teachers who have not mastered the language well themselves. The coping strategy of teachers is often to code-switch between a familiar language children master and the foreign language which is supposed to be the language of instruction (Brock-Utne, 2007b; Mwinsheikhe, 2007; Vuzo, 2007). This practice is not allowed. If secondary school students give correct answers in national exams, e.g., after Form Four, but they give them in Kiswahili (the national language) instead of English (the official language of instruction), they are given a mark of zero (Brock-Utne, 2000).

Norwegian linguists, missionaries, volunteers working in secondary schools and Norwegian academics working at universities in Africa have been concerned by the fact that the foreign language used as the language of instruction prevents African children from learning subject matter and from developing their own language. It acts as a barrier to knowledge. Though we are just five million Norwegians, we use Norwegian as the language of instruction all the way through primary and secondary school and the first years of university education. We shall later see that Norwegian as an academic language is increasingly being threatened by English at master and doctoral levels. We still mostly retain our own language as the language of instruction. Children of asylum seekers and other immigrants coming to Norway have to learn Norwegian, the language we speak. Though various Norwegian governments have said that they want more of the Norwegian development budget to go to education, there is little evidence that at governmental level Norway has supported developing countries in their struggle to retain their mother tongues or familiar languages as languages of instruction.

There has, however, been research in this area by Norwegian academics working with counterparts in Africa through the NUFU program (in, e.g., Zimbabwe, Ethiopia, Mali, Tanzania and South Africa) (Brock-Utne and Skattum, 2009). While the official reason for the new cooperation between universities in the North and the South through the so-called NORHED[1] programme has been to build capacity in the South, it does not work that way as long as NORAD is in control and can stop the collaboration at any time they like (Brock-Utne, 2019a). The programme also puts less emphasis on research and NUFU projects like those described by Brock-Utne and Skattum (2009) are not likely to take place. One of the few official recognitions of the problems experienced by children in Africa since they have to learn through a language in which they are not fluent comes from the Norwegian Councilor Johan Meyer (2019)[2] stationed in Mali. He notes that it is good that we use 50 million Norwegian kroner to further Norwegian literature at the Frankfurt book fair. 'But what about using 50 million Norwegian kroner for teaching material in local languages in Africa?' he asks. He mentions that Norway is generous with development aid, but thus should be in the forefront among donors seeking to secure the use of mother tongues in the schools in Africa. Unfortunately, we are not.

The rhetoric of English and development

Broadly, English is projected as a global language (Graddol, 2000) or a language needed for maintaining a competitive edge in a globalized world. Yet, as Coleman (2011,104) notes:

Globalisation and competitiveness are associated with a need for Engish and then with a need to use English as a medium of instruction, although the logical relationships between these concepts remain unclear.

Mohanty (2017) drawing on his work in respect of English in Indian society and education discusses the processes through which English in India has become dominant, disadvantaging other language communities and perpetuating social discrimination in India. He shows that while some groups benefit from English, most do not (Mohanty, 2017, 266).

In the struggle for Indian independence, Mahatma Gandhi warned that English represented cultural alienation. Nehru, the first Prime Minister of India (educated at Cambridge University and imprisoned by the British before independence) was very concerned about the language question in India and how the choice of English as the language of instruction perpetuated a strongly stratified society. As leader of the socialist part of the Indian Congress party, he had fought against the caste system of India. He saw that a new caste was being developed: an English speaking caste, separated from the rest of the people. In a letter, he stated that he was 'convinced that real progress in India can only be made through our own languages and not through a foreign language. I am anxious to prevent a new caste system being perpetuated in India – an English knowing caste separated from the mass of our public' (cited in Gopal, 1980, 25). Robert Phillipson (2003, 6) comments:

> In fact, an English-using caste has emerged, because the management of multilingualism in India has largely been left to market forces. These strengthen the position of users of English, here as elsewhere. Roughly 30 million Indians are fluent users of English, but they account for under 5 per cent of the population.

He goes on to mention (2003) that there are elites in Africa and India who speak exclusively English to their children. Ali Mazrui (1978) called them the Afro-Saxons. It is not uncommon for Indian grandparents, who do not speak English, to have no language in common with their grandchildren. Thus Phillipson (2003, 75) further laments 'The young upwardly mobile, internationally oriented generation of Indians and Africans have more in common with "global" culture than with the mass of inhabitants of India and Africa'.

Mohanty (2017, 275) notes that even though Prime Minister Nehru feared a development of an 'English knowing caste' in India, he was not able to stop this development. Mohanty writes that in fact there are now English speaking sub-castes in India, differentiated on the basis of their competence in English: those with excellent English who have been schooled in very expensive private schools with excellent teachers; those with average

English who have also gone to private schools but less expensive ones and the pupils with poor English acquired at low-cost private English-medium schools. He questions the practice of low-fee private schools, which claim to be providing English-medium education, but which fail to teach English and fail to teach the subjects which are supposedly being delivered through English (Mohanty, 2017, 275). He asks 'Whose development does English promote?' The same question could be asked in the other so-called 'anglophone' countries in Africa, where only about 5% of the population are fluent speakers of English, as well as in the so-called 'francophone' countries in Africa where only about 5% of the population are fluent speakers of French

Referring to the role of 'the superimposed international languages' in the African context, Kathleen Heugh points out that 'these languages serve only the interests of the elites' (1999, 306). Thus, any claim of a positive role of English in development, according to Heugh, cannot be taken to be a universal phenomenon. She does not see English as a culturally neutral medium that puts everyone on the same footing; it empowers some and disempowers many. But in the so-called anglophone countries it is not only English that poses a threat to the indigenous and smaller languages but also the larger national languages.

On the Indian Subcontinent, Ajit K. Mohanty and Minati Panda (2017) write about the 'double divide' – the hierarchical relationship between English and the major national/regional languages and the other divide between the major languages and the Indigenous tribal minority ones (ITM). English is promoted along with the major national regional languages, while the ITM languages are grossly neglected, as is reflected in the public/private division between schools. This situation is rather similar to the one we find on the African continent where there is a double divide between the former colonial languages English, French and Portuguese and the larger regional languages like Kiswahili, Hausa, Oromo, Amharic on the one hand and the regional languages and community languages on the other. The Tanzanian linguist Martha Qorro and I describe the double divide in Tanzania between English and Kiswahili on the one hand and Kiswahili and the many community languages on the other (Brock-Utne and Qorro, 2015).

The international year of indigenous languages

At the 55th plenary meeting of the United Nations, which took place on 17 December 2018 the following year, 2019, was declared the International Year of Indigenous Languages (Brock-Utne, 2019b). On the 17 December 2019, a high-level event for the closing of the International Year of Indigenous Languages was organized at UN Headquarters in New York. The official website[3] stated that there were at least 2600 indigenous languages in danger of disappearing. The same website also stressed that the survival of these languages will depend on the prosperity and political influence of the language users and their ability to speak and use the languages in all spheres of life.

The fate of the Sami in the Nordic countries is very similar to the fate of many other indigenous peoples in the world. The relationship between the Norwegian, Swedish and Finnish states vis-à-vis the Sami is colonial in origin as the former president of the Norwegian Sami Parliament, Ole Henrik Magga (1996) described it. However, during the 1970s, the ethnopolitical Sami movement gained strength (Huss, 2017). Today, official language acquisition planning in Norway, Sweden and Finland includes explicit protection and promotion of indigenous and minoritized languages, regarded as part of the national heritage of these countries.

Huss (2017) reviews studies which have compared the education in and of the Sami language in Sweden, Finland and Norway and comes to the conclusion that all these countries have taken steps forward, but the school has not yet become a sufficient counterforce to the far advanced language shift among the Sami. She noted that the terms of learning Sami and maintaining Sami identity through school education varied considerably from country to country while Norway stood out as offering the best terms in all respects. She also noted that the fulfilment of Sami language rights through compulsory school education was least satisfactory outside the official Sami administrative areas and also was most pronounced with regards to the smaller Sami languages such as South Sami, Lule, Inari and Skolt Sami.

Outakoski (2015) studied literacy development among 9- to 15-year-old North Saami learners in the core Sami areas of Finland, Norway and Sweden. She found that all these schoolchildren were exposed daily to at least three languages – North Sami, English and the national majority language, Norwegian. Their exposure was not only through the school but also via the media, popular culture, tourism, literature and the home. The languages were, however, unevenly distributed in these contexts and North Sami could easily be sidelined by the other languages. While the pupils found plenty of written material in their national languages as well as in English, there was less to be found in their Indigenous Sami language. Nevertheless, Leena Huss (ibid., 378) also maintains that while the speakers and potential speakers themselves have a central role to play in revitalization work, it is also the responsibility of the Nordic states to strongly support its continuation.

Legal protection of the Norwegian languages

The use and survival of the Sami language in Norway has been given legal protection. In section three of the law protecting the rights of the Sami people, as defined in 1987, but put into effect from 24 February 1989 (and further amended in 2008), the right to have the Sami language as the language of instruction is guaranteed. One of our law professors, Professor Ola Mestad, has proposed giving the Norwegian language similar legal protection in our Constitution as France has done for the French language. It seems high time that Norwegian is accorded such legal protection since the language, especially as an academic language, is under threat. The law on Norwegian higher education of May 1995 contained the following paragraph: 'The language of instruction in Norwegian universities and colleges is normally Norwegian' (§2.7). The paragraph had come into the law after pressure from the Norwegian Language Council. At one point, the Ministry of Education tried to delete the paragraph, but Parliament reinserted it. In 2002, a new law for Norwegian higher education was proposed. Here it was again suggested to do away with paragraph 2.7. There were protests against the deletion of this paragraph from the University of Tromsø, from the Norwegian Language Council and from some academics. Yet the paragraph was taken out of the new law of August 2005. It was argued that the paragraph had to be taken out because of the current internationalization of universities (Kristoffersen, 2005). Without this important paragraph, we cannot demand from non-Norwegian speaking university professors that they learn the Norwegian language in order to teach and tutor our students in our language and in order not to force the academic staff to hold their meetings in English.

This development is also a threat to Norwegian as an academic language

In the summer of 2008, the Norwegian Ministry of Culture and Church presented a white paper to Parliament on Norwegian Language policy[4]. I found the paper disappointing on two counts and wrote an article in the largest Norwegian newspaper, *Aftenposten*, about this (Brock-Utne, 2008). This article led to a radio debate between the Minister of Culture, Trond Giske from the Social Democratic Party, and me on the 21 July 2008. At that time (2008), the Norwegian government – the so-called red-green government – was a coalition consisting of the following three parties: the Social Democrats, the Centre party and the Socialist Left party. These three parties together with the support of the Christian People's party had Parliament adopt the paragraph: 'The language of instruction in Norwegian universities and colleges shall as a rule be Norwegian' as part of the Law of Universities and Colleges in 1995. But the bourgeois coalition government at the beginning of the new millennium – consisting of the Conservative party, the Liberals and the Christian party saw to it that this paragraph was taken out of the University law of 2005, even though Norwegian is more threatened as an academic language to-day than it was in 1995. One would have expected that the red-green government would argue in their white paper on Norwegian language policy for reinserting this paragraph in the Law of Universities and Colleges. The white paper 'Mål og meining' does mention that the Norwegian Language Council had previously (2006) suggested reinserting this paragraph. However, the white paper argued against the Language Council as the Minister of Culture had done against me on the radio debate, maintaining that deletion of this paragraph was a consequence of the 'internationalization of higher education'. But it is exactly the pressure from the internationalization of higher education which requires legal protection of the Norwegian language in places of higher learning. In 2001, the Legal Court of the EU denied Iceland the right to have lower rate of taxation for Icelandic literature than literature written in foreign languages – a practice Iceland had embarked on to protect their own language. Knowing about this, I asked our Minister of Culture whether he was afraid of sanctions from the EU if Norway wanted further promotion of the Norwegian language through legal measures. The Minister chose not to answer that question.

The current government has proposed a language law to protect the Norwegian language. The law proposed has been scrutinized and debated by several organizations. The deadline for comments on the proposal was 15 November 2019. The law was passed by Parliament in the spring of 2020. The intention of the law as formulated in the first paragraph is to strengthen the Norwegian languages.[5] Norway has a multitude of dialects, which are oral, and two official written forms of Norwegian. These written forms are compulsory subjects in all primary and secondary schools. If you in the state administration get a letter in the one form, you are required to answer in that form.[6]

Privatization and language of instruction in Norway

After the change to a blue/blue government in 2013, the issue of private schools resurfaced. A few months after its instatement, a temporary amendment to the Private Schools Act was suggested. This would allow the Ministry to approve private schools that did not fulfil the criteria in the present law. The provisional amendment, which was approved by Parliament in June 2014, indicates the urgency with which the present government sought to encourage more private schools. A more liberal private education law was adopted by Parliament during spring 2016. The greatest change between this law and the previous ones is that § 3 in the law on private schools of 1985 with its clear restrictions as to what type of schools would be accepted as eligible for state support was deleted. Now any private school could be eligible for state support, not only those that built on another pedagogical idea (like Montessori or Waldorf schools) or more religious schools.[7]

An incident connected with the choice of school for the Norwegian princess Ingrid Alexandra illustrates the strong position of the public community school, the egalitarian values among the general public and the scepticism towards private schools in Norway. In June 2014, it became known that crown-prince Håkon and crown-princess Mette-Marit had decided to send their daughter, princess Ingrid Alexandra (then ten) to Oslo International School (OIS), an extremely expensive international school catering for the children of diplomats and for the richest capitalist families in Norway. The current fee for attending the school is 250 000[8] NOK (£23 311) per year. This choice has several disadvantages for the princess herself and for the perception of the royal family as part of the general public. The pedagogical choice of the royal family has not been subject to much debate. But the choice made by the crown-prince and his wife has been debated from a political viewpoint. It is looked upon as a threat to the monarchy. It marks a break with the earlier schooling of the royal family. Both the king and the crown-prince went to regular public Norwegian schools. The Norwegian monarchy has been based on assuming that the royal family is part of the people. There is a famous picture of the former King Olav sitting on the tram to Holmenkollen with his skis during the oil crisis paying the conductor for his ticket. This is the way Norway wants to picture the royal family.

The language of instruction at OIS is English from the first grade. The choice made by the crown-prince and the crown-princess for the princess is also pedagogically an unwise choice. In a chapter on 'Language Policy in Education' the well-known linguist Bernard Spolsky (2017, 3) writes: 'In spite of the growing evidence-based knowledge about language education, implementation of such obvious principles as teaching in a language the pupils understand continue to be blocked by ignorance and inertia'.

Of course, Ingrid Alexandra would learn subject matter more easily were it taught her in Norwegian, the language she speaks every day. The choice made for her has probably been both out of sheer ignorance and from the wish from her parents to have their daughter belong to an international elite and to the Norwegian rich upper-class. It has been said that they want her to learn to think in English. In all breaks and in the school-yard, the language of communication at OIS has to be English. But she is supposed to become the Queen of Norway, not of England! The choice made by her parents for her has decreased her opportunity to develop more academic Norwegian. For each subject one learns, one also learns thousands of words belonging to that subject. Learning these vocabularies in a language other than your own will make it difficult for you to communicate about the subject in your own language. She is also likely to learn a version of English which is not the optimal one since 60–70% of the children attending OIS neither have Norwegian nor English as their first language. Fortunately, her parents had her attend a Norwegian public school the last couple of years of her lower secondary school and she has now started in a regular Norwegian school for her upper secondary education.

An unfounded experiment in a Norwegian public primary school

For the first time in Norway, a public primary school offers the same type of curriculum using English as the language of learning as the private international schools. The difference is that this offer is free, which means that it is not only available for rich parents. But it is likely to have detrimental effects for the 80 pupils participating in this unfounded experiment. In 2016, an experiment using English as the language of instruction from the first grade in primary school and in all subjects started at Manglerud School in Oslo. The project was accepted by the Directorate of Education for a four-year period. The municipal county of Oslo argued that it was important that the offer would be available for more students and had to be free. The Language Council was worried and said it was unacceptable that a public school transfers the teaching of Norwegian to the home. The Director of the Language Council Åse Wetås (2016) in the newspaper *Aftenposten* notes that the Councilor for Education, Tone Tellevik Dahl, in the municipality of Oslo revealed an astonishing lack of knowledge about the importance of building a firm foundation in the Norwegian language from an early start. The Councilor, however, praised the project and claimed that it would give the pupils easier access to the global labour market. Dahl makes the same mistake as many parents I have met in Africa not knowing the difference between learning a language as a subject and having that language as the language of instruction. In the latter case, the language becomes a barrier to learning. The Director of the Language Council Åse Wetås (2016) tried to tell Dahl that small children, who are going to live in Norway, first and foremost need competence in the Norwegian language. They need to develop their vocabulary both in oral and written Norwegian. Thomas and Breidlid (2015) argue that insufficient attention has been paid to the impact of the proliferation of English on minority educational attainment and what this portends for their future. They mention figures for 2013 from the Municipality of Oslo indicating that 54 of Oslo's 125 primary and lower secondary schools (compulsory 10-year schooling) that year had a majority of students from minority/immigrant backgrounds (mainly from the Global South). Sixteen of these schools have over 80% students from minority/immigrant backgrounds. These children need instruction in both their own mother tongues and also to become fluent speakers of Norwegian. The use of English as the language of instruction is not likely to benefit these children and their life in Norway. At Manglerud School, more than 25% (in 2012) of the pupils have a minority/immigrant background.

In February 2015, the Ministry of Education gave Hordaland County permission to start experiments with teaching in English in social science, natural science and geography at Nordahl Grieg Secondary School in Bergen. And at Knarvik Secondary School in the municipality Lindås, one of the largest secondary schools in Hordaland County, the Ministry of Education gave permission for the school to use English as the language of instruction in the teaching of history.

Anglification of Norwegian higher education

The privatization of Norwegian education has not witnessed substantial growth, even under the neo-liberal policy of the current government. The increase in the use of the English language both as the language of instruction in higher education and even more so in academic publishing has, however, been so rapid that this growth now is a real threat to the survival of the Norwegian language as an academic language. These changes have occurred rather rapidly within the last couple of decades. They have occurred under each and every government that has held office and have occurred in all the Nordic countries, in fact all over most of Europe, with the exception of France. Thomas and Breidlid (2015, 354) quote the former British Prime Minister Gordon Brown from an article he published in the Wall Street Journal in 2008 where he argues for the indispensable role of English in defining the 'special' Anglo-American relationship: 'So, finally, I propose that together Britain and America strive to make the international language, that happens to be our own, far more freely available across the world. I am today asking the British Council to develop a new initiative with private-sector and NGO partners in America, to offer anyone in any part of the world help to learn English'.

His wish was already promoted through the Bologna Declaration. The intention of the European Union with its Bologna Declaration[9] was to streamline educational standards in Europe. The streamlining also had the consequence of strengthening English as the language of instruction. According to Luc Soete, the Rector of Maastricht University, 'National languages were perceived as a hindrance for student mobility akin to customs barriers, so the creation of an open market in English is another way for them to sell their educational products' (cited by Thomas and Breidlid, 2015, 350–351). Some years back, I was involved in organizing a European Master's Degree Programme involving three universities, one in Belgium (Leuven, where the languages of instruction are Flemish and French), one in Finland (Oulu, where the language of instruction is Finnish) and one at the University of Oslo. The language of instruction of the whole Master's Program was to be English, whatever university the students visited.

When I taught at the University of Dar Es Salaam (1988–1992), many of my students said they wanted to come to Norway and continue their Ph.D. studies at my university. I had to tell them that if they wanted to do so, they had to learn Norwegian. At that time we did not have any Ph.D. courses in English. Neither did we have any such master courses. But this has changed as witnessed in Table 10.1.

Schwach and Elken (2018, 20) state that since the percentage of foreign students at Norwegian universities and colleges is only 10%, there are

Table 10.1 Studies in English at all Norwegian universities and colleges

Year	2007	2012	2016
Number of studies, all places of study	2,379	4,543	5,798
Percentage of studies, all places of study	8.9	15.7	19.6

Source: Schwach and Elken (2018, 61).

Table 10.2 Number of registered «hoved»/master's dissertations at Norwegian universities and colleges according to the language in which they were written in 1986, 2006 and 2016

Year	1986	2006	2016
Norwegian	1,081	4,403	3,449
English	115	2,238	2,675
German	13	27	11
French	3	27	2

Source: Schwach and Elken (2018, 61).

many native Norwegians taking courses taught in English. In 1997, I took the initiative of organizing an M.A. in Comparative and International Education at the Institute for Educational Research at the University of Oslo. The course started in 1998 and I was in charge of it for ten years. It was intended to be mainly for our students from Africa, Asia and Latin-America but some few Norwegian students also enrolled. I noticed that the Norwegian students actually commanded written English better than, e.g., the Tanzanian students. And for the Norwegian students, it was the first time they were exposed to the use of English as the language of instruction while the Tanzanian students had used that language for at least nine years.

Academic publishing – In whose language?

The Swedish language activist Per Åke Lindblom (2009) noted that during the period 1960 to 1979 90% of Ph.D. theses delivered at the University of Copenhagen were written in Danish and 10% in English. From 2000 to 2004, 100% were written in English! (Lindblom, 2009). Schwach and Elken (2018, 51) noted that in 2017, 90.8% of the Ph.D. theses examined at Norwegian universities were written in English. Only 8.5% were written in Norwegian. Of these, 7.9% were written in the urban variety of Norwegian, *bokmål* and only 0.6 % in the more rural variety of Norwegian, nynorsk.[10] At the level of Masters' theses, there has been a clear increase in the number of theses delivered in English over the last 20 years; illustrated in Tables 10.2 and 10.3.

We also see that the number of theses written in German and French has been on the decline.

Higher rewards for academic publications in English

In 1991, Norwegian state institutions were given the possibility of introducing a 'performance salary' (merit payment) as a part of local salary negotiations. Before that all associate professors had the same salary and so did all professors. The whole reward system fits well with the commercialization of higher education, which has also hit European universities (Brock-Utne, 2001; 2002).

Table 10.3 Registered «hoved»/ master's dissertations (in percentage) at Norwegian universities and colleges according to the language in which they were written in 1986, 2006 and 2016

Year	1986	2006	2016
Norwegian	89.19	65.77	56.20
English	9.49	33.43	43.59
German	1.07	0.40	0.18
French	0.25	0.40	0.03

Source: Calculation from Schwach and Elken (2018, 61).

In 2004, the Norwegian Association of Higher Education Institutions published a dossier called: *Vekt på forskning*[11] (UHR, 2004). This publication institutionalized a reward system dividing journals and publishing companies into three levels, level 0 (no payment was given to the institution or researcher – most publishing companies in developing countries belong to this category – even if they publish in English), level 1 (reward given), level 2 (higher reward given – normally three times higher than level 1).

On the internet one can find a list of 486 ranked publishing companies. Of these 55 companies are ranked at level 2, while 431 companies are ranked at level 1. No Norwegian publishing company is ranked at level 2, not even the University Publishing Company or other academic publishers like Fagbokforlaget, or Gyldendal Akademisk, Cappelen Akademisk or Tapir Akademisk. More than 80% of the publishing companies ranked at level 2 are based in the United States.[12]

Points are given for single-authored books produced by a publishing company ranked at level 1 (five points), and single-authored books from a publishing company ranked at level 2 (eight points). Chapters in books published by a publishing company ranked at level 1 are rewarded with 0.7 points, at level 2 with 1 point. In 2006, each point represented a reward of 40 000 NOK (US$6,500) which goes to the university centrally. Normally, the central university retains 25% and distributes the rest to the faculties in which the academic contributors are employed. The faculty keeps some of the money and distributes the rest to the different departments. The departments decide how much of the income received will go to the academic staff member who has written the article/chapter/book and how much will be part of a research fund to which those holding tenured posts at the university can apply. At my institute, the academic staff member who has generated the points will get about a tenth of the sum for her or his own research purposes. This applies both to tenured and non-tenured staff such as emeriti professors.

When it comes to academic journals, a list of 1,758 ranked journals is given, among which a tenth are ranked at level 2 and the rest at level 1. The list is collated by a group of high ranking academics. Only three of the many peer-reviewed academic journals published in Norwegian have been ranked at level two – *Tidsskrift for Rettsvitenskap* (Journal of Law[13]), *Edda* (A name from the Norse Saga[14]) and *Maal og Minne* (Oral and written literature[15]). The peer-reviewed academic journal *Historisk Tidsskrift* (Journal of History), mostly published in Norwegian, is the longest running academic journal in Norway. It has since its first issue in 1871 been the central channel for Norwegian historians, read by researchers and students as well as teachers of history. *Historisk tidsskrift* is the journal of the Norwegian society of historians, a society for those who have had at least two full terms of study of history at a Norwegian university and are engaged in historical research or dissemination of such research. For some years, the journal was recognized as a level 2 journal. The editorial board fought hard to maintain this recognition. But they had to give in and in 2018, the journal was downgraded to level 1. In the field of Educational Research no academic journal, where any of the articles is written in another language than English, has been ranked at level 2.

Norwegian researchers defending our language as a language of research

Norwegian academics seem to be more prepared to defend the Norwegian language as an academic language than colleagues in some other European countries like the Netherlands and Denmark.

On the 5 May 2006, a petition signed by 223 well-known Norwegian professors from the humanities and the social sciences was published in our largest newspaper *Aftenposten*, the newspaper which also had been the leading news channel for the debate. The petition was called: *To the defence of Norwegian as a language of research*. The text referred to the publication '*Snart to hundre*' (Soon two hundred[16]) from the University of Oslo where it was stated that the universities have a fundamental responsibility to preserve and further develop Norwegian as an academic language. That publication launched as a principle that there should be no connection between financial reward and choice of language of publication. The petition supported this principle and argued that it had to be established as a norm for the whole of the university and college sector. The professors who signed the petition challenged academic Norway to rethink the reward system. The social sciences and humanities need provisions which do not discriminate against Norwegian. The petition has, however, had no effect. The reward system continues.

The engagement of many Norwegian academics in the defence of Norwegian as an academic language can be contrasted with the attitude of many Dutch academics. In 1989, Prof. Ritzen was appointed the Minister of Education in Holland. Minister Ritzen, who has a doctoral degree both in economics and physics, and had studied in the United States, had felt frustrated as a professor of economics in Holland because of the use of Dutch in the academia. As a Minister, he now proposed that English should be the sole medium of instruction in all Dutch universities. His proposal met with overwhelming support from academia but met with harsh critique when it was presented in Parliament. Parliament insisted on regulating the language issue because it didn't trust the Minister[17] and the academics. Therefore, Parliament passed an amendment to the university law now saying that no courses could be offered in another language if it were not also offered in Dutch. This was seen as a step backwards for those professors who wanted more English language instruction in Dutch higher education. However, there has still been a steady growth of Masters' courses taught in English within Dutch higher education.

Some years back I felt that there was an acute need for a textbook in comparative and multicultural education written in Norwegian and took the initiative to edit such a book which appeared in 2006 (Brock-Utne and Bøyesen, 2006). With two exceptions, all the authors were native Norwegians, but they all did most of their academic writing in English. Most authors, including myself (Brock-Utne, 2006), had problems finding academic terms in Norwegian describing phenomena they normally wrote about in English. Not long after the book was published, my institute decided that the course in comparative and international education at the Bachelor level, which had been taught in Norwegian, should henceforth be taught in English. That may be one of the reasons why the book has not achieved the sales figures we had hoped for.

The Norwegian case shows how a smaller European language like Norwegian is threatened as an academic language. When Norwegian academics are discouraged from publishing in Norwegian, it means that academic Norwegian will deteriorate and its semantics will not develop further. We shall reach a situation similar to that which African academics are in when they have difficulties discussing academic matters in African languages because the appropriate academic concepts have not been developed in them. All languages develop through use and they also fail to develop or stagnate through disuse. The Norwegian case also shows the threat to Norwegian publishing houses. The language policy of Norwegian universities and colleges is in Norway, as in developing countries, a political question which has to do with distribution of power between social classes, between the elites and the masses.

Notes

1. The Norwegian Programme for Capacity Development in Higher Education and Research for Development (NORHED) is a programme which was launched by Norad in 2012. See: https://norad.no/NORHED
2. https://www.bistandsaktuelt.no/arkiv-kommentarer/2019/norge-bor-sikret-morsmalets-plass-i-utdanningsbistanden/
3. https://www.un.org/development/desa/indigenouspeoples/news/2019/11/high-level-event-iyl/
4. The White paper was called *Mål og meining. Ein heilskapleg norsk språkpolitikk* (*Language and meaning. A holistic Norwegian language policy*).

5. The intention of the new Norwegian language law §1.
   \# The intention of the law is to strengthen Norwegian in order for the language to continue as a fully-fledged and strong language in Norway. The law shall promote equality between the two written forms of Norwegian and seek protection and status of the languages for which the state is responsible.
   \# Public institutions have a special responsibility to use, develop and strengthen Norwegian language. This includes a responsibility to promote the Norwegian language used the least as a written language.
   \# Public institutions have a responsibility to protect and promote Sami languages.
   \# Public institutions have a responsibility to protect and promote the Kven, Romani, Romanes and Norwegian sign language. (My translation).
6. The one form, in Norwegian called 'bokmål', is most used in the cities and has developed from Danish. In the 400 years, Norway was occupied by Denmark; Danish was the official written language in Norway. After our independence from Denmark in 1814, a new written form of Norwegian, called 'nynorsk' was created on the basis of many Norwegian dialects.
7. The new law was adopted on 19August 2016 and called **Friskoleloven** [the law of Free schools] (full title Lov om frittståande skolar). In the period between January 2007 and 2015, the law was called **Privatskoleloven** [The law of private schools] (full title 'Lov om private skolar med rett til statstilskot'). The greatest change between the laws is that § 3 in the law on private schools of 1985 with its clear restrictions as to what type of schools would be accepted as eligible for state support was deleted.
8. The yearly tuition fee is: 212 500 NOK (£18,327), the registration fee: 15 000 NOK (£1,278) and the facility fee 11 500 NOK (£980) per term.
9. The **Bologna declaration** (in full, Joint **Declaration** of the European Ministers of Education convened in **Bologna** on 19 June 1999) is the main guiding document of the **Bologna** process.
10. See footnote 6 about the two varieties of written Norwegian.
11. In English: Emphasis on Research.
12. See below for the website dealing with the ranking of publications: https://dbh.nsd.uib.no/publiseringskanaler/Forside
13. All laws in Norway are written in Norwegian. *Tidsskrift for Rettsvitenskap* has since its first issue in 1888 been a channel for Nordic academic law studies and builds links between lawyers in the Nordic countries. This is the academic journal where interpretations of laws and discussions around them take place. The journal also publishes reviews of current books
14. Edda was the name of a book of stories and tales written by Snorre Sturlason around 1200. The journal *Edda* was founded in 1914 as a Nordic journal for the academic study of Nordic literature. The journal is one of the leading journals within studies of literature written in the Nordic languages.
15. The direct translation of *Maal og Minne* is 'Language and Memory'. The journal publishes articles which deal with Norwegian language and Norwegian oral and written tradition like literature from the Middle Ages, names of places in Norway, folk tales and oral literature still alive among people in remote areas. *Maal og Minne* publishes two numbers each year. It publishes articles mostly in Norwegian, Swedish and Danish but also some in German and English.
16. Referring to the fact that the University of Oslo, which was founded in 1811, soon would be two hundred years old. The publication came from a committee which had been appointed to look at the language issue at the University of Oslo.
17. Former Minister Ritzen later worked in the World Bank in Washington DC.

References

Brock-Utne, Birgit. 2019a. "Models of Cooperation Between a University in Norway and Two Universities in Africa: An Autoethnographic Report." In *Sharing Knowledge, Transforming Societies: The NORHED Programme 2015-2018*, edited by Tor Halvorsen, Kristin Skare Orgeret, and Roy Krøvel, 379–403. Cape Town: African Minds.

Brock-Utne, Birgit. 2019b. "Engelsk-språklig kastesystem?" [An English Speaking Caste?]. *Klassekampen*, 21 June, pp.16–17.

Brock-Utne, Birgit, and Martha Qorro. 2015. "Multilingualism and Language in Education in Tanzania." In *Multilingualism and Language in Education: Sociolinguistic and Pedagogical Perspectives from Commonwealth Countries*, edited by A. Yiakoumetti, 19–31. Cambridge: Cambridge University Press.

Brock-Utne, Birgit. 2008. "En sprikende språkmelding." [An Ambivalent White Paper on Language Policy]. *Aftenposten*. 21 July.

Brock-Utne, Birgit. 2007a. "Worldbankification of Norwegian Development Assistance to Education." *Comparative Education* 43 (3): 433–449.

Brock-Utne, Birgit. 2007b. "Learning Through a Familiar Language versus Learning Through a Foreign Language: A Look into some Secondary School Classrooms in Tanzania." *International Journal of Educational Development* 27 (5): 487–498.

Brock-Utne, Birgit. 2006. "Innviklet utdanning for utvikling." [Difficult Education for Development]. In *Å Greie Seg i Utdanningssystemet i Nord og Sør: Innføring i Flerkulturell og Komparativ Pedagogikk, Utdanning og Utvikling [How to Survive in the Educational System in the North and in the South: Introduction to Multicultural and Comparative Education, Education and Development]*, edited by Birgit. Brock-Utne, and Liv Bøyesen, 221–236. Bergen: Fagbokforlaget.

Brock-Utne, Birgit. 2002. "The Global Forces Affecting the Education Sector Today – The Universities in Europe as an Example." *Higher Education in Europe* 37 (3): 283–300.

Brock-Utne, Birgit. 2001. "The Growth of English for Academic Communication in the Nordic Countries." *International Review of Education* 47 (3–4): 221–233.

Brock-Utne, Birgit. 2000. *Whose Education for All? The Recolonization of the African Mind?* New York/London: Falmer.

Brock-Utne, Birgit, and Ingse Skattum. 2009. *Languages and Education in Africa: A Comparative and Transdisciplinary Discussion*. Oxford: Symposium.

Brock-Utne, Birgit., and Liv Bøyesen. 2006. *Å greie seg i Utdanningssystemet i Nord og Sør: Innføring i Flerkulturell og Komparativ Pedagogikk, Utdanning og Utvikling. [How to Survive in the Educational System in the North and in the South: Introduction to Multicultural and Comparative Education, Education and Development]*. Bergen: Fagbokforlaget.

Buchert, Lene. 1997. *Education Policy Formulation in Tanzania: Coordination between the Government and International Aid Agencies*. Paris: International Institute for Educational Planning.

Coleman, Hewel. 2011. "Allocating Resources for English: The Case of Indonesia's English Medium International Standard Schools." In *Dreams and Realities: Developing Countries and the English Language*, edited by Hewel Coleman, 89–113. London: British Council. http://www.teachingenglish.org.uk/transform/books/dreams-realities-developing-countries-english-language

Galabawa, Justinian. C. J., and N. R. Alphonse. 1993. The National Education Trust Fund: Implementation, Initial Take Off, Constraints and Sustainability. A Consultancy Report Prepared for NORAD (Dar es Salaam: NORAD).
Gopal, S. 1980. *Jawaharlala Nehru. An Anthology.* Delhi: Oxford University Press.
Graddol, D. 2000. *The Future of English.* London: British Council.
Heugh, Kathleen. 1999. "Language, Development and Reconstructing Education in South Africa." *International Journal of Educational Development* 19: 301–313.
Huss, Leena. 2017. "Language Education Policies and the Indigenous and Minority Languages of Northernmost Scandinavia and Finland." In *Language Policy and Political Issues in Education*, edited by Teresa L. McCarty, and Stephen May, 367–383. New York: Springer International Publishing.
Kristoffersen, Gjert. 2005. "Vil norsk fagspråk forsvinne?" [Will Norwegian Academic Language Disappear?] *Aftenposten* 28 November.
Lindblom, Per-Åke. 2009. "Are the Nordic Languages Threatened as Academic Languages?" In *Language is Power. The Implications of Language for Peace and Development*, edited by Birgit Brock-Utne, and Gunnar Garbo. Oxford. African Books Collective. Dar es Salaam: Mkuki na Nyota
Magga, Ole Henrik. 1996. "Sami past and present and the Sami picture of the world." In *Awakened Voice. The Return of Sami Knowledge*, edited by E. Helander, 74–80. Guovdageaidnu/Kautokeino: Nordic Sami Institute.
Meyer, Johan Kr. 2019. "Fransk eller hausa? Om morsmålets betydning i skolen." [French or Hausa? The Importance of Using the Mother Tongue as Language of Instruction] *Bistandsaktuelt.* 20 December.
MOEC (Ministry of Education and Culture). 1995. The Tanzanian Education and Training Policy. Dar es Salaam.
Mohanty, Ajit. 2017. "Multilingualism, Education, English and Development: Whose Development?" In *Multilingualism and Development*, edited by Hywel Coleman, 261–281. London: British Council.
Mohanty, Ajit K., and Minati Panda. 2017. "Language Policy and Education in the Indian Subcontinent." In *Language Policy and Political Issues in Education*, edited by Teresa L. McCarty, and Stephen May, 507–519. New York: Springer International Publishing.
Mwinsheikhe, Halima Muhammed. 2007. Overcoming the Language Barrier: An In-Depth Study of Tanzanian Secondary School Science Teachers' and Students' Strategies in Coping with the English/Kiswahili Dilemma in the Teaching/Learning Process. Ph.D. Dissertation, University of Oslo.
Outakoski, H. 2015. Multilingual Literacy among Young Learners of North Sami. Contexts, Complexity and Writing in Saapmi. Ph.D. Dissertation, Department of Language Studies, Umeå University.
Phillipson, Robert. 2003. *English-Only Europe? Challenging Language Policy.* London & NewYork: Routledge.
Prah, K. K., and Birgit Brock-Utne, B. (eds). 2009. *Multilingualism – An African Advantage: A Paradigm Shift in African Language of Instruction Polices.* Cape Town: CASAS
Schwach, Vera, and Mari Elken. 2018. *Å Snakke Fag på et Språk andre Forstår. Norsk Fagspråk i Høyere Utdanning og Arbeidsliv. [To Speak on Academic Matters in a Language Normal People Understand. Norwegian Language in Higher Education and Work].* RAPPORT 20/2018. Oslo: NIFU-STEP.

Spolsky, Bernard. 2017. "Language Policy in Education, Practices, Ideology and Management." In *Language Policy and Political Issues in Education*, edited by Teresa L. McCarty, and Stephen May, 3–17. New York: Springer International Publishing.

Thomas, Paul, and Anders Breidlid. 2015. "In the Shadow of 'Anglobalization', National Tests in English in Norway and the Making of a New English Underclass." *Journal of Multicultural Discourses* 10 (3): 349–368. DOI: 10.1080/17447143.2015.1041963.

UHR (Universitets og Høgskolerådet – the Norwegian Association of Higher Education Institutions). 2004. Vekt på forskning. Nytt system for dokumentasjon av vitenskapelig publisering. [Emphasis on Research. A New System for Documentation of Scientific Publishing].

Vuzo, Mwajuma. 2007. Revisiting the Language of Instruction Policy in Tanzania: A Comparative Study of Geography Classes Taught in Kiswahili and English. Ph.D. Dissertation, University of Oslo.

Wetås, Åse. 2016. "Engelskspråklig Skoleklasse Presenteres Som et Solskinnsprosjekt. Språkrådet er Oppriktig Bekymret." [An Experiment Using English as the Language of Instruction in a Norwegian Primary School is Presented as a Good Thing. The Language Council Voices its grave Concern]. *Aftenposten*. August 23.

Index

Italicized and **bold** pages refer to figures and tables respectively, and page numbers followed by "n" refer to notes.

Aasen, P. 62, 63
academic publications in English 223–225
Africa 211–216, 221, 223, 226
agency 39, 40, 81, 82, 101–102, 110, 113, 123, 172, 174, 175, 189
Amharic 216
Andrews, T. 89, 98, 99, 111
Archer, M. S. 1–4, 6, 14, 39, 41, 42, 45, 47, 49, 54, 55, 70–72, 81, 83, 88, 101–104, 113, 123–126, 128, 134–137, 140, 163, 168, 181, 189–191, 204, 206; centralized state educational systems 55–61, 65; decentralized state educational systems 55–61, 65; morphogenetic approach 156–159
A realist theory of science (Bhaskar) 53
Arnesen, A.-L. 62–64, 71
Australia 49, 62, 151, 195
autonomous reflexives **125**, 126, 136–142, 191, 195, 198, 201–206

Bæck, Unn-Doris K. 5, 6, 123
Baird, Jo-Anne 149, 152, 153, 155
Basic Education Reform Act of 1997 160
Bauman, Zygmunt 122, 123
Beck, Ulrich 122
Bergesen, Helge Ole 164, 165
Bhaskar, Roy 4, 53, 54, 72, 73n2, 81, 82
Bieber, Tonia 148
Bologna Declaration 9, 222, 227n9
Bologna Process 161, 162, 170
Breakspear, Simon 150
Breidlid, Anders 221, 222
Brock-Utne, Birgit 8, 9, 214
Buchert, Lene 213

Buckley, Walter 39
burgher schools 21

case municipalities 105–106
Cathedral School 4, 13, 41–46, 48
Central Agency for Flexible Distance Lea 170
centralized state educational systems (SES) 3, 4–7, *16*, 17, 24, 26, 29, 31, 54–65, 71, 72, 88–89, 91, 101–104, 112, 114–116, 155–158, 173, 175
'Choice of Education' 132
Clemet, Kristin 163, 164
Coastal Valley 126–128, 130, 138–140
Coleman, Hewel 214
communicative reflexives **125**, 126, **134**, 135–137, 139, 141, 191, 195, 198, 199, 201
The Conservative Party 163, 166, 167, 173, 175, 218
continuous reflexive deliberations 132–134
Corbett, M. 79, 80, 94, 98, 106
Critical Realism (CR) 5, 34n1, 36n26, 53–54, 73n1, 79–82, 124, 172, 189; generative mechanisms 82–84
cultural institutions 107–108
Culture For Learning 63, 164, 166, 169, 170

Danermark, Berth 53, 157, 192, 193
Danish decentralized educational system (DES) 3, 17, 23, 31
decentralized state educational systems (SES) 3, 4, 7, *16*, 17, 19, 23, 24, 31, 54–65, 68, 70–72, 88–90, 102, 103, 104, 116, 155–158, 171, 173

decision-making authority 60–64, 67, 69–71, 81, 103, 123, 128, 129, 191; family and friends 131; modes of reflexivity **134**; school personnel 131–132
Denmark's state educational systems (SES) 17, 19–27, 34
'de-sectorization' of education 67
differentiated collection of institutions 17, 25, 55, 103
differentiation 3, 16, 30, 56, 58, 65, 66–68, 70, 71, 88, 89, 103, 156–159, 161, 163, 171
distance to school 129–131, 135, 136, 138, 142

economic resources 107–108
education 5, 14, 26, 30, 34, 43, 44, 48–50, 63, 66, 67, 69, 79, 80, 94, 100, 105, 149, 160; contextualization of 2–4; 'de-sectorization' of 67; interaction and practice 7–9; privatization of 212–213; in school leadership 170
Education Act of 1998 162
educational decision-making process 131
educational development, contextualization of 2–4
educational institutions 2, 14, 19, 44–45, 48, 57, 87, 89, 93, 103, 129, 211
educational interaction: in centralized systems 57; in decentralized systems 58; and practice 7–9
educational landscapes 5, 82, 86–88, 90, 91, 94
educational mechanisms, spatial context of 4–6
educational project 129–131
'Education and Training Policy' 213
Eggen, Astrid Birgitte 187, 204
elementary schools 2, 4, 19, 20, 23, 25, 29, 48, 105
Elken, Mari 222, 223
Elstad, Eyvind 153
'English knowing caste' 215
English language 214–216; in academic publications 223–225; in Norwegian universities and colleges **222**
English-medium education 216
European Commission 64, 73n7, 148
European Higher Education Area (EHEA) 161, 162, 170
extensive unification 56, 65, 68, 156, 160–163, 168
external transactions 7, 8, 58

Fletcher, A. J. 82
Folk High Schools 16n16, 25, 135
fractured reflexives **125**, 126, 128, 138, 190, *191*
The Free School Act of 1855 20–21, 24

generative mechanisms 13, 18, 53, 80, 82–85, 87, 89–94, 172, 175
Giddens, Anthony 122
global educational competition 30–31
'Great School Commission' 19
Green, B. 79
Green Paper 162, 163, 167, 168, 170
Grek, Sotiria 148, 149
Groff, Ruth 54, 73n1
Grønnvik 104–108, 110–116
Grundtvigian Free Schools 21, 25
Gulson, Kalervo N. 98
Gunnulfsen, Ann Elisabeth 184, 205

Hammond, Hans 38, 41, 45, 47
Hanson, E. M. 60, 61
Hanushek, E. A. 187
Hattie, John 100
Haug, B. 62
Hausa 216
Helgøy, I. 64
Heltberg, Elias 46
Heugh, Kathleen 216
higher education 7, 25, 30, 106, 128, 132, 136, 138, 139, 159–163, 170, 171, 221–223
high-quality education 107, 111, 114, 116
Homme, A. 64
Huss, Leena 217

imperative of reflexivity 136
'Improving School Leadership' 171
India 215
indigenous languages 216–217
indigenous tribal minority ones (ITM) 216
intensive unification 56, 65–68, 103, 156, 161, 162, 171
Internal Conversation Indicator (ICONI) 128, 136, 137, 141, 206
internal initiation 7, 8, 58
international competition 32–34
International Largescale Assessments (ILSAs) 154, 155
International Monetary Fund (IMF) 60, 213
International Year of Indigenous Languages 216–217

Jenkins, Edgar 186

Karlsen, G. E. 62, 90, 91
Kiswahili 213, 214, 216
The Knowledge Promotion Reform 63, 68, 169, 170, 184
Korsgaard, Ove 27
Kven 105, 126, 142n1

Labour Party 29, 158, 163, 164, 166, 167, 173
language of research 225–226
'Language Policy in Education' 220
Lash, Scott 122
Latin Schools 20, 21
Leadership Development in School (LUIS) 159
Leadership in School (LIS) 159
Leadership in Upper Secondary School (LEVIS) 159
Learned School Act of 1809 21
Learned Schools 19–22, 24, 25, 27, 36n19
Lingard, Bob 150
Lund, Eirik 103
Lund, Morten 46
Lundahl, L. 62–64, 71

Magga, Ole Henrik 217
Making Our Way Through the World (2007) (Archer) 101, 124
management by objectives (MbO) 62, 63, 66, 67, 74n13, 158, 163, 182
Martens, Kerstin 148
Mausethagen, Sølvi 153–155, 182, 184
Mazrui, Ali 215
meta-reflexives **125**, 140–141, 195, 198, 202
Meyer, Johan 214
Middle School 21–24, 27
Million, A., T. 87
Ministry of Education and Research 109, 164, 166, 170
Missionary Collegium 2, 38–47, 50
Mohanty, Ajit 215, 216
Møller, Jorunn 205
morphogenetic approach 15–17, 39, 42, 45, 49, 55, 81, 123, 156–157, 189
morphogenetic cycles 2–4, *16*, 34, 156–158
Morris, Paul 149
multinational production 31–32
Municipal Act of 1992 112, 163, 171
municipality administration 109, 110, 112

municipality board 109, 112
municipality-funding system 99, 111–115, 151
municipal school owners involvement 109–110

National Curriculum 62, 63, 66, 70, 88, 153, 158–161, 176n5, 182, 198, 199, 203, 205, 206
national educational policy 32, 187
National Education Trust Fund (NETF) 212, 213
National Quality Assessment System (NQAS) 167–169, 172, 173, 185, 188, 195
National Tests 168, 183, 184, 195, 205
'natural kinds' 54
'The Neglect of the Educational System' 13–14; morphogenetic approach 15–17; SESs 14–15
neo-liberal education policy 6, 90–92
New Public Management (NPM) 67, 159
'The Nordic Model' 1, 2, 13, 17–19, 29, 36n28
Nordkvelle, Y. 89–91
Norman, Christopher 46
Northern Norway 40, 42–44, 84, 98, 100, 105, 108, 122, 127, 142n1
Nortvedt, Guri A. 154, 155
Norwegian Agency for Development Cooperation (NORAD) 212
Norwegian Association of Higher Education Institutions 224
Norwegian Directorate of Education and Training 168, 202, 206
Norwegian educational policy 154, 155, 202
Norwegian educational system 4, 6, 7, 55, 62–65, 72, 79, 88, 114, 154, 155–158, 167, 169, 173, 183, 185, 187, 188, 191, 194, 202, 204, 205, 207n1, 211, 221; centralized state educational systems 61–65; decentralized state educational systems 61–65; development in 22; efforts to decentralize 89–90; mother tongue instruction 213–214; SAC 13; as structured and centralized 102–104
Norwegian Education Association 188
Norwegian Language Council 218
Norwegian languages: development of 218–219; instruction of 219–220; legal protection of 217–218

Index

The Norwegian Ministry of Church and Education 62
Norwegian Network Council 161
Norwegian state educational systems (SES) 7, 19–28, 30
Nyerere Educational Trust Fund 213
Nyhus, L. 89–91

Olsen, Isaac 46, 49
opportunity structures 82, 86–89, 91, 94, 100, 106, 116, 123–125, 128, 131, 136, 141, 142
Organization of Economic Co-operation and Development (OECD) 7, 8, 31, 32, 60, 62, 63, 70, 72, 91, 95n1, 147–149, 151–153, 158, 163, 165, 167, 168, 171, 173–175, 181, 183, 185–187
Oromo 216
Oslo International School (OIS) 219, 220
Outakoski, H. 217

Panda, Minati 216
perceived work opportunities 130–131, 138, 142
Phillipson, Robert 215
PISA Governing Board (PGB) 150
political manipulation 7, 8, 56, 58
Pons, Xavier 151, 152
The possibility of naturalism (Bhaskar) 54
potential powers 92–93
Primary School Act of 1827 20, 26
Pring, R. 90
Private Proprietary Schools 19
privatization of education 212–213, 219–220
Program for International Student Assessment (PISA) 3, 7, 8, 31–34, 72, 73n7, 91, 147, 185–189; accountability and learning 181–185; educational structures 162–163; internal conversations *193*; international comparisons 148–152; in Norway 152–155; reforms 154, 155, 157; Shock 163–166; structural elaboration 167–171; systemic structures and processes 158–162
public primary school 220–221
pupils' decision-making process 131–132

Qorro, Martha 216
qualified teachers 110–111
Quality in School 170, 171

Rachlöw, Rasmus 46
Realist Social Theory: The Morphogenetic Approach (Archer) 101
Real Schools 20–25, 27, 34, 35n16, 36n22
reflexive deliberations 101, 125, 129, 189
reflexivity 122–125, 142, 181, 189–190, 193; autonomous 137–138; concerns, constraints and educational projects 134–137; modes of **125**, 190, 193–199; upper secondary school 132–134
reward system 223–225
Ringarp, J. 150
Rød, Daniel A.V. 6
Rothland, M 150
rural school 91, 98, 100, 106–108, 111, 116, 126, 128, 131

Sámi language 43, 44, 46, 48, 49, 126; legal protection 217–218
Sami Mission 2, 4, 43
Sámi people 1, 2, 39, 44, 45, 48, 217
Sayer, A. 53, 54, 81–83, 92, 93
Scandinavian languages 1, 35n4
school autonomy 4, 5, 61, 62, 65, 71, 72, 73n7, 73n8
school leaders 7, 8, 100, 109, 110, 151, 154, 159, 163, 167, 169–171, 176n6, 181–185, 182–185, 187, 188, 190–192, 190–197, 199, 201–206, 207n1, 207n7; importance of 181; reflexive modes *193*
school leadership group 109, 110
Schwach, Vera 222, 223
Sellar, Sam 150
Seminarium Domesticum 44–46, 49, 50
'The Seven Stars' 41, 43
Sivesind, Kirsten 153, 154, 155
Sjøberg, Svein 186, 187
Skattum, Ingse 214
Skedsmo, Guri 205
Skinningsrud, T. 2, 4, 13, 16, 39, 88–90, 102, 156, 158
Skjelmo, Randi H. 3, 40
Social Democratic Party 17, 18, 28, 29, 31, 212, 218
Socialist Left Party (SV) 164
'social kinds' 54
Social Origins of Educational Systems (Archer) 15, 27
social structure, culture, and agency (SAC) 13, 16, 30, 34n1
'soft governance' 153, 174
Solstad, K. J. 89, 98, 99, 111
Space and Time in Education (STED) 1

spatial education analysis 92
specialization 3, 16, 26, 27, 30, 31, 56, 58, 59, 65, 68, 71, 88, 103, 138, 156–158, 160, 163, 171
standardization 3, 9, 65, 68–70, 88, 91, 94, 149, 161, 163
state educational systems (SES) 2, 3, 7, 13–19, 23, 24, 26–31, 30, 33, 34, 79; Denmark 19–27; Norway 19–27; systemic developments 27–29
Steiner-Khamsi, Gita 154
Stenseth, Anna-Maria 6, 123
Stronge, James H. 100
structural adjustment policy (SAP) 60
structure, culture and agency 101–102
support functions, lack of 107–108
Symes, Colin 98
systematization 3, 16, 25–27, 56–59, 65, 88, 103, 156–159, 161–163, 170–173, 175

Tanzania 212–214, 216
teacher education 107, 110, 113, 116, 150, 151, 153, 158, 159, 160–163, 168, 170, 171
Teacher Education Council 161, 162
teachers' motivations 107
teachers' work experiences 98, 100, 102
teaching staff 29, 44–45, 110, 195
Telhaug, A. O. 90
Thelin, Annika Andræ 111
Thomas, Paul 221, 222
Tromsø 1, 45, 98, 105, 106, 108–110, 116, 127–129, 131, 218
Tveit, Sverre 183, 184, 205

unification 3, 24–27, 57–59, 65, 68–70, 88, 103, 114, 115, 156–163, 168, 171, 173, 175; extensive 56; intensive 56
upper secondary education 6, 31, 65, 66, 67, 79, 80, 82, 133, 137, 141, 159, 162, 163, 169, 220; educational structures in 127; reflexive deliberation 132–134; students' experiences of 84–86
Upper Secondary Education Reform of 1994 159
urban school 98, 106–108, 116, 135

vocational education and training (VET) 79, 84, 86, 95n1, 127
Volckmar, N. 64
von Westen, T. 3, 4, 38–40, 50; achievements 46–47; missionary work achievement 42–43; mission organizing 43–44; source of knowledge 47–49

Waldow, Florian 154
Wedde, Elise 103
Weiler, H. N. 71
White Papers 22, 63, 66, 68, 69, 150, 151, 153, 154, 158, 159, 162, 164, 166, 169–171, 218
Wiborg, Susanne 27, 64
Wight, C. 83
World Bank (WB) 60, 212, 213
Wossmann, L. 187

Yin, Robert K 192

Zajda, J. 61